Hospitality Industry Growth and Development

HOSPITALITY INDUSTRY GROWTH AND DEVELOPMENT

Arohi Kanchan

CENTRUM PRESS
NEW DELHI-110002 (INDIA)

CENTRUM PRESS
H.O.: 4360/4, Ansari Road, Daryaganj,
New Delhi-110002 (India)
Tel: 23278000, 23261597, 23255577, 23286875

B.O.: No. 1015, Ist Main Road, BSK IIIrd Stage,
IIIrd Phase, IIIrd Block, Bengaluru-560085 (INDIA)
Tel: 080-41723429

Email: centrumpress@gmail.com
Visit us at: www.centrumpress.com

Hospitality Industry Growth and Development

First Edition, 2013

ISBN 978-93-81460-14-6

PRINTED IN INDIA

Printed at **Balaji Offset, Delhi.**

Contents

Preface

As per a report published by the World Travel and Tourism Council, India stood 18th as far as business travel was concerned and it featured alongside the top 5 most visited destinations in 2010. According to ASSOCHAM Medical Tourism is really gaining momentum in India and soon it will become the highest foreign exchange earner for the nation. India over the last few years has become a favourite medical tourist spot for millions and is just after countries like Thailand, Philippines, Singapore, Malaysia, Hong Kong and Columbia. According to a study conducted by the World Travel and Tourism Council the hospitality industry in India is all set to grow at a steady rate of 15 percent per annum. However the growth rate will shoot up in the next few years considering the number of rooms required by both luxury and budget hotels. The growth in the next two to three years is surely going to be stupendous with almost 2, 00,000 rooms added to the existing 110,000. Dwelling perfectly on the principle of ATITHI DEVO BHAVA' (GUEST IS GOD) the hotels in India are just the apt concoction of luxury, humility and unparallel hospitality. The hotels in India are known for offering the best of products and services at absolutely pocket friendly rates. As per expert hoteliers the hotel industry in India is estimated to grow at a rate of 8.8 percent between the years 2007-16. This will place India on the second position in the list of the fastest growing tourism industries in the world. The phenomenal growth of the hotel industry in India would not have been possible without the Initiatives taken the government. The open sky policies and the enormous infrastructural investments made by the Indian government have only fastened the development of the hospitality sector in the country.

The Indian hotel industry is affecting the economy both directly and indirectly. The growth of the hotel industry in India has created employment opportunities for millions of Indians.

According to estimates almost 20 million people are employed with the hotel industry in India. Over the last decade and half the mad rush to India business opportunities has intensified and elevated room rates and occupancy levels in India. Even budget hotels are charging USD 250 per day. The successful growth story of 'Hotel Industry in India' seconds only to China in Asia Pacific. 'Hotels in India' has a supply of 110,000 rooms. According to the India tourism ministry, 4.4 million tourists visited India in 2009 and the figure went upto almost 10 million in 2010. 'Hotels in India' has a shortage of 150,000 rooms fueling hotel room rates across India. With tremendous pull of opportunity, India is a destination for hotel chains looking for growth. The World Travel and Tourism Council, India, data says, India ranks 18th in business travel and will be among the top 5 in this decade. Sources estimate, demand is going to exceed supply by at least 100% over the next 2 years. Five-star hotels in metro cities allot same room, more than once a day to different guests, receiving almost 24-hour rates from both guests against 6-8 hours usage. With demand-supply disparity, 'Hotel India' room rates are most likely to rise 25% annually and occupancy to rise by 80%, over the next two years. 'Hotel Industry in India' is eroding its competitiveness as a cost effective destination. However, the rating on the 'Indian Hotels' is bullish.' India Hotel Industry' is adding about 60,000 quality rooms, currently in different stages of planning and development and should be ready by 2012. MNC Hotel Industry giants are flocking India and forging Joint Ventures to earn their share of pie in the race. Government has approved 300 hotel projects, nearly half of which are in the luxury range. Sources said, the manpower requirements of the hotel industry increased from 7 million in 2002 to 15 million in 2010. With the USD 23 billion software services sector pushing the Indian economy skywards, more and more IT professionals are flocking to Indian metro cities. 'Hotel Industry in India' is set to grow at 15% a year. This figure will skyrocket in 2010, when Delhi hosts the Commonwealth Games. Already, more than 50 international budget hotel chains are moving into India to stake their turf. Therefore, with opportunities galore the future 'Scenario of Indian Hotel Industry' looks rosy.

The book looks at the impact hospitality has on the economic, social, and cultural status of the travel destination.

—Author

1

Marketing and Planning of Hospitality Sector

Steps to Sustainable Tourism

Sustainable tourism development meets the needs of present tourists and host regions while protecting and enhancing opportunities for the future. It is envisaged as leading to management of all resources in such a way that economic, social and aesthetic needs can be fulfilled while maintaining cultural integrity, essential ecological processes, biological diversity and life support systems.

World Tourism Organisation

Environment refers to ecosystems, and also to cultural qualities and characteristics of places. *Heritage* embraces our natural, Indigenous and historic inheritance – what we think our descendants should, and would want to, inherit.

Generally, these two terms are interchangeable. Environment and heritage are valued differently by different people. Those working in tourism recognise them as assets of mainstream and niche tourism products and are in a position to do much to educate visitors about the values of our natural and cultural heritage places.

Achieving sustainable tourism requires motivation, determination and a systematic approach. Its core is proper planning. The 10 steps form an entire planning process that can be applied from start to finish, or can be used in part if more appropriate. It can be followed in large planning exercises such as a 'big picture' regional planning process or by small interest groups or individuals wanting to promote a single attraction. Following these steps thoroughly will assist you meet the needs of the visitor, the environment, business and the local community. There can be a sustainable future for them all. The 10 steps can be used in many different ways. They can help to:

- develop audits, scoping projects and preliminary assessments of tourism development potential in regions
- identify tourism and heritage issues which need to be considered in management, regional or business planning
- develop regional heritage and tourism strategic plans and action plans
- assist in developing business plans for new or existing heritage tourism products
- foster more effective planning for infrastructure development at heritage places
- evaluate options and establish a stronger business case for an idea or proposal.

Sustainable Development

Sustainable development needs to address economic, social and environmental issues. Many businesses now include social and environmental factors as part of their performance measurement. Sometimes referred to as 'triple bottom line' measurement and reporting, this approach focuses on accountability, transparency, commitment to stakeholder and community engagement and systematic measurement and reporting.

Tourism and Heritage Principles

An important complementary publication to this framework is *Successful Tourism at Heritage Places*. It sets out principles, guidelines and case studies that illustrate success factors in tourism at natural and cultural heritage places.

The principles from *Successful Tourism at Heritage Places* underpin this framework and should be a starting point for discussions and collaboration. They are:

1. recognise the importance of heritage places
2. look after heritage places
3. develop mutually beneficial partnerships
4. incorporate heritage issues into business planning
5. invest in people and place
6. market and promote products responsibly
7. provide high-quality visitor experiences
8. respect Indigenous rights and obligations.

Appropriate Tourism Development

Sustainable Tourism sets out an approach to help develop appropriate longterm solutions for tourism at places with natural and cultural heritage values. It also seeks ways to support growth in the tourism industry while ensuring that conservation needs are met.

Tourism will not be an option for some environments or heritage places where it is incompatible with the special values or management objectives of a place. Using the process in this guide will enable you to assess whether this is the case.

What do we want to do?

This step will help you to:

- define your aims
- understand the context.

Whether you're using this process in relation to a region, a particular place or a tourism product, your first step is to determine what you would like to achieve and to understand the context of your project.The statement of aim that you produce will become an important reference for briefings, consultation, media communications and proposals, as it will help others to clearly understand what you're trying to achieve. If a number of people are involved, you must all agree on your aims before going any further.

What are Your Aims?

A clearly defined aim will guide the work ahead. It can be as simple as you like and can be worded many different ways such as in a vision statement, mission statement or statement of purpose. Invest a little time in making sure this statement is tight, clear and achievable.

In developing your aim, consider:

- what are we aiming to achieve
- in the short term?
- in the long term?
- why do we need to do this?
- what time frames are we working to?
- What is the context for your region, place or project?

To help you and others better understand the context of the region, place or project, you will need to set the scene in a brief overview statement. This statement should cover:

- social setting
- economic conditions
- current political climate
- natural environment setting *and*
- cultural considerations.

Some of the key questions you may need to answer succinctly are:

- what are the key natural and cultural assets for tourism?
- what are the current visitor numbers?
- what is the potential for future growth in visitor numbers?
- how well is the current situation working?
- is the place or region appropriate for tourism use and development?

If at all possible clearly identify common ground or potential areas/points of conflict between those interested in the place/ project. Defining common ground early in the process can be important in assisting progress. How to manage issues and conflicts will be explored in later steps.

Who is, could be or needs to be Involved?

This step will help you to:

- identify stakeholders
- consider when and how people should be consulted and involved
- work out how to develop effective working relationships.

It is important to find out who is concerned about and responsible for tourism, environment and heritage issues relating to your place or region. If you systematically and strategically identify and involve those with a stake in your place, region or tourism product, you will:

- ensure the right people are involved in planning and future activities
- help determine heritage significance of places involved
- help make sure all the important issues are considered
- help to decide what future actions are realistic and will best meet everyone's needs and
- help build support for regional plans, management plans and development proposals.

This step is important as it will underpin all future steps and will need to be revisited and updated continually. Initially, everyone who is, could be or needs to be involved or considered in future decisions should be identified and the nature of their interest noted. From here, various forms of consultation, as appropriate, can be considered and this can then lead some form of involvement in the process, project or business.

Who are the Stakeholders?

Determine who is, should or could be involved by listing all potential stakeholders.

You can identify stakeholders by:

- talking to people
- reading existing reports *and*
- if necessary, publicly or formally seeking interested persons or organisations.

Start using existing networks and communication forums to identify the people who

might be involved. Ask your colleagues:

- who else should I talk to?
- who is not involved who should be?

Some or all of the following questions may help you to identify the people, groups and organisations who may need to be informed, consulted or involved in some way. Understanding the nature of the interest of each stakeholder helps, whether it is statutory, professional, economic, cultural or personal. Depending on their interest, stakeholders may just need to be kept in mind in future steps, others will need to be included in some form of consultation and a smaller set will need to be involved. The essential or key stakeholders should be identified as early as possible.

How to Consult and Involve People

Informing and involving people can be challenging and time consuming but can make a huge difference to successful projects, plans and tourism products. Consultation processes can be targeted at your key stakeholders for specific purposes, or might be designed to generally inform the community, build support and seek willing involvement. There are many different consultation techniques. Choosing the best one for you will depend on the context, type of people involved and the available human and financial resources. Some techniques are formal, others are targeted and specific. The range of techniques includes, but is not limited to:

- community meetings
- interviews
- public exhibitions, displays and information sheets
- advisory committees
- media placements seeking input
- written submissions
- telephone polls and surveys
- focus groups
- open days

- guided information tours
- conferences or workshops
- residents' feedback sessions
- visual mapping
- pictorial and photographic illustration.

If you would like help in developing your consultation approaches, you may like to engage someone who is trained or experienced in consultation techniques. Additional resources detailing consultation methods are listed in the references section. Working out the appropriate people to involve is often a matter of common sense, but it can be important to involve people other than the usual suspects. Sometimes these people can be a breath of fresh air, and bring with them new and interesting perspectives.

How to Develop Effective Working Relationships

Several other factors may make a big difference in establishing or developing effective working relationships, such as:

- identifying the 'drivers' or champions
- identifying the key people to be involved in regular communication *and*
- identifying important partnerships.

Drivers and Champions

Every project or process needs someone to coordinate activities, bring people together and be the central contact point. This individual may be the initial person to get the process rolling before handing it on to others, or they could be nominated as the coordinator by superiors or a project team. This person, along with other contact people, should be clearly identified, and all key stakeholders notified of their role, and provided with their contact details.

Project Teams, Working Groups or Steering Committees

Where possible, use and build on existing communication mechanisms to coordinate work. If a suitable consultative group does not already exist, it may be useful to set up a working group to address issues relevant to your region, place or tourism product.

The aim of the working group should be to communicate across organisations, integrate the needs of tourism, heritage and the environment and foster support for the process.

Possible Participants for a Working Group

Appoint members and use them as conduits for information into the group and out to the broader community. Your group can be as formal or informal as you like. It can provide a focal point for reporting and communication between people, accessing information, exploring options, making decisions and communicating to the broader community. It should reflect all key interests, and should involve key people or organisations at the core of decision-making.

Developing Partnerships

Successful tourism often requires resources that no one organisation can offer so partnerships can be an effective tool when dealing across tourism and heritage issues. They can help to build support, and to coordinate rather than duplicate efforts. Taking a partnership approach early on, may help you when seeking approvals and may ensure that you have all the right information as a project progresses. The key steps to developing partnerships are:

1. identifying what key partnerships will help you to achieve your goals
2. identifying the people who are or should be involved
3. building the relationships (using this document is a good start)
4. developing mutual understandings of issues and the natural and cultural heritage involved
5. jointly developing goals and objectives
6. expressing commitment to the partnership, and to implementing agreed future actions.

What is Known?

This step will help you to:

- identify existing studies or sources of information relevant to your process or project

- locate and summarise available information on the current and potential market for tourism
- determine the heritage assets, their heritage values and themes Information is a powerful tool so drawing together relevant facts and figures will provide a solid grounding for future decisions. As you look for material on planning and managing tourism at heritage places, and the current and potential tourism market, you may find that much useful information already exists.

Where to look

You might have a look at books, newspaper articles, sound recordings, council records, tourism brochures, annual reports, tour operator records, park management plans and research reports. Information can also be found:

- by talking to knowledgeable individuals and through observations, interviews, questionnaires and focus groups
- in local and state libraries
- in private collections
- on websites
- through various local or regional organisations
- in universities
- at heritage site management authorities
- at state and Australian Government departments
- with tour operators.

Questions to Ask

Are there any:

- regional plans for economic development?
- relevant local government plans?
- expressions of community aims/aspirations?

If you can, also try to identify what areas of information seem to be missing as these might be important parts of the overall picture and may need to be obtained some other way if they are important for making future decisions.

Other Sources

Environment and Heritage Information

A useful starting place for environment and heritage information is through the internet at sites such as the Australian Heritage Directory. The websites of the Australian Government Department of the Environment and Heritage, and state environment, park and heritage agencies are also useful.

What makes this Region, Place or Product Special?

In this step you need to identify the important values of your place, region or product, and the ways in which they are understood and communicated. Places can be special for all kinds of reasons — they may be important to the local community or to the world as a whole. Tourism, heritage and local community interests will benefit from developing a common understanding of what is significant so that they have a unified approach to presenting local and regional heritage to visitors.

Identifying Natural and Cultural Heritage Values

Natural and cultural heritage places are often the key assets for tourism. The unique qualities of a place, or its values, can be a large part of a tourism business and its key selling points.

Understanding the values of your heritage places is essential for effective product development, planning, marketing, management and interpretation. It is also important when considering the appropriateness of introducing or expanding tourism activities at your heritage place. This understanding helps to ensure that future development is as compatible as possible with the ongoing care of the values.

You may find that the values have already have been documented by natural and cultural heritage specialists or are known to locals. Heritage professionals have developed considerable expertise and have structured methods (including criteria) for assessing the significance of a place. Information they can offer on aesthetic, historical, scientific, social and spiritual significance will be valuable. Hunt out this information. A good place to start is to check local, state or national heritage registers.

Identifying other Values

Other values, aside from those formally recognised by heritage specialists, are also important. These may be the less tangible aspects that make a place, region or experience special to the local community or to visitors. They may relate to its cultural, community, recreational and economic uses.

The Tourism Perspective

Stories based on heritage values, particularly those provided by local people, are often what make a place attractive to visitors. These stories are also what visitors take away with them and share with others when they return home. The combination of values, stories and landscapes, can create a total 'experience' for the visitor.

What are the Issues?

This step is about identifying all the important issues or factors that might affect what happens in the future. This means talking to people and looking at the information you have collected to date. Tease out the important matters that are unresolved or that will impact on your place, region or tourism product. Before you start, remember:

- issues are not always problems — they can be worked on and with
- identify conflicts in perspectives or issues — flag these for further clarification and analysis so that you can find ways to address them later
- focus on the issues and not the people raising them
- if people have identified issues, make sure these are considered through the next steps. People's views need to be reflected in the process and individuals should also be able to see their input
- in identifying issues, you may come across some which require expert advice or further investigation. This could include professional assessments of the condition of places, market potential, and visitor management and interpretation. Obtaining professional advice or digging out extra information may help to build a sturdier

foundation for planning future work, forecasting budgets and preparing for any necessary approvals

- a thorough knowledge of issues will also help you to develop performance measures and monitoring indicators as you address the issues over time.

Ways to Identify Issues

Identify issues clearly and thoroughly. Where necessary, consider using professional skills and approaches, such as those offered by facilitators experienced or trained in techniques for working with stakeholders and identifying issues. If you are undertaking this step yourself, think of running separate meetings or separate parts of meetings, so that people have a chance to think and talk about issues concerning them. Record what people say. Ensure everyone has an opportunity to express their view.

Further checks that can help you to identify important issues are:

- *Revisit step* 2 (who is involved?) and consider the issues that might come from different perspectives and stakeholders. If you don't have an understanding of issues from their point of view, how might you find this out?
- *Revisit step* 3 (what do we know?) to consider issues raised previously. Are there any recommendations that have been made before?
- *Revisit step* 4 (what is special?) and consider issues that arise when we understand what makes a place, region or tourism product special.

Identifying Issues

To help consider and cover the range of issues relevant to both tourism and heritage, it may be useful to consider:

- consumer/visitor experience
- community experience
- environment/heritage management and impacts
- infrastructure issues
- market/marketing issues

- tourism product availability
- economic cost/benefit issues
- training/capacity building
- strategic and resource context
- approvals and regulation.

Sometimes an issue is broadly identified, but not enough information exists on which to base a reasonable judgement. In this case, either you need to gather more information about the issue, or use some sort of analytical technique to develop a clearer picture.

Various types of analysis appropriate for tourism, heritage and business planning are detailed in the next step.

Handling Conflicts

It is important to identify areas of conflict, as these can reappear later as barriers to progress or action. Looking beyond the conflict of different ideas and people and getting to the root cause can often help to resolve the issue. Conflict is often inevitable. It can make ideas or projects unworkable, but it may also present opportunities for innovative solutions.

Various methods of conflict resolution and mediation processes exist. Rather than focusing on the particular individuals and their views and creating an adversarial situation, there are ways of working with interests to acknowledge views, explore issues and develop solutions cooperatively.

In some cases informal cooperative and collaborative approaches will be successful, others may require more formal approaches such as negotiation, arbitration or mediation. Using the services of a professional and 'neutral' facilitator can produce a good result.

Keys to managing and resolving conflicts include:

- having an inclusive participatory process
- maintaining open and effective communication
- being responsive and adaptable *and*
- building consensus between a majority of stakeholders.

Analysing Issues

Now that the issues have emerged from the last step, you may need to delve further to clarify what is going on. Important issues need to be fully understood if the right decision is to be made about a particular course of action.

Concentrate your efforts on analysing priority issues. If resources are limited you may need to make a judgement based on available information and analysis. Analysis may simply be a matter of presenting a reasoned judgement about an issue with justification of how you came to that position and citing what data or information supports this. More sophisticated analysis may help you to make better business and management decisions, but this can also be time-consuming and costly, so compromises may have to be made. In any case you should clearly state how you have reached your current understanding of the situation.

Many of the methods of analysis described below are standard approaches used in strategic planning. Some of them, such as market analysis, are essential components for business plans. You will need to decide what types of analysis are relevant or appropriate to your situation. The aim of using any analytical technique is to better understand factors at play in what might be a very complex situation. Analysis will also help to further identify and prioritise fundamental issues.

Key analytical methods may include, but are not limited to the following:

- market analysis
- heritage conservation analysis
- SWOT analysis
- situational analysis
- cost–benefit analysis
- priority analysis.

Market Analysis

A number of market-related issues would have emerged in the previous step. A market analysis is an analytical summary of how your region, place or product fits into the marketplace. It takes into account the saleability or profitability of a product or service, based on information about the product and the potential market. Market analysis may include an assessment of how your region, place or tourism product compares with existing competition.

- Are there others around competing for a similar market?
- What are their strengths?
- What are yours?
- Is the market big enough for people to share?
- How can your region, place or product be presented in the marketplace to maximise the fit between what you can offer and what people want?

Basically a market analysis should assess the supply and demand for tourism product, accommodation, transport and associated services relating to your situation. This type of analysis helps in positioning your product intelligently in the marketplace. You can estimate the market potential for a product using information on sales volumes for similar products or in similar regions. Industry statistics collected regularly across Australia may also be available from you state or territory tourism organisation (refer to contacts information).

Market analysis often includes a forecast of where the market is going. Trends over time may indicate how your product or service may fare in the future. In the summary of your market analysis you should explain the potential for future development opportunities based on market and trend information.

Heritage Conservation Analysis

In Step 4 you identified the factors that make your place special – its heritage values. In some cases, when the implications of tourism on a heritage place become clearer, you may need to revisit this question with further specific studies on the heritage values, or on particular technical issues that may affect how the site is used. One important type of conservation analysis is a condition analysis. This method uses trained heritage conservation experts to look closely at buildings, Indigenous sites or natural features and assess their physical condition, and their capacity to withstand visitors or other possible indirect impacts.

Situational Analysis

This is a description of the context in which tourism is currently occurring. It includes the main determining factors such as the seasonal or geographic flow patterns and the functional relationships at play. Understanding the situation is the first step in designing the response. A situational analysis involves analysing needs and assets, understanding what works well and what doesn't and the capacity of those involved. Including others in situational analysis helps to build a better understanding of the context or situation.

SWOT Analysis (Strengths, Weaknesses, Opportunities and Threats)

This is a very standard way to help identify and consider the issues identified in Step 5. A SWOT analysis is a simple and useful part of many types of strategic plans, including business plans.

In this process you will need to consider the *present* strengths and weaknesses of your situation and *future* possibilities for opportunities and threats. Remember, that the weaknesses and threats can become strengths and opportunities if addressed. This analysis will help you to get an overview of key issues, and will help to articulate issues that may not have come out in other ways. It is useful to undertake SWOT analysis after you have collected and considered information from issues identified in the last step.

Cost–benefit Analysis

This is a relatively simple and widely used technique. As its name suggests, simply add up the value of the benefits of a particular approach or idea and then subtract its associated costs. Costs are either one-off or ongoing. Benefits generally accumulate over time.

Costs and benefits can be financial, environmental and social. Putting a financial value on intangible costs and benefits can be more challenging and highly subjective. Cost–benefit analysis is linked to the concept of the 'triple bottom line' which is used as a framework for measuring and reporting performance against three key areas – economic, social and environmental.

Cost–benefit analysis can be done formally, using quantified financial measurement, or informally. A simple way to do this is to list in a table all of the expected costs and benefits.

Some cost–benefit analysis questions that could be asked in relation to a region, place or project:

Priority Analysis

You can determine priorities in many different ways, but one simple way is to look at the importance and urgency of the issues.

Consider each issue and its place on the chart. Issues that are judged to be both very important and urgent will obviously need to be addressed as a top priority.

The priorities for issues which fall elsewhere on the chart will depend on the issue and context.

The following questions may help you consider priorities, and place issues on the chart:

- are there options or actions that address important needs or gaps?
- which options or actions advance and support set priorities or responsibilities?
- is there a particular action that, if not taken, would result in negative consequences?
- what opportunities present themselves that should be pursued?

Ideally, you should do this analysis with a group of your stakeholders so that you develop a common understanding of your key issues. It will help point towards particular options and future courses of action, and will also help to build agreements between stakeholders on possible future directions.

Principles or Objectives to Guide Action

Now that you have an understanding of tourism and heritage values and the key issues at play, you need to consider more specifically what you want to achieve. This should be a balance between looking after heritage and developing tourism if, and where, appropriate.

In Steps 2 to 6 you drew together all the relevant background material and knowledge. Using this as your foundation you now need to consider where you want to go in the future. In this step you will develop specific objectives, or if appropriate, a general set of principles, to guide future work.

These principles or objectives, need to deal with the realities of tourism while maintaining and protecting what is special about the area's natural and cultural heritage.

It is very important that principles or objectives are agreed by key stakeholders and that they have a high level of ownership. Implementation of the principles works best when people feel they have played an important part in their development.

Principles

In some cases a general set of principles is the most appropriate way to guide the direction and breadth of future work. Principles can be expressed in the form of guidelines, protocols or policy statements.

For example, a tourism business might develop a set of responsible tourism principles, or a set of protocols might be developed with Indigenous communities covering issues relating to Indigenous heritage and tourism.

In historic heritage conservation plans, you can often find a statement of 'conservation policies'. Where these policies exist, they should be included in the principles as they are likely to guide the development of heritage tourism.

Objectives

Setting objectives is one of the most common ways of planning for the future. Objectives are sets of short statements that are like goal posts. They are something to aim towards, and can give a clearer focus to your plan and efforts.

Objectives should be written in clear language, be specific, measurable, realistic, and have a time frame. They are an important part of many planning documents, including business plans.

Objectives are created by thinking how you want the future to look. Build into your objectives words which reflect economic and community aspirations as well as the intention to take care of heritage. Objectives should be developed and owned collectively by stakeholders or business partners.

They can be written in several different ways. One approach is to state your intent, for example, *"to improve directional signage at..."*. The other way is to state the desired end result, for example *"signs installed at all..."*. The form you use will depend on personal preference and the context in which they are to be used.

You can measure whether or not you have met your objectives by developing indicators or tangible evidence of attaining your goals. You may also want to think about what milestones would help to break down your work into achievable stages. As your work proceeds, any reporting should focus on your progress towards achieving your objectives.

This is the means by which you and others can monitor performance.

Example of Objectives

- To develop a regional tourism strategy focusing on key areas which are linked by a particular theme
- To build relationships and communication between tourism operators, attractions and regional managers of natural and cultural heritage places through regular reporting meetings
- To improve the regional directional and interpretive signage relating to tourist and heritage attractions
- To maintain and enhance the region's international profile as an ecotourism destination
- To ensure that educational materials are available relating to the values of particular places
- To secure increased financial resources to promote the distinctive natural and cultural heritage assets of the region
- To build the capacity in the local community to support and participate in tourism through awareness raising and training activities
- To increase market share from 2% to 5% within two years.

What are your Ideas and Options?

You will have generated ideas and concepts as you have progressed through Step 3 (what information is there?), Step 4 (what makes this region, place or product special?), Step 5 (identifying issues) and Step 6 (analysing issues). The aims and objectives identified in Step 7 can help you to develop ideas and options in this step.

It's likely that you will have many different options and pathways to your final goal or goals. If you are working in a region or community, you may need to consider many possibilities before making a final decision. In planning for tourism the feasibility of one or more options may need to be tested and presented before funding or approvals are granted.

This step will help you to clarify your ideas and options, make decisions and prepare you for taking action.

Consider options by...

1. developing ideas
2. presenting ideas or options for testing
3. analysing issues further, if needed
4. developing recommended option/s
5. seeking agreement on preferred option/s.

Developing Ideas

As you have worked through this process, many ideas will have emerged or will have been put forward by the people with whom you have been working. Now you can bring those ideas forward and show how they might work. You may need to bundle together specific ideas into packages or groups of actions. You will need to take into account key issues and to ensure that you maximise opportunities and manage any threats. If clear ideas and options do not emerge at first, you may need to develop them through discussions, brainstorming sessions, focus groups or workshops.

In general, ideas and options should include:

- the visitor experience
- community engagement

- care of heritage assets
- infrastructure
- marketing
- product development
- stakeholder communication
- training and capacity building *and*
- necessary resources and support.

Consider Questions

Visitor Experience

- What will help improve the visitor experience?
- What specific interpretation activities could be undertaken to improve visitor experience?
- How are we meeting demand for the particular natural and/or cultural heritage experience being offered?
- How will interpretation be delivered/improved? (*Successful*
- *Tourism at Heritage Places* provides guidance on this)
- What heritage themes will be used?
- What activities will visitors undertake?

Community Engagement

- How can community engagement be maximised?
- Can community representatives be included in key decision making processes?
- How can the community be involved in tourism at a heritage place?
- What sort of regional cooperation will be pursued?
- Who will be involved in developing tourism?
- What partnerships could be further explored?

Care of Environment and Heritage

- How can heritage assets be best cared for?
- How will visitor impacts on values be managed?

- Will it be necessary to limit use of a place?

Assets

- What activities will directly contribute to maintaining a heritage place/asset?
- What steps will be taken to work cooperatively with park managers, site managers etc?
- What sort of actions will be taken to ensure the appropriate people are consulted in relation to Indigenous tourism, gender protocols, intellectual property etc?
- Are there significant plant or animal species requiring protection?
- Are there significant landscape values at the place —are they acknowledged or protected, how accessible are they and are they sensitive to visitor impacts?

Infrastructure

- How can you best plan for infrastructure?
- How can tourism planning integrate with current local/ regional planning?
- What will be pursued in terms of transport, waste, water and other services in order to meet visitor demand?
- What signage will be developed?
- Will the proposed infrastructure use sustainable energy sources, practices and technologies?

Marketing

- How can marketing be more effective?
- How will visitors find out about the product/place?
- Can marketing be done cooperatively at a regional level?
- What key information, such as minimal impacts on heritage values, can be communicated?
- How will marketing of Indigenous tourism be strategic and coordinated?
- A What is the marketing strategy?

- What are the place, regional and national themes?
- Will the product be promoted in visitor centres?

Product Development

- How can tourism products be developed?
- Is there good match between the product and the market?
- How will your product/experience complement regional tourism product/experiences?
- How can a better understanding of heritage values lead to new tourism products and marketing opportunities?

Communication

- What is the best way to maintain, maximise and improve communication between interests?
- Are new communication forums needed?
- How will you report progress on achieving aims to people who need to know or who might be interested?
- What representation should be sought in government and industry forums? and capacity building
- What capacity building is needed in the community and in individuals?
- What skill levels will be needed for staff to perform at the standard required?
- What business skills need to be developed?
- Can formal training, industry development or accreditation programs assist?

Resources and Support

- What resources and support are needed?
- What advice may be needed at different times and where can this be found?
- What best practice environment and heritage management
- will be adopted?
- What research is desirable or useful?

Baseline Data and Monitoring

- What data is needed about the physical condition of the environment or heritage places that will assist in monitoring potential positive and negative outcomes for conservation?
- What data is needed about and from visitors to ensure that in the future we can determine how effectively we are meeting customer demand and expectations?
- What data is needed about local community attitudes, issues, amenity and social conditions that will enable effective monitoring of the potential positive and negative effects of tourism?
- Who is responsible for collecting baseline data?
- What specific monitoring will be undertaken to ensure that significant impacts on environment and heritage assets, community health and business development are identified?
- What indicators might be necessary as a measure of performance for sustainable practice?

Presenting Ideas or Options for Testing

Once you have put together your ideas into a package or proposal that you think will work you can then present this to a group of informed people, a business or project team or a stakeholder group.

Use their knowledge and experience to test how your ideas might meet the needs of key interests while also addressing the issues and opportunities of the situation. When presenting the options you should give a realistic assessment of their feasibility and include information on proposed timing and required resources.

Analysing Issues Further, if Needed

When developing your ideas or options, you may discover that you don't have a clear picture of some important elements. If so, go back to Steps 5 and 6 to gather more information or further analyse your situation. If you have several possible scenarios, you can test how each scenario might fare in light of your market analysis. You might even want to conduct specific market testing of your ideas or product.

Developing Recommended Options

Once you have tested your ideas and gathered any extra information that you need, you can then develop your preferred options. These should be backed up by a clearly reasoned statement supported by the information you have collected in the steps so far. These options can then be presented in a proposal, feasibility study or strategic plan. Good communication and people skills can make a big difference when it comes to convincing others of the benefits of your recommended option/s.

Seeking Agreement on Preferred Options

Negotiating over the best course of action can be complicated by tensions between competing interests. Different stakeholders are likely to have different but equally legitimate priorities. At this point it is important to focus on the positive mutual interests that can link tourism, heritage conservation and communities and that can form the basis for cooperation.

Once a particular idea or option looks like meeting most people's needs, your next step will be to seek agreement through the necessary formal and informal processes. As you obtain agreements and support, make sure you document this for future reference.

How to do it?

The preferred options or ideas from the previous step now need to be turned into actions that you can implement! Making new projects or ideas happen may involve many stakeholders, organisations and groups. Even if implementation is the responsibility of one organisation or business, you will probably need to gain the support or approval of others. Whatever your situation, a clear implementation plan is essential. This not only makes sound business sense but is standard practice in project management. This plan can also be called an action plan or a work plan. In addition to developing this plan, each participating organisation may need to look at its own planning documents to ensure that the implementation plan links to existing planning documents. It may be worth having an overall implementation/ action plan for heritage tourism issues as a common agreed framework.

Additional Factors

Additional factors that are crucial to address include:

- strategies for political support
- communication
- capacity building
- making links
- staging
- influence.

Strategies for political support — consider and include actions that help build political support for what you want to achieve. Lobbying can be a legitimate and necessary activity.

Communication — good mechanisms for communicating are vital in bringing together diverse interests and helping them to work together. Consider and include any actions or activities that will make this happen. Too often these communication activities are not given the resourcing or attention that they deserve.

Capacity building — while training and staff or community development may be included as an objective of the plan, you may also want to think carefully about whether implementing the plan will need specific training or capacity building. What support or additional capacity do individuals or groups need to participate and play an effective role in implementation?

Making links — consider how different activities can link together to create a whole which is greater than the sum of its parts. Often the most efficient use of resources comes from piggy-backing on other initiatives and pursuing activities with multiple outcomes.

Staging — consider how actions can build up in stages over time to reach the desired result. At times you may need to reach one stepping stone before reassessing where to go next.

Influence – gain the support of other key players and influence other plans or activities to increase your ability to make a difference. Ways of gaining support need to be considered and included in your planning and activities.

Keeping on Track

Any strategic plan, development plan or action plan needs to be followed and referred to regularly to be kept relevant. The best way to use a plan is to constantly check and report on progress. You can do this through:

- performance measures or indicators
- monitoring and reporting *and*
- evaluating and reviewing.

Performance measures or indicators – these can be used to monitor progress and identify what is being achieved They help to demonstrate how well an organisation, program or strategy is meeting its objectives or when actions are not proceeding as planned. They can also show where performance can be improved.

Performance indicators can use qualitative and quantitative information. They should be relevant to the program's desired outcomes and objectives, be quantifiable, verifiable and free from bias. Indicators can be relatively simple, cheap and easy to measure.

You can develop these yourself or use existing indicators. Monitoring and reporting – build into your implementation plan key points at which to check your progress. It is a good idea to give formal progress reports to the group with responsibilities across both tourism and heritage interests. This will help keep attention on what has been achieved and what still needs to be done.

Timeframes for monitoring and reporting are important and should be carefully thought through. You need to allow enough time to determine if the outcomes are successful or whether you have made a significant impact. If unforeseen obstacles arise you may want to report sooner rather than later to avert negative consequences. You also need to consider how much time it takes to collect and collate monitoring data.

Evaluating and reviewing – your plan should also include a timeframe (three to five years is typical). A major evaluation and review should be conducted at the end of this time. This may lead to the plan being refreshed or the process being repeated to produce a new plan. Keeping track of progress means that efforts can be redirected and management continually adapted to suit changing circumstances.

Statement of Directions

If you are writing up a plan, this step is simply like the conclusion or executive summary. It summarises in as succinct a form as possible:

- the key heritage and tourism assets of the region, place or product
- the key issues *and*
- the agreements and outcomes reached between parties.

If you are using this process to run a meeting or series of meetings, or a major project, this step comes at the end so that all the people involved can see what they have achieved and can be clear about the outcomes. There may also be other creative ways to present your outcomes through images or other forms of communication. Whatever case, you will find this summary very useful for briefing colleagues, superiors and for including in newsletters, electronic information or media materials.

Planning for Tourism Marketing

Many businesses nowadays are working towards incorporating sustainability into the core of their products. Quite often these products are the result of a well thought sustainability concept, and yet the entrepreneurs behind it fail to reach the marketplace, because they lack marketing expertise and knowledge of the tourism industry's distribution channels. These tourism companies, and particularly small firms from developing countries, suffer from poor targeting, market segmentation and positioning, low consumer product knowledge, and consumer risk perception.

Distribution channels are key to increase the exposure of sustainable suppliers, and to capitalise on the latent market demand for sustainability by changing behaviour in non-sustainable firms. Each channel has strengths and weaknesses which are reviewed with a range of examples showcasing good practice. These channels are analysed from the point of view of the supplier for equity, cost-benefit, market penetration and normalisation potential. The results show that few channels have high equity, but many of them offer a good cost-benefit ratio, hence efforts are needed to provide opportunities for businesses. The market penetration and normalisation potentials show the channels with the greatest overall scope.

Policies should encourage industry associations and individual distribution channels to introduce sustainability criteria for their suppliers. A stepped approach could first introduce criteria where eco-savings can be made, and where sustainability is part of the quality evident to the client, as well as customer education. This first step aims to allow companies with low access to training and know-how to repay their investment through the eco-savings, and develop a proactive culture. A second step would require industry associations to introduce more complex standards such as labour and other fair trade specific issues, as well as deepening into the many aspects of sustainability that the clients may not notice during their visit, but will have great importance to the long term wellbeing of the destination.

Destination management organisations and tourist boards are useful to create destination brands and can act as sales portals. They can strengthen their role by setting standards and providing training. Tour operators are key sales channels that allow tourism companies to sell large volumes, usually at a lower price than if selling direct. Large operators, but also increasingly smaller ones are setting sustainability standards for their suppliers as well as support mechanisms. Guidebooks are very successful marketing tools but they require products to be unique and a long lead time, and as such are mid-term investments.

Media can be a powerful tool for consumer education and the challenge here is to feed interesting unique stories to the press that change consumer behaviour, as suchfor example a public relations clearinghouse on sustainability would be an attractive tool. Certification schemes are increasingly setting standards for tourism firms and providing guidance, but their implementation is not widespread and with low equity and low consumer recognition they are a tool for business to business lobbying. As such the recommendation is to experiment with their implementation.

Travel fairs are useful venues to for learning about the market and renewing contacts but their negative costbenefit means they are not accessible to most, and they should, therefore, be seen more as events to educate suppliers on marketing, and be packaged by tourist boards as part of training for developing companies. Internet retailing has the potential to reach a broader market but for the inexperienced tourism firm much training is needed, with priorities such as managing risk perception of consumers if operating their own website, to possibly paying high commissions for discounted last minute travel sites. More regulation of internet retailing will increase consumer trust and particularly help small firms. Finally, consumer organisations are powerful brands to endorse products, but as in the case of guidebooks, are mid-term investments and require clearer sustainability criteria, as well as a stronger contribution to consumer education.

Marketing Sustainable Tourism Products

Many entrepreneurs fail to understand the nature of the tourist industry as a marketplace, and assume that because they have an authentic and exciting tourism product, clients will find them. Many donors and policy makers also make the same mistake, funding conservation projects expecting that tourism will generate sufficient revenues for the long term survival.

Underestimating the challenge, as well as the cost of distributing tourism products is a key reason why new tourism ventures fail, and why many donor projects do not survive beyond the initial subsidised period. The challenges mentioned here apply in the majority both to sustainable and non sustainable tourism products. Reviewing the key stages of a marketing plan provides some background to this report. The first stage is a thorough analysis of the market, resources, competitors and the business environment. The second stage is to decide on the strategic choices of how to segment markets, to determine the markets to be targeted, and to plan an appropriate product positioning.

The latter part is to determine the marketing mix, which in its most basic sense means how the product will be offered to tourists, the price that will be charged, how the product will be communicated, and how it will be distributed.

It is through examining the requirements of these promotion and distribution channels that projects and firms face the reality check of what the market wants.

Key Stages of the Marketing Plan

Three key issues are highlighted below that influence the success of marketing efforts by tourism companies.

Many of these cannot be solved by individual tourist firms or even through collaboration at a destination level; it is however important to be aware of them to consider how they will affect the promotion and distribution of tourism products.

Analysis

- Market
- Resources
- Competitors
- Environment.

Strategy

- Segmenting
- Targeting
- Positioning.

Marketing Mix

- Product
- Price
- Promotion
- Distribution.

Three key issues are highlighted below that influence the success of marketing efforts by tourism companies. Many of these cannot be solved by individual tourist firms or even through collaboration at a destination level; it is however important to be aware of them to consider how they will affect the promotion and distribution of tourism products.

Targeting, Segmenting and Positioning

There are many examples of sustainable tourism products that are not viable because the supplier has failed to understand market needs, often through a failure to engage the industry in product development. This is sometimes the result of agencies working with host destinations that have suffered the negative impacts of unsustainable development, and then fail to involve operators, on whom marketing success often ultimately depends.

Resource based Instead of Market Led

Sustainability means authenticity, which in turn suggests that the tourism product should not be changed just to please tourists. But in doing so tourism products often do not take into account the expectations of tourists and the needs of tour operators.

Targeting International Markets

Too many businesses expect international markets to become the key source of income. This should be balanced with filling a good percentage of the capacity with domestic and short haul regional markets. This is partly to mitigate a destination's exposure to the vagaries of international tourism trends, but also because advertising in regional markets is almost always more cost effective.

Sustainability as Unique Selling Proposition

Marketing on the basis of sustainability is not going to suffice for most tourist segments and products, even when sustainability could be at the core of the product itself, and could be one of the determining attributes that the tourist looks for. For the vast majority of consumers, sustainability will only be a consideration when other criteria, such as price, choice of accommodation and availability of activities have all been satisfied.

Sustainability as Part of Quality

In the past, too many sustainable products in tourism and elsewhere, have performed worse in the basic quality attributes. Tourists are willing to purchase sustainable once the basic attributes of product quality are met. The win-win products in the sustainable, organic, fair trade sectors are those that provide added value.

Consumer Product Knowledge

If a tourist market knows the product well, the type of promotion can emphasise characteristics of the product or place that are meaningful to the tourist, whereas first time tourists will need more information about the product as prior knowledge cannot be assumed. Also repeat tourists are more likely to buy directly from suppliers that first time tourists.

Inexperienced Product Users

Tourists that buy a certain type of holiday for the first time are more open to education, but it is also less likely that their behaviour will be in-keeping with that of locals. First time tourists on a package such as trekking, diving or homestays have specific awareness raising and education needs before and during their experience, that will mark their behaviour for future trips. The product and the message to these first time users will need to be tailored to emphasise safety and customer care, whilst also communicating the need for cultural sensitivity and respect – insofar as tourism involves interactions that necessarily include an active and a passive experience.

Price Sensitive First Time Visitors

Many tourists experiment with destinations, visiting just once, making it hard for the service providers to communicate product quality, and relying on price alone to secure sales. Uniqueness and authenticity need to be reinforced for these first time visitors who lack the knowledge to demand them for themselves. Information sources that can be trusted such as travel guides and signs of quality for example are good vehicles to reinforce such messages.

Repeat clients encourage sustainability. Repeat clients are more likely to appreciate the unique characteristics of a place, usually related to sustainability. Lack of loyalty to destinations often means service providers do not see a short term benefit from providing the required services of quality, as those tourists leaving will not come again, and others just as gullible will follow.

Risk Perception

Tourists often do not want to book directly with service suppliers because they perceive risk. Small firms are perceived as more risky because they do not have strong brands to support them, and for this reason they will need to work in partnership to ensure purchases. Sustainable tourism products will have to work on reducing the perception of risk, by tackling the following:

Risk of the Unknown

A large volume of internet sales at present are repeat sales once the client knows the business, and they are mainly for airline tickets, car rental and hotel rooms in global companies with standardised products. This increases when travelling to countries for the first time, particularly when these countries are very different to the country of origin of the tourists.

Risk of Fraud

Secure purchasing systems that can give confidence to clients are necessary for small tourism firms to sell directly. At the moment a large percentage of direct sales are with large firms. The perception of potential fraud from giving credit card details to companies outside the tourists' home country is high, also raising concerns about data protection and the possibility of identity theft.

Risk of Virtual Companies

Tourists are less likely to want to book with small companies because of the perceived threat that these might not be real companies, the client has paid in advance for the service but once they arrive at the destination the company does not exist. Small tourism firms need the backing of stronger brands to provide reassurance to the client that they are sound companies. Retailing through a link at the national tourist board, or having the backing of consumer organisations can provide the kind of quality assurance that will increase bookings.

Risk of no Consumer Protection

Purchasing directly from tourism suppliers means that clients will not have the same legal protection as when they purchase a product from a tour operator in their own country. This is clearly the case in Europe, where the Travel Packages Act places responsibility for the quality of the product including health and safety on the tour operator. There is little regulation and only very limited consumer protection against false claims made on the internet by direct suppliers.

Distribution Channels: Current Practice and Prospects

The tourism marketplace is made up of a large number of tourism service suppliers trying to reach a multiplicity of tourist markets. They do so targeting the tourists directly, developing positive messages about their product through promotion channels, and working with intermediary distribution channels that will sell a range of services tailored to the market's needs.

Business to Consumer (B2C)

Tourism service suppliers can use a range of direct marketing channels such as database and internet marketing to attract tourists. The advantage is having a greater control over the message sent and the type of tourist attracted. The disadvantages are that this is done at a greater financial risk, with potentially high start up costs. Box 2 includes a summary of main channels for direct marketing.

Business to Business (B2B)

The main focus of this report is for suppliers to trade through intermediaries that take the role of either selling individual services, packaging them or doing the marketing and booking. Tourism suppliers benefit from outsourcing the cost and risk of marketing. The advantages are diversification of markets that reduce risk, a potentially secure level of business, and fixed commissions that facilitate financial planning. The challenges are less control over marketing messages, markets and income streams.

Most often, tourism suppliers combine the two: direct (B2C) and via distributors (B2B). In the latter case, intermediaries are used to provide a baseline level of business that ensures minimum occupancy rates or load factors, which provides a contribution towards fixed costs of capital repayment and salaries. Direct marketing is used to capture repeat visitors, particular market segments and for specific promotions. The balance between the two types of marketing is determined by how entrepreneurial the company is, the availability of knowledge and funds, and the interest of intermediaries to work with it. Promotion strategies are the consequence of the distribution strategy, with some of the promotion tools used to generate direct sales, or to increase the interest of distribution channels in working with these suppliers.

This section reviews the potential and challenges faced by different promotion and distribution channels to contribute to the marketing of service suppliers that are sustainable.

While eight distribution and communication channels are reviewed here, some of these (particularly tour operators) are much larger than the others, whereas some of them only have an impact on a niche market, or are highlighted here because of their potential for the future.

Direct Marketing Channels

Database marketing. This is more likely for national than for international clients, and few small companies hold databases of past clients. These can work with specialist outbound tour operators to be included in their client reminder newsletters, usually generated as part of database marketing tactics, by providing up to date copy on the product and destination.

Internet marketing. Service providers frequently try to promote individual products without any coordination. Too often, suppliers perceive all others as competitors, when in fact key consumer motivators are 'choice' and 'range', which means that products are only enhanced by demonstrating links to other local products and suppliers. Whereas some confident travellers would be happy to seek out extremely remote products, many would prefer to know that they form part of a more substantial product cluster in the chosen destination.

Affiliate marketing. One of the most effective forms of marketing is for suppliers to establish relationships with other organisations, often unrelated to tourism, who can market their products to their own customers. This might be through special interests, such as wildlife, heritage or sports, or through particular groups, such as clubs and associations or faith groups. Sometimes these can be arranged simply by identifying that a satisfied customer is involved in a particular group and that they would be enthusiastic about promoting the product to fellow members.

Joint marketing portals. National and regional tourist boards and incoming tour operators need to pull together different services through joint marketing portals. Selling individual products, however sustainable, will not get tourists to a destination.

To be meaningful, these products need to be grouped by their appropriateness to specific market segments and price ranges.

Repeat business and word of mouth. Established companies fulfil a large percentage of their capacity through repeat business, as it generally accepted that it costs five times as much to gain a new customer as to maintain an old one. At its most sophisticated, this can involve a powerful multi-media CRM (customer relationship management) system, but it can simply be the good practice of maintaining a record of all customers' (and enquirers') contact details-albeit subject to relevant data protection legislation, which should not be underestimated.

Destination Management Organisations (DMOs) and Tourist Boards

DMOs are agencies or marketing consortia (normally publicly funded, sometimes supplemented by membership subscriptions) that promote a 'destination' to outbound tour operators and both domestic and foreign consumers through a variety of media, and provide information on local products and suppliers. Sometimes, suppliers (e.g. subscribed members) receive preferential treatment.

The challenge for destinations is to identify the environmental constraints and impacts of tourism development, and to then engage local destination suppliers, buyers (foreign and domestic) and all visitors in embracing sustainability as a key element of the tourism proposition. The opportunity is to make excellent environmental management part of consumer motivation, in order to help ensure the sustainable development of tourism.

Some destinations have marketed themselves as being totally sustainable, although in reality this often reflects an emphasis on natural heritage, rather than indicating product sustainability. Tourism New Zealand's campaign "100% Pure New Zealand" is a good example of this approach, where this DMO concentrates on presenting a consistent message to position New Zealand as a sustainable destination.

There are examples of tourist boards giving additional promotion to firms that have met certain standards of sustainability. Places as far apart as Scotland and Costa Rica are promoting companies certified as sustainable, either by highlighting certified suppliers with an additional logo in their promotional material or by creating a separate dedicated brochure for sustainable products.

Oman's Ministry of Tourism, which is responsible for developing and promoting the country's tourism product, has designed a policy that places 'sustainable tourism' at its heart. But, whilst many foreign tour operators are enthusiastic about 'ecotourism', sustainability of the product is not really a consideration-their key requirements are the availability of airconditioned tourism facilities, 4x4 vehicles and 5* accommodation. Local expertise is generally focused on the physical environment, rather than an appreciation of the cultural and social dimensions of sustainabiiity in tourism.

The challenge for DMOs is often less about marketing sustainable tourism products, but more about raising awareness of what the sustainable development of tourism means for suppliers, which in turn will help to ensure the more sustainable development of tourism products. Remarking that the term "'responsible tourism' is more meaningful to suppliers", Oman's Dr. Aziz stated that the development of "the responsible tourism sector is one of the guaranteed ways of achieving sustainable development for the Sultanate of Oman." Thus the motivation for sustainable tourism products is national self-interest, and the opportunity is to encourage and facilitate more sustainable supplier practices. Oman is working to achieve this outcome through a programme of training and awareness raising, and by offering preferential terms to suppliers that adopt more sustainable practices. The former will be achieved through a national training programme, primarily targeted at tourism SMEs, whilst the latter will involve a schedule of discounts on marketing activities, including attendance at international tourism fairs. There can be other priorities that DMOs must tackle before they can even begin to focus on sustainability issues, but such circumstances can bring benefits, allowing DMOs to approach product development as a 'blank canvas'. Although it has a tremendous product, Yemen has been the subject of much negative publicity in recent years and has been considered by tour operators and consumers alike to be too outlandish a destination for mainstream tourism. This means that the focus has been to rebuild the country's image as a viable tourism destination. In fact, this challenging marketing environment also enables Yemen to highlight the sustainability of its products, adding real value to the destination. This involves all the *usual marketing activities, such as organisation of familiarisation visits for journalists and tour operators, production of promotional media in paper and electronic formats and attendance at major international tourism fairs.*

With a particular emphasis on cultural and nature-based tourism, the main themes being promoted are 'ecotourism' and activity tourism, especially diving, deserts, mountains and climbing, which are attractive to tour operators. With 70% of visitors coming from the MENA region (Middle East & North Africa), the Yemen Tourism Promotion Board (YTPB) is focusing on several key foreign markets and plans to develop a new multi-lingual website. This will be in Arabic, English, French,

German and Italian and in the future also in Japanese and Russian, in order to communicate directly with the consumer. According to the YTPB's Director, "sustainable tourism is fundamental, because it helps the economy of Yemen through the creation of jobs and investment; tourism is Yemen's future". With many diverse products and micro enterprises, YTPB's challenge is simply to "get Yemen into tour operators' brochures". Marketing sustainable tourism is not simply a marketing exercise, but requires integration across all social and economic sectors. Thus, echoing the approach of Oman's Ministry of Tourism, Yemen's General Authority for Tourism Development (GATD) is focused on the sustainable development of tourism. Observing that Yemen's tourism product is essentially its "environment and culture", the

GATD stated that the challenge is to keep this "intact", because "if changed, then Yemen loses". The aim of sustainable tourism is therefore to "encourage investors, reduce poverty and preserve cultural and natural heritage". However, since there is limited understanding of 'sustainable tourism', the GATD puts a lot of energy into engaging key stakeholders, especially community representatives, to promote the principles of sustainable tourism. It will support those communities that choose tourism as a development strategy, but critically, it will also respect those that choose to resist tourism. When introducing foreign investors, it will encourage them to promote local employment, and to use local food and building materials, again adding value to the product and helping to satisfy consumer demand for the 'authentic' local product.

Natour Communications has run a series of short online campaigns to change the negative perception of Venezuela as a tourist destination, using a database of over 8,000 e-mail addresses of travel agents, operators, media interested in the natural world and tourism. The campaign consisted of between 8 and 10 issues over three months depending on the specific messages, to promote the country's natural attractions and activities, and generating interest for a familiarisation trip for 24 international media and operators.

Familiarisation visits ('fam trips') bring invited press and selected operators to destinations to sample the product. These are especially of value to emerging destinations and to showcase new products in more established destinations. Tourist boards tend to sponsor and support these, and in some instances run them. Typically a fam trip takes 8 to 12 weeks to set up because it requires targeting participants, raising awareness, organising logistics and tailoring the trip to their particular needs. Natour Communications run a fam trip to the Caribbean island of Trinidad coinciding with the 3rd annual Shandy Carib Adventure Festival to showcase adventure, nature and cultural opportunities.

Tour Operators

These are organisations that sell holidays and travel products to consumers, taking a commission or margin on the product (or package of products) sold, which they have purchased from suppliers or are selling (as an agent) on behalf of suppliers. Additional income is gained through the sale of other travel-related products, such as travel insurance and foreign currency. In some cases, they will establish a 'partnership' relationship with their suppliers, working collaboratively with them on destination management, product development and direct marketing activities.

The key tool for tour operators is the 'service agreement', the contract between operator and supplier, whether an airline, accommodation or excursion provider or ground handler. It defines the service standards, including quality as well as health and safety requirements. The results of customer satisfaction questionnaires in areas such as food, facilities, staff and overall quality, often determine bonuses being added or compensation being paid if the supplier varies significantly from the required standard.

Some tour operators are starting to introduce environmental standards, but with only limited consumer demand, few are yet willing to link these to contractual obligations and financial penalties. The general approach is one of encouragement, with operators identifying key suppliers that might need to improve their environmental performance and are consequently offered mainly training and advice, and in fewer instances financial incentives. A large proportion of the work done by large tour operators to improve the sustainability of their service providers is by promoting the economic advantages of reducing water, waste and energy costs through being more environmentally friendly.

There are fewer examples of tour operators engaging their suppliers in improving their socioeconomic records, for example by providing better labour relations, support to communities or the use of local produce. For many specialist tour operators, sustainability is part of the product quality sought by tourists. In this case there are few examples for supplier development, but usually because a minimum sustainability requirement was part of the selection criteria.

Most tour operators are not likely to pay a higher price to their suppliers for sustainability. Generally they argue that sustainability is an element of the expected quality, and that it will also bring (in particular in the area of environmental practices in the accommodation sector) major cost savings. Supplier development initiatives are generally voluntary, with few examples of tour operators making them mandatory. Several large tour operators have reported that between 10 and 25% of suppliers have met the voluntary 'sustainability related' standards (for example Kuoni Switzerland, TUI, MyTravel Northern Europe, First Choice, Hotelplan). Tour operators are most successful in convincing long-term suppliers, and those that are owned or managed by the same parent company. Few tour operators highlight those suppliers that are more sustainable in their brochures.

The Reiseanalyse 2002 survey in Germany showed that tourists demand such information, but it is likely that many tour operators will not want to do so until a certain volume of their products have met the necessary standards, and they can send a positive reassuring message to the market.

The large German tour operator LTU Touristik distributed 16,000 environmental management manuals to accommodation suppliers in German, English, French, Italian, Spanish, and Greek. Impacts are rated by time and cost required to make a significant improvement. The manual is the result of long term development involving suppliers and destinations, and LTU Touristik requires feedback from hoteliers on the manual's usefulness and the hotels' performance. Hotels implementing this manual best are those managed by LTU itself and those where LTU brings a high percentage of their business.

Hello Tuscany promotes to young people a positive experience of sustainable tourism: the Summer Camps in Tuscany. Summer camps seem to be a very pleasant experience, since they combine the attraction of natural parks, a real interaction with a beautiful environment, and with local people with their own historical traditions. Kel 12 is a small Italian tour operator specialising in adventure holidays mainly in Africa, even though their presence is now widespread everywhere from the Sahara to China to South America.

It promotes the marketing of sustainable tourism products by working with destination agencies that share the same philosophy, including sustainability as purchasing criteria, running conservation and community projects in the field, and engaging consumers in projects. Examples of projects include protecting part of the Gabon forest, buying the rights on territories instead of the concessions involved in cutting wood, as well as a Sahara project to prevent accumulating big amounts of plastic waste using plastic tanks for water instead of plastic bottles.

The Dutch Tour Operator Association ANVR requires members to appoint and train a responsible tourism coordinator; develop and implement a responsible tourism policy; report annually to ANVR on at least one sustainability measure per each of five areas (accommodation, transport, recreation/excursions, consumers information and internal sustainability); and not offer travel products that are forbidden according to the developed list of irresponsible travel products. Similar requirements are being introduced in the UK through the Federation of Tour Operators.

Guidebooks

Most guidebooks are produced by independent commercial publishers. Although some guides might be openly commissioned as marketing tools by individual travel companies, guidebook publishers are generally independent of the travel industry. They identify products and destinations, giving objective opinions (both good and bad), and are sold to consumers, including conventional tourists and business travellers. These guides rely on the quality and objectivity of their messages to be trusted by travellers. Additional revenue can be earned from advertising and the production of associated online editions, but the most trusted guidebooks keep their information independent from commercial ties.

Freelance travel writers are commissioned to write individual books. In general, the appointed writers receive a very specific brief by the guidebook editing team, which outlines the guide, the structure to follow, including the characteristics of the companies to be included in the guide. The authors also receive (in particular if their task is an 'update') all the information collected on the country and in particular on hotels and tourism services that they will have to personally review. The briefs are developed taking into account the specific target audience. In general however, travel guides are increasingly including sustainability charters, as well as sections on environmental and socioeconomic issues at the destinations.

These writers research hotels, restaurants and attractions following the criteria of the travel guide according to their market positioning and unique selling proposition. Many guidebooks emphasise unique, exciting and interesting products that are aligned to the principles of sustainable tourism, although few will use explicit criteria for the selection of what towns and companies are to be included, and the final decision depends on space and a balance between different destinations and types of product. Sustainability is often referred to as far as it is part of the exciting and unique attributes that the independent tourist is seeking.

The companies publishing traditional guidebooks are evolving to produce customised guidebooks, spin-off guides and unique travel information, licensed use of web engine or travel information, and to selling photographs. Travel information is now not only coming in the typical guidebook form, but also increasingly in electronic form, whether on websites or in phone/PDA formats. All of these provide new niche opportunities for tourism companies and destinations. Highly professional guidebooks are now also being produced by non-governmental organisations and campaign groups, for which the motivation is development assistance, rather than commercial profit. The focus is increasingly shifting to the consumer, since publishers are discovering that these publications meet a market need, giving objective (and entirely noncommercial) advice on obscure community-led tourism products, offering consumers access to 'authentic experiences' with less of the more negative aspects of tourism. By being produced by not-for-profit organisations, consumers treat contents as a strong seal of quality assurance, which helps increase sales of sustainable tourism products, which in turn promotes best practice in tourism and across the industry.

As in the case of travel media, the ability to be included in a guidebook depends on whether the product can be presented as being exciting, quirky and unique. Sustainability is sometimes the reason why a product is interesting, but the message has to be tailored with the tourist experience as the centre of attention. The guidebooks support sustainable tourism products within the limits of having to honestly report about quality of the services provided, and when a company with a sustainable ideology provides sub-standard services, this has to be highlighted.

Over 100,000 Lonely Planet travellers use the electronic Thorn Tree travellers' bulletin boards on a regular basis, where travellers can exchange information on destinations and experiences, and plan their next adventure. This makes Lonelyplanet.com a vibrant heavily trafficked global travel resource. Lonely Planet also sends a monthly email newsletter to thousands of readers.

Lonely Planet's Shoestring guides have a large readership amongst young people travelling for the first time. These guides include extensive information on responsible behaviour in their travels, and the choices of places to visit reinforce this *philosophy. Lonely Planet has however been questioned for publishing a guide that encourages tourism to Burma* (Myanmar (Burma). *8th ed., 2002.), despite their claims that the guide raises awareness and supports the type of firms that will least* support financially the oppressive regime.

Sustainability is at the core of Lonely Planet, although this has so far happened more intuitively than strategically. The company is now examining how they formalise their commitment to sustainability. Their French branch has produced an Ethical Charter, and Lonely Planet Europe would consider explicit sustainability guidelines for both their authors of guides, and for the suppliers of services to be featured. In their own forecast they estimate that in 10 years, 40 to 50% of the products listed in their guides could have verified sustainability credentials.

Tourism Concern, which "campaigns for ethical and fairly traded tourism" is currently planning the third edition of it's the Good Alternative Travel Guide. *Working through its large international network of tourism stakeholders, known as the 'Fair* Trade in Tourism Network', it is able to identify a wide range of sustainable tourism products, including community-based tourism initiatives primarily and responsible tour operators.

With Access to Extensive Language skills, the Organisation is not constrained by having to communicate in English, and is able to research many products in often remote and marginal destinations. Products that pass a preliminary review are sent a questionnaire (in an appropriate language), which is used as the basis of assessment and to determine which products meet sufficient criteria of fair trade and responsibility to be included. There is no fee for inclusion, although there is some income from advertising, and those that are rejected are offered advice and guidance on best practice, since "the objective is to change the industry". Two hundred products were included in the guide's second edition, of which 10,000 copies have been sold, and which is supplemented by promotion at trade fairs and online listings. Tourism Concern's website receives 9,000 unique site visits each month, making this a highly effective medium. Feedback from suppliers has been extremely positive, with over 100 new suppliers contacting

Tourism Concern in the past twelve months seeking inclusion in the next edition, reflecting the recommendations and value placed on the medium by existing suppliers. According to Tourism Concern, the guide is particularly valued by suppliers, because the organisation "shares information across its network", promoting best practice and contributing to the development of 'fair trade in tourism'. Whilst for consumers, *who are "a bit more socially responsible" and "want to take a different kind of holiday", its value is that it is "not just a marketing tool", but is* "effectively *a certification scheme". Some consumers seek product endorsement, whilst suppliers* recognise the benefits of working with an independent organisation with fifteen years of international network experience. Insofar as the guide is a tool for normalising sustainability and promoting best practice, Tourism Concern describes the guide's contents as "tourism that's developed in the context of sustainable development".

Media

Media includes the travel section of mainstream newspapers and consumer magazines, as well as dedicated travel magazines. Most income comes from advertising revenue, whilst the content primarily consists of stories, reviews and features about particular destinations and products. Newspapers also offer commercial opportunities through affiliate marketing initiatives (endorsing and featuring holiday offers in the newspapers for a commission for the newspaper instead of paying a price for the advert). The travel pages of newspapers are the key promotional channel for specialist tour operators other than word of mouth.

But, just as the point of newspapers is to sell news, the point of travel journalism is to promote travel. Therefore, according to *The Independent,* sustainability is "not an issue", because ultimately "people want to go on holiday, even if they want to travel more *thoughtfully*". The newspaper has certain values, which means that it will tend to encourage community-led tourism and promote small guest houses, cycling and public transport, but it also has a commercial need to gain advertising revenue, which cannot be constrained by considerations of sustainability, on which there is no specific policy. The editorial view is that for consumers, the theme of 'sustainable tourism' is "boring... like travel insurance", but that at the same time 'sustainable tourism products' are generally "more interesting", (said the freelance journalists interviewed for this report).

Travel pages of newspapers have a small team of staff editors that commission the work from freelance editors, who have to pitch ideas that are original, new, interesting and also good ideas for holidays. Freelance writers look for ideas that will sell. Funnelling interesting stories from the tourism provider and the travel media is the gap. Training tourism companies on how the media operates, and how to identify the relevant freelance journalists with the right stories is crucial. Original, quirky, interesting stories of exciting and unique places to go and things to do have the greatest potential to be featured in the travel pages. The emphasis sought by freelance journalists and travel editors is on why these are good holidays. Giving money to charities, investing in schools, saving turtles all play a part in the feature, but not in the opening paragraphs. In doing so the media contributes to consumer education in a more subliminal way. A feature on the importance of responsible tourism per se would only be a story once, while this way there is a way to keep communicating the underlying principles.

Tourism firms need to plan the message to be communicated, emphasising first why it is exciting and unique. They require thinking from the point of view of the consumer, and not focusing first on conservation, and they first have to make an interesting travel proposition.

Messages need to be newsworthy, so products are easiest to be featured when they are new. For products that have been on the market for some time, companies need to think of ways to reinvent messages in the public relations tradition to ensure their products have maximum exposure. For example, the UK project promoting bicycle routes 'Sustrans' had already received extensive exposure for their work in the 1990s, and yet they are being featured again for introducing public artwork along their routes to attract more families to cycling. Celebrities visiting a sustainable tourism company and supporting the cause is another way of getting repeated exposure. Several newspapers run travel awards that highlight good practice and have become great marketing methods for the few companies winning. *The Times* dedicated four pages to the winners of their Responsible Tourism Awards (organized by the online travel agent responsibletravel.com, in association with *The Times*, World Travel Market and *Geographical Magazine*). Many independent tour operators use their winning status to promote themselves, and a number of sustainable tourism products have dramatically increased their bookings and reputation through winning one of these awards.

The Guardian *newspaper in the UK runs a monthly column called The Green Light, featuring responsible holidays, based on market research that identified a gap in the market. "Go diving with octopuses" was the incentive to read about an* Earthwatch project in Costa Rica monitoring octopuses and their habitat. The tour operator Discovery Initiatives was featured in two mainstream UK television travel programmes, The Holiday Programme and Wish You Were Here. In both cases the productions were well received and stimulated a great deal of interest. The Holiday Programme feature was further repeated in at least one revised format suggesting recognition by the producers of the value of this type of holiday.

Certification Schemes

Certification schemes highlight sustainable tourism products. They have a dual function of helping tourism suppliers to raise their sustainability standards, and providing market mechanisms to increase trade gained from having the brand of the ecolabel. There are over 60 initiatives, targeting mostly the accommodation sector, and mainly in Europe. Most of them have started since the mid 1990s, with 20 more in development at present.

These schemes have the dual role of increasing industry performance by providing guidelines on how to be more sustainable, directing applicants towards sources of help and in some cases providing advice directly, and at the same time providing marketing benefits. As the certification programs grow, they are promoting the certified companies to both distribution channels and to consumers.

However, there are too many labels, with few certified products each, to have an impact on the market. Consolidation of current labels for international recognition, and repositioning of the labels as being an extension to traditional product quality (particularly for ecotourism markets) are obvious avenues forward. In only a few instances will sustainability be a unique selling proposition that can be meaningfully branded.

The certified product is not meaningful to the consumer for two reasons: firstly, lack of awareness, and secondly, the perception that it does not have significantly different attributes. Consumers cannot tell from the available information whether a certified product is better than the average product, on the points that matter to the tourist. The small number of certified companies, and the fact that the basic quality attributes are very different (a 5 star hotel and a guest house can have the same environmental label) means that choosing providers based on an ecolabel is not likely. This is partly attributed to the fact that certification programs have no in-house marketing or communications specialists.

VISIT is the acronym for 'Voluntary Initiatives for Sustainability In Tourism', the result of 10 ecolabels uniting forces to raise standards across Europe and to benefit from the economies of scale of joint marketing and lobbying. The EU funded project Tourlink supports tour operators to standardise their sustainability checklists with those of certification programmes. This will create more transparent and cost-effective distribution systems for certified companies, and reduce technical barriers to trade from multiple but similar standards.

Green Travel Market offers tour operators a tool for receiving reliable, up-to-date information on more sustainable tourism products currently available on the market, screened for quality and sustainability. Amongst others it includes over 1000 certified accommodation providers in Europe. The Sustainable Tourism Certification Network of the Americas aims to make sustainable tourism firms more competitive by providing market advantages through certification. The goal is to involve 175 enterprises in certification by 2007.

Technical assistance to suppliers to date includes 21 trainers trained, 507 entrepreneurs trained, and 1686 introduced to best management practices through seminars. This effort is being implemented in four pilot countries by Rainforest Alliance-Costa Rica, Alianza Verde in Guatemala, the Ecuadorian Ecotourism Association (ASEC),and Programme for Belize.

Consumer and Trade Fairs

Travel and tourism suppliers ranging from individual products to national tourist boards use fairs to present their goods and services to travel trade buyers and consumers, including prospective tourists and business organisations. Key sectors of the fairs market include leisure tourism, independent travel and MICE (Meetings, Incentives, Conferences & Exhibitions although in North America and Asia Pacific, the 'C' is usually 'Conventions').

The number of specialised fairs addressing the topic of sustainable, eco and responsible tourism is increasing, while traditional national fairs are developing these themes as well by offering specific events or pavilions and forum of discussions. Individual companies are unlikely to attend many fairs, particularly small providers, for cost reasons. Learning about the market is useful, particularly at the early stages of developing a company. The majority of firms will not be able to justify the cost, even when they are selling under the umbrella of the national tourist board's stand.

Business travel, as evidenced by the MICE sector, has traditionally not been considered particularly relevant to sustainable tourism, but this is changing. With the growing importance of 'corporate governance' in business and the associated shareholder exposure to corporate risk, buyers are increasingly seeking out suppliers that have strong sustainability credentials, and are asking to see companies' environmental policies and evidence of 'corporate social responsibility'.

The Centre for the Promotion of Imports for Developing Countries, an agency of the Netherlands' Ministry of Foreign Affairs, sponsors community based tourism and NGO's under certain conditions and provides marketing assistance prior, during and after the Vakantiebeurs' Fair in Utrecht, Netherlands, such as brochure and website design and negotiation skills, as well as organising meetings with relevant tour operators.

Reisepavillon is the alternative travel fair running annually in Hanover, Germany, attracting 250 stands from 50 countries in 2004 (the 13th year of operations, up 10% from 2003). There is a high exhibitor turnover, with 39% of new exhibitors, and 20% of non returns. Networking of experts provides the edge to this fair, with parallel meetings and project briefings by associations and institutions such as Ecotrans, Bund für Umwelt-und Naturschutz, Viabono, WWF, Naturfreunde and GTZ, the German Agency for Environmental Co-Operation. GTZ supports the fair by organising the industry networking and training event, Tourismus Forum International (TFI), and also bringing 20% of the stands by showcasing developing ecotourism projects from developing countries.

Consumer fairs such as Chicago and New York have rebranded from specialist adventure shows to more mainstream to attract a broader public and companies. In doing so they have attracted first time buyers for specific product types such as adventure and eco tourism because the fairs showcase products not usually found in travel agencies, with actual sales made on the show. These fairs are days out, with 22,000 people paying USD 15,00 each to enter the New York Adventure and Travel Expo. The activity holidays and shortbreak tour operator Inntravel organises a day long travel fairs where suppliers from all over Europe are invited to the UK to meet directly with customers. The fairs are held every three years in different parts of the country, with the most recent in

December 2004 in North Yorkshire. About 120 suppliers (including hotel owners, restauranteurs and service providers such as ski-hire companies) presented their products and services to 1000 customers and potential customers. Attendance is by ticket only because of the high demand, although tickets are free. Inntravel staff – including directors, product managers and sales staff are on hand to answer enquiries and take bookings.

IMEX is the leading MICE fair held each year in Frankfurt, with three schemes to showcase best practice and to promote corporate social responsibility in its sector. These are gaining in prestige and each year attract a growing number of applications. The Programmes of Purpose Award for Social Responsibility "recognises meeting organisers who have put together meetings or incentives benefiting the local community – undertaking charitable acts can be inspirational to participants as well as lastingly beneficial to the community concerned".

The Environmentally Responsible Meetings Award (in association with IHEI and Oceans Blue Foundation) "recognises environmental awareness amongst meeting organisers, highlighting the opportunities that now exist to stage business tourism events in 'green-minded' venues, whilst also planning an agenda in which sustainability issues have been taken fully into account". The Free Wild Card Places is one of the most innovative awards, enabling emerging destinations with MICE potential to participate and access new markets.

Internet Retailers

These are on-line retailers, in some cases complementing conventional operators and agents, but usually they are a global distribution system for mainstream products. This category also includes holiday auction sites and over-branded in-house websites used to sell distressed stock. There are very few sites that are selective and control their product according to strict quality criteria, and sometimes they act as 'matchmakers' between suppliers and operators. Retailers act as sales agents and sell products direct to consumers, and also via travel agents. Income is mainly from commission, and also advertising revenue and registration fees. The distinction between 'matchmakers' and 'sales agents' is both practical and legal. Whilst both might gain a commission from the transaction, a 'matchmaker' introduces potential clients to suppliers (and sometimes vice versa), whilst an 'agent' sells the tourism services of a supplier directly to customers, although consumers might be under the impression that they are dealing directly with the supplier.

Internet retailers can also be divided into two categories: high volume-low margin and low volume-high margin. The large internet retailers compete on price and supply a commodity market, whilst the many small ones focus on specialist products, particular niche markets or are dedicated to a small number of suppliers, sometimes in a single destination. The smaller retailers therefore gain tremendous expertise, but at the expense of a balanced portfolio, which would reduce their exposure to the risk of an unexpected fall in their chosen field.

The websites of vertically integrated tour operators, such as TUI, Thomas Cook and MyTravel, and those of other large tourism service providers, such as international hotel groups, airlines and car hire firms, are not considered here. This is because such websites are an extension of conventional retailing, rather than representing a specialist distribution channel.

However, unlike holidays booked through tour operators (whether online, by telephone or through a travel agent), consumers will often not have the same protection provided them by the Council Directive on package travel, package holidays and package tours (90/314/EEC of 13 June 1990). Thus, whilst the larger internet retailers have developed fairly comprehensive contractual and regulatory frameworks that offer a measure of protection to consumers, the smaller ones have adopted a more precautionary approach, to protect both their customers and their own businesses. Many have therefore adopted more of a 'matchmaking' role, so that their legal agency (and liability) is limited, but their ability to freely make a much wider range of specific recommendations is enhanced. Consumer confidence in the smaller retailers thus becomes a function of commercial independence and transparency.

One of the fastest growing internet retailers is the UK-based responsibletravel.com, which has grown by 250% each year since its launch in April 2001. It acts as an 'introducer' for suppliers, matching suppliers to customers and also bringing together suppliers and operators. Its 260 suppliers in 140 countries are known as 'partners' or 'members' and between them offer 2,000 individual products; its customers are primarily in English-speaking markets, with 80% in the UK, but this is changing.

Every supplier is carefully screened and each product must fulfil specific criteria that include environmental, social and economic policy. This process typically takes 7-10 days. All partners must have the capacity to respond to email enquiries in English within 48 hours. Each partner pays an annual fee, which ranges from nothing for community-led enterprises to more than £5,000 for the largest tour operator, plus commission per converted enquiry, which is never more than 10%. The company insists that it is "not a middle man, because the supplier knows best". Thus, it generates booking enquiries for its partners, who are then responsible for converting these into sales.

With a strapline inviting visitors to "Find 1000's of holidays to 100's of places not ravaged by mass tourism", the company distinguishes itself from the larger internet retailers, like lastminute.com and Expedia, both of which have huge brand recognition but which lack the capacity to deal so individually with customers. Its objective is to "market responsible tourism as a different and better product than less responsible tourism". Many of responsibletravel.com's "best sellers are wildlife trips, walking holidays... [and] more adventurous family holidays". Given that such products are nowadays in fact very mainstream, this indicates that the online marketing of sustainable tourism is no longer a niche activity. A leading UK tour operator has reported that it achieves more sales through responsibletravel.com than through any other internet retailer.

Consumers of such products however inevitably require a lot of information which only the supplier can furnish. A customer identifies a product through the company's website (with every page individually subjected to highly sophisticated search engine optimization) or through one of its increasingly numerous newspaper supplements, sends an enquiry (via the website) to the supplier, who responds with full information and booking details.

Such a service could not be offered by large retailers, if only because enabling such communication would put their commission at risk, but it is part of the unique proposition of responsible travel.com. This process is, of course, subject to audit which is possible for a relatively small operation.

Known primarily as a B2C agent, responsibletravel.com is particularly proud of some of its B2B activities: enabling tiny community tourism businesses to engage with leading international tour operators, helping numerous journalists to identify some excellent sustainable tourism products, generating significant PR opportunities and additional business for its members. It has rarely lost a member, because it offers good value for money and has created a community of suppliers and customers that value authenticity and the direct approach. Apart from offering all the usual add-on products, such as flights, travel clothes and insurance, the company also offers 'Tips for responsible travellers'.

Consumer Organizations

Consumer organisations promote the rights and interests of their members, through product testing, policy lobbying and conducting information campaigns. Consumer organisations whose mandate is to protect consumer rights are increasingly showing interest in the sustainability of products as part of their overall quality, and as such are reporting quality and sustainability standards to their members.

These communicate and distribute a range of information to their members that influences purchasing behaviour, and in many cases they also provide holiday accommodation and booking services. Consumer organisations' recommendations to their members are powerful marketing tools because of high member loyalty and because their assessments are perceived as independent.

In addition to general consumer organisations, there are 'membership' associations such as automobile and caravanning associations. The Alliance Internationale de Tourisme (AIT) and the Federation Internationale del' Automobile (FIA) have more than 42 million members in Europe, and 100 million plus members globally. They are champions of the 'mobile consumer', with the focus of their public policy agenda being sustainable mobility, road safety, consumer protection and testing, environment and tourism. Their work has focused on increasing the quality and safety of driving, and within this, driving holidays. These clubs promote cleaner emissions, reducing road congestion and increasing safety.

Promoting sustainable tourism has to be seen within the remits of both organisations. For automobile clubs this means they are information providers within the mandate of consumer protection. They have enormous media resources and reach with strong brands and reputations. The ADAC association in Germany is considered more credible by young people than the Church and Green Peace, while in the Netherlands three out five households have ANWB membership. The services these consumer organisations provide to their members include hotel guides, camping and caravanning guides, maps, holiday guide books and route planners amongst others based on the clubs' own inspections, evaluations and assessments which take some sustainable practices into account.

Camping and caravanning associations, in particular, have engaged with a range of environmental actions for their own sites, and setting criteria for other sites. In the UK the Caravan Club has an alliance with the Royal Society for the Protection of Birds as 11% of CC members are members of RSBP. AIT & FIA conduct environmental audits for camping and caravan sites, support for the new European tourist accommodation Eco-label, and the monitoring of European Bathing Water Quality.

The Consumers Union (USA) is considering sustainability certification as the criteria for including tourism suppliers in their travel directory. This is within their organisational remit of providing unbiased product testing and consumer information to protect the interests of consumers. Their publications have 6 million subscribers in the United States alone, and are part of the Consumers International global network of 250 organisations in 110 countries. The Alliance Internationale de Tourisme & Federation Internationale del' Automobile would consider a policy to increase the coverage of sustainable tourism issues in the magazines of their national member associations within Europe. *The Camping and Caravanning Club (UK) operates over 100 club sites, and is starting to operate franchised sites. With over 400,000 loyal members, the club provides one of the strongest camp site brands. One of their most recent acquisitions in the Lake District has been renovated to the gold standard in the Cumbria for Excellence 2004 awards in the Caravan Holiday Park category, and was quoted by* The Guardian *newspaper as possibly the greenest camp site in the UK.*

Analysis

Traditionally governments, inter-governmental organisations and non-governmental organisations have encouraged sustainable tourism by focusing mainly on the supply side of the tourism industry, or on promoting responsible citizenship through consumer education, with the aim of increasing demand. Matching supply and demand is the missing link. Specific policies should then be designed to support the linkage between sustainable consumers and sustainable tourism products by strengthening the opportunities offered by the various distribution tools. The four issues used to assess each of the eight distribution channels under consideration are designed to indicate the relative value of each tool. It is generally recommended that policies should be based on the ability to promote change of tourism suppliers that is equitable, with potential for market penetration, a positive cost-benefit analysis, and normalization or mainstreaming potential.

Supplier equity: High/Low-'High' indicating that this tool/ channel is extremely accessible on fair terms to a wide range of suppliers Market penetration potential: Strong/Weak-'Strong' indicating that this tool/channel has significant reach (B2B or B2C) Cost benefit analysis (supplier perspective): Positive/Negative- 'Positive' indicating that the receipts and other business benefits produced by this tool/channel can reasonably be expected to outweigh any costs associated with participation Normalisation potential: Strong/Weak-'Strong' indicating that this tool/channel has the potential to be used to promote and encourage a more sustainable development and environmental management of travel and tourism products

Supplier Equity

Equity, understood as the ability of companies to have the same opportunities to access knowledge, loans, distribution channels, and to promote their products, is the first attribute used to analyse these tools. Public sector intervention in the marketplace has usually been justified on the basis of promoting equal access. Policy makers should promote equitable tools, and contribute to the equity of the different tools, because otherwise the danger is that only a few privileged companies will be able to market themselves as sustainable, through no fault of the remaining companies.

Destination management companies, tourist boards and guidebooks have the highest level of equity in as far as all companies can have the same access to use these channels. Communicating and distributing through tour operators and internet retailers have varied equity because it depends on the ability to set commercial relations with them, and to accept the commissions they charge. Media, travel fairs and certification schemes have low equity, because they require capital investment usually with little guarantee of return, only few companies can be featured, or there are no schemes available.

Training at an early stage is crucial to support product and destination planning. Marketing training will help to set realistic targets, and to create more level playing fields that will make all instruments more equitable. Policies should support companies and destination management organisations to learn about their markets, particularly about expectations and purchasing patterns, and how this affects the marketing and service delivery. Development plans should be realistic and market the marketable, as part of a plan for sustained and balanced growth.

Market Penetration Potential

Some distribution channels have the potential to make a considerable contribution towards changing the behaviour of the market they target. For all these markets, the greatest potential is to change behaviour in the adventure, ecotourism, nature tourism markets where sustainability is part of the quality of the product both experienced and expected, as the potential market is already sympathetic to the philosophies of sustainable tourism.

DMOs and tourist boards rarely reach the actual markets, although increasingly internet marketing portals are achieving where print publications failed. These are custodians of the destination brand and as such can create interest in a certain destination. Providing an internet sales portal that allows efficient bookings increases the potential for market penetration.

Suppliers can achieve considerable market penetration through tour operators, with many examples in the past of over relying on few operators, that subsequently meant suppliers losing entrepreneurial skills and self-control. Travel guides are important marketing tools because they reach a large number of people within one given target market, and the readership of these travel guides use the information to make purchasing choices.

However, individual suppliers need to consider working with travel guides as a mid-term investment, as there is no guarantee that they will be featured, and there is a considerable lead time between preparing information and the publication date. The media can generate short-term interest in specific destinations and provide a boost to companies starting with creative, unique concepts. But media has a short self life and cannot be relied on.

Certification has limited potential for market penetration at present because the marketing know-how as well as resources of certification programs are insufficient to reach consumers. The focus should therefore be on business to business marketing and lobbying tour operators that certified products can guarantee sustainability.

While progress is being made in this respect, it is too early to say what the potential actually is. Travel fairs have very limited potential for market penetration, particularly business to consumer. They are better tools to reaffirm current working relationships with distribution channels, and to learn about market trends. Internet retailers also have a high potential for market penetration, although this depends on the type of product and market targeted, and there is often a high commission to pay for internet retailers. "Dynamic packaging" that allows consumers to pick and choose different components of a holiday from the same travel site to form a personalized package. Finally, direct marketing has good potential for niche marketing, and to encourage repeat purchases.

Companies should think about promoting to the domestic market, and the extension of current products, before trying to attract new "hard-to-reach" international tourists. Donor-funded projects in particular should be realistic about the ability to generate markets from small interventions. Many funded projects cannot be self-financed in the long run through poor understanding of market needs, simply incorporating tourism as a form of income generation for conservation projects without developing the necessary skills, or market-led product planning which sets unachievable expectations.

Cost-benefit Analysis

Cost-effectiveness is the third key issue reviewed here to consider the suitability of different tools. These are considered both from the point of view of government intervention as well as the investment for tourism companies. DMOs and tourist boards are cost-effective ways for small firms to market themselves, membership costs are usually low for the service received as these organisations receive central funding to contribute to their fixed costs.

Most governments undertake economic impact assessments that suggest that public sector investment in marketing functions generates a return on investment into the economy through tourism revenues in the region of 8 to 1. Policy makers are also increasingly being asked to contribute to the running of certification programs, as an extension of their duties in quality assurance.

The challenge here is that all these programs require substantial subsidies, and despite individual examples of good practice, the impact on the market is not sufficient to justify the investment. These certification programs need to move towards being self-financing. In the same way, many travel fairs require subsidies and growth is hindered by the potential benefits they can deliver, and by how many fairs one company can attend.

Distribution tools that do not require public financial support include tour operators, guidebooks, and internet retailers. Marketing to tour operators is also a cost-effective method to reach markets. There are directories of outbound operators for most key markets, and the national tourist boards of the destination country should provide the necessary market inteiligence to support targeted campaigns. In the same way, marketing to internet retailers is cost-effective if the company can survive with the commissions charged, and if reasonable yield management arrangements are made. Guidebooks are a cost-effective method for unique products with a high chance of being included. However, as there is no control of how the product is featured, the supplier might not agree with how they are portrayed. Getting a good review in the media can make a significant difference to the launch of a product. But spending too long on a media campaign could be cost ineffective if the product does not have uniqueness. Finally, direct marketing can be cost-effective for specific markets and to capitalize on consumer loyalty.

2

Techniques and Strategies in Development of Hospitality Industry

Although the hotel, catering and tourism (HCT) sectors produce an estimated 3-4 of GDP in most of the world economy and employ approximately 3 percent of the world's total labour force, its workers earn "on average at least 20 percent less than workers in other economic sectors," . And while technology, deregulation and globalization are fuelling growth prospects in some up-market segments of the tourist trade, the prospects for smaller and medium-sized enterprises (which produce most of the employment benefits) are increasingly unclear.

The wage differential is due to the "higher proportion of unskilled workers" employed in the HCT sector, where working conditions are often characterized by part-time or low-paid jobs. "Up to half the workers in the industry are under 25 years old and up to 70 percent are women,".

Migrant workers are another vulnerable group which tends to be overly-proportionately employed in the sector, with migrants concentrated in lower paid and less stable segments of the job market due to such factors as language or unfamiliarity with the host culture.

Often very young children work in the tourism sector, particularly in small, family-based enterprises, but often on their own as vendors or helpers: "The worst form of child labour in tourism is seen in the sex trade," the report notes. Though the problem is widespread, the report notes the increasing indignation of the international community at this exploitation and highlights "the increasing participation of international employers and workers' organizations and the World Tourism Organization in combatting child prostitution in tourism".

Other labour problems affecting the industry are high staff turnover, irregular working hours, low levels of unionization (less than 10 percent) and intense pressure on human and environmental resources as tourism becomes increasingly competitive and reaches into far flung destinations where institutional resources are weak or inadequate.

The true scope of the economic and employment importance of tourism becomes even larger when one considers that each job in the sector, generates an estimated one-and-a-half additional (indirect) jobs in tourism related sectors and in some regions tourism provides direct employment to as much as 10 percent of the workforce.

If both direct and indirect employment is taken into account, "the total tourism related economy has been estimated to produce as much as 11 percent of GDP and to employ 8 percent of the labour force worldwide," according to the World Travel and Tourism Council.

In recent years, the highest annual growth rates have been registered in South Asia (9 percent), the Caribbean (7 percent) and Eastern Europe (5 percent). In contrast, Europe is growing at around 2 percent and Asia Pacific by only 1.4 percent in the aftermath of the Asian financial crisis.

Cross-border tourism has grown faster than tourism overall, and is expected to increase by 4.5 percent over the next 20 years. "During the year 2000," the report notes, "almost 700 million tourists crossed a border and spent over US$500 billion while abroad". The deregulation of air transport and resulting fall in air fares is a major contributing factor to the globalization of tourism: "In developing countries no less than 80 percent of international tourists arrive by air."

The quality of tourism services is also changing rapidly, with travel becoming a regular part of the lifestyle of populations in wealthier nations and the better-off in developing countries, the ILO report finds.

Trips are becoming shorter but more frequent, with new market niches, such as nature tourism, ecotourism and adventure tourism flourishing in response to consumer demand and often yielding substantial benefits to populations in remote rural areas where agricultural incomes tend to be declining. According to the ILO report "the spread of information technologies enables tourism providers to cater more efficiently for a more diversified clientele". However, these benefits are not evenly spread. The report cites concerns about "the relatively low participation of developing countries in electronic distribution and reservation systems run by large air carriers, which do not sufficiently take into account the needs of small and medium-sized enterprises (SMEs)".

While large hotel chains are constantly increasing the scope and efficiency of their operations through mergers, franchising arrangements and increased linkages between air carriers, hotels, travel agencies and retail distributors, "independent enterprises tend to be left behind,". This is troublesome because it is precisely the SMEs that "employ at least half the sector's workforce and represent a majority of its enterprises".

Tourism in the Developing World

Although often underestimated, the tourism industry can help promote

- peace and stability in developing countries by providing jobs, generating income, diversifying the economy, protecting the environment, and promoting cross-cultural awareness. Tourism is the fourthlargest industry in the global economy.
- However, key challenges must be addressed if peace-enhancing benefits from this industry are to be realized. These include investments in infrastructure and human capacity, the development of comprehensive national strategies, the adoption of robust regulatory frameworks, mechanisms to maximize in-country foreign currency earnings, and efforts to reduce crime and corruption.

- The case studies of India, Kenya, and Nigeria reveal several important points. First, relative peace and a degree of economic development are preconditions for a successful tourist industry. Second, although it has the capacity to help promote peace and prosperity, tourism can also cause a great deal of harm unless it is carefully developed. Third, to deliver optimal benefits, tourism must be respectful of the environment and mindful of cultural and social traditions. Fourth, tourism must be supported by a coherent national strategy and robust laws.
- For tourism to help deliver prosperity and stabilize communities effectively, specific action must be taken by three main constituencies: host communities, host governments, and foreign stakeholders. Host communities should work to leverage their competitive advantage, improve service delivery, and protect their environment and culture. Host governments should establish supportive strategies, introduce and implement necessary regulations, remove bottlenecks, and adopt internationally recognized tourism standards. Foreign stakeholders could prioritize tourism as a viable economic force, direct investment to this sector, and facilitate knowledge and technological transfers.

Tourism is a vital part of the global economy. Generating roughly $1 trillion in global receipts in 2008 (up 1.8 percent from 2007), international tourism ranked as the fourth-largest industry in the world, after fuels, chemicals, and automotive products.

1. The breadth of international travel also has greatly expanded in recent years to encompass the developing world. In 1950 just fifteen destinations—primarily European—accounted for 98 percent of all international arrivals. By 2007 that figure had fallen to 57 percent.
2. Once essentially excluded from the tourism industry, the developing world has now become its major growth area. Tourism is a key foreign exchange earner for 83 percent of developing countries and the leading export earner for

one-third of the world's poorest countries. For the world's forty poorest countries, tourism is the second-most important source of foreign exchange after oil.

The economic might of the tourist industry has helped transform societies, often for the better. Tourism has several advantages over other industries: It is consumed at the point of production so that it directly benefits the

- communities that provide the goods.
- It enables communities that are poor in material wealth but rich in culture, history, and heritage to use their unique characteristics as an income-generating comparative advantage.
- It creates networks of different operations, from hotels and restaurants to adventure sports providers and food suppliers. This enables tourist centres to form complex and varied supply chains of goods and services, supporting a versatile labour market with a variety of jobs for tour guides, translators, cooks, cleaners, drivers, hotel managers, and other service sector workers. Many tourism jobs are flexible or seasonal and can be taken on in parallel with existing occupations, such as farming.
- It tends to encourage the development of multiple-use infrastructure that benefits the host community, including roads, health care facilities, and sports centres, in addition to the hotels and high-end restaurants that cater to foreign visitors.

With these benefits in mind, the United Nations has identified the development of tourism as one of the methods poorer countries might use to meet the Millennium Development Goals (MDGs). For the first MDG—alleviating poverty—the merits of tourism are evident. It can provide jobs and generate income for communities that, in some cases, lack viable alternative means of employment. In an assessment of Nigeria's potential for tourism, Francesco Frangialli, the former head of the UN World Tourism Organization, argued that with its "capacity to spread its socioeconomic benefits to all levels of society ... tourism can be a leading industry in the fight against poverty." With its tendency to produce flexible labour markets and offer diverse working opportunities, tourism can also help realize a second MDG, that of promoting gender equality.

In Mali, the World Tourism Organization's Sustainable Tourism for Eliminating Poverty (ST-EP) program has supported an effort to train the female artisans of Djenne, one of Mali's oldest and most visited towns. In Costa Rica, women's handicraft cooperatives catering to the tourist market have flourished, providing many women, for the first time, with both independent incomes and improved self-esteem.

If carefully managed, tourism can also be an important part of promoting a sustainable environment, another of the MDGs. Frangialli identified tourism's potential for not only protecting the natural environment, but also "preserving historical, archaeological, and religious monuments; and stimulating the practice of local folklore, traditions, arts and crafts, and cuisine."

Finally, as tourism by definition involves the transfer of people, culture, and ideas, it is ideally placed to foster effective global partnerships, the eighth MDG. In addition to advancing development goals, some have credited tourism with helping to build and sustain peace.

Among them is Wangari Maathai, the Nobel laureate and founder of the Green Belt Movement, who highlights tourism's potential as "a great vehicle for peace promotion." Whether tourism can actually bring about peace or whether the relationship is better described as mutually reinforcing, Corazon Gatchalian and Cindi Reiman conclude that through its tendency to promote "communication between nations and cultures," tourism is an instrument that "creates a global language of peace."

That said, while tourism can bring positive benefits, good does not necessarily follow. In recent years, tourism has tended to be a delivery mechanism for some of the darker effects of globalization: health pandemics and terrorism. International travelers enabled the outbreaks of severe acute respiratory syndrome (SARS) and swine flu to spread rapidly across borders. And holiday destinations, tragically, have become a popular target for terrorists, who want to maximize civilian casualties and publicity for their actions. In recent years, Mumbai, Bali, Sharm el-Sheikh, Dahab, Mombasa, and Casablanca have come to be associated as much with mass bombings and killings as with tourism.

Ecotourism

While conventional mass tourism often negatively affects host environments, other forms of tourism have emerged in recent decades that are more sensitive to their surroundings and offer tangible benefits to the local labour force.

These newer forms of tourism have come to be known as ecotourism, an umbrella term best defined as responsible travel to natural areas that conserves the environment and improves the well-being of local people.

Since it first emerged in the late 1970s, ecotourism has spawned several other travel concepts that are, in essence, variations on the same theme. These include geotourism, pro-poor tourism, sustainable tourism, responsible tourism, and travelers' philanthropy.

They are united by the simple idea that tourism should offer a benefit—and not incur a cost—to the host community. They reflect the desire of many holiday goers to give something back to the places they visit, or at the very least, avoid doing them harm. A number of countries have tailored their tourism industries adeptly to reflect this desire and have reaped economic rewards while minimizing the environmental and social impacts of growth. Costa Rica led the way in developing the ecotourism concept, followed closely by Ecuador, Tanzania, Kenya, and Nepal.

Kenya, Nigeria, and India are three developing countries with tourism industries at different stages of maturity. Kenya has a long-established and highly successful tourist sector catering to the conventional and ecotourism markets. As the table demonstrates, international tourism is a lucrative source of income for Kenya, accounting for 2.24 percent of the nation's gross domestic product (GDP) in 2006. By contrast, Nigeria barely has a tourist industry at all, reflected by tourism's paltry contribution to national wealth, just .02 percent of GDP in 2006. India has several tourist centres but, given its vast size, it has yet to realize tourism's economic potential. International receipts from tourism made up just 0.35 percent of its GDP in 2006. In Kenya, which has had a longer time to finesse its strategy, ecotourism is starting to bring about the progress that Honey describes. Conservationist David Western, the author of a study of Kenya's tourism industry, explains how Kenya learned from some of the mistakes it made when it began building its safari-based tourism industry.

He discusses how Kenya became the first country in Africa to establish both an ecotourism society and a framework for assessing the social and environmental impact of resort developments. He also illustrates the importance of generating domestic tourism by offering free or heavily discounted national park fees to its citizens.

Most important, he shows how Kenyan communities have benefited directly from tourism by running their own wildlife conservation areas. However, the picture he paints is not overwhelmingly rosy. While pockets of good practice exist, a fair share of Kenya's tourism tramples on local customs, is indifferent to conservation, and fails to pass on economic benefits to host communities.

Planning in Tourism

Planning is the dynamic process of determining goals, systematically selecting alternative courses of actions to achieve those goals, implementing the chosen alternatives and evaluating the choice to determine if it if successful. The planning process regards the environment which includes political, physical, social and economic elements as interrelated and interdependent components which should be taken into account in considering the future of a destination area.

Reasons for Tourism Planning

Tourism planning is greatly needed. The stagnation and decline of a destination or attraction may be due to the lack of planning or poor planning.

Good Practice Guide On Planning for Tourism

Tourism, in all its forms, is of crucial importance to the economic, social and environmental well-being of the whole country. The planning system has a vital role to play in terms of facilitating the development and improvement of tourism in appropriate locations. This chapter is designed to:

- ensure that planners understand the importance of tourism and take this fully into account when preparing development plans and taking planning decisions;
- ensure that those involved in the tourism industry understand the principles of national planning policy as they apply to tourism and how these can be applied when preparing individual planning applications;
- ensure that planners and the tourism industry work together effectively to facilitate, promote and deliver new tourism developments in a sustainable way.

The Local Value of Tourism

Tourism can bring many broader benefits that will contribute to the economic and social well being of local communities as well as to individuals. It can:

- be the focus of regeneration of urban and rural areas, as has been demonstrated by its success in Birmingham and in many seaside resorts;
- provide a catalyst for growth in an area, raising its profile and stabilising out-migration;
- provide opportunities for retraining for the resident workforce and help to diversify over-specialised economies; and
- help maintain and expand underused sports and recreation facilities in urban areas; and

The revenue generated by tourism can help to:

- support and enhance local services and facilities such as shops and pubs, particularly in rural areas;
- secure the retention or upgrading of public services such as public transport, health centres and libraries;
- support a broader and more vibrant and active community by attracting arts, sports or cultural events;

- aid diversification within the rural economy; and
- underpin the quality of the local environment and facilitate further enjoyment of it by residents and visitors.

These benefits can be particularly valuable in rural areas as they may provide amenities that people would otherwise not have access to. Tourism depends heavily on the natural and built environment and can also be the key to maintaining and enhancing the environment:

- The economic benefits of tourism in particular can help to sustain and improve both the natural and built physical environment.
- Derelict land and buildings may be brought back into use and the countryside can be better maintained.
- Visitors to historic buildings, archaeology and landscapes can provide income or voluntary effort which help maintain and conserve such assets.
- In rural areas the health of the environment and of the community depends on the viability of the local economy. So areas which attract visitors for their scenic beauty and which enjoy income from tourism will be better able to afford to sustain the local environment.
- Proposals involving high quality design improve the visual and environmental experience for visitors and the local community alike.

Planning for Tourism

The planning system, by taking a pro-active role in facilitating and promoting the implementation of good quality development, is crucial to ensuring that the tourism industry can develop and thrive, thereby maximising these valuable economic, social and environmental benefits. At the same time, the planning system aims to ensure that these benefits are achieved in the most sustainable manner possible.

The example below gives an overview of how one local authority, the London Borough of Greenwich, has worked actively through the planning system to underpin the development of tourism in its area.

Good Practice Guide on Planning for Tourism

The work of the Planning Department has been crucial to its success. This work has included:

- dedicating specific parts of the development plan to tourism and its promotion. This followed from consultation with the tourism sector including the World Heritage Site Steering Group;
- consultation with stakeholders on planning applications and involvement with partners in the preparation of planning briefs;
- preparing a hotel strategy that actively promoted sites to hotel operators & developers. This has led to two new hotels being built and increased visitor spend in the local economy;
- lobbying with private sector partners for improvements in public transport. This has helped secure investment in light rail, underground and river transport services;
- active engagement with small hoteliers and owners of bed and breakfast establishments to give advice on planning matters;
- securing contributions to tourism initiatives throughs 106 agreements, and voluntary contributions for marketing; and
- working with developers and operators to secure local employment and business opportunities

A Planning Framework for Tourism

Principles of the Planning System

Tourism is an important industry. Its future development will be secured by tourism developers engaging with the planning process and by those operating the planning system recognising that importance. This section sets out the principles of the English planning system which governs all forms of development including planning for tourism.

Sustainable development is the core principle underpinning planning. At the heart of sustainable development is the simple idea of ensuring a better quality of life for everyone, now and for future generations. The planning process provides the opportunity to help to make new development more sustainable, both through the preparation of development plans and when decisions are taken on specific schemes. The outcomes should be developments which:

- provide well-designed, safe and accessible development, and create new opportunities that will improve the well being of individuals and the regeneration of communities;
- result in the more efficient use of land and bring forward sufficient land to meet a wide range of expected needs;
- provide a supportive framework for economic growth and successful business;
- create vibrant, vital and viable town centres;
- reduce the need to travel; and
- protect and enhance the natural and built environment and safeguard natural resources.

Plan-led System

The planning system in England aims to realise these objectives of sustainable development through a 'plan-led' system of development plans prepared by regional planning bodies and local planning authorities. These plans lead the subsequent development by setting a framework which helps to provide both an overall strategy for that development and policies for the determination of individual development proposals. Where these plans contain relevant policies, applications for planning permission should be determined in line with the plan unless material considerations indicate otherwise.

These plans have a number of key characteristics:

- they provide developers, businesses and communities with certainty and predictability about future development in an area;
- they are transparent so that users can readily understand them and the information and assumptions upon which they are based;

- they are flexible so that they can be adjusted to meet changing circumstances and priorities. Planning authorities must ensure that plans are kept up to date and report annually on how their plan's policies are being achieved; and
- they are drawn up with community involvement and present a shared vision and strategy of how the area should develop to achieve more sustainable patterns of development.

Development plans should reflect and build upon the Government's statements of national planning policies. The development plans prepared by regional planning bodies and local planning authorities are known respectively as regional spatial strategies (RSS) and local development frameworks (LDFs). Planning policy statement (PPS) provides advice on the preparation of RSS and planning policy statement (PPS) provides advice on the preparation of LDFs.

The preparation of RSS is a statutory requirement. They:

- provide a broad development strategy for the region for a fifteen to twenty year period;
- should contribute to the achievement of sustainable development;
- are locationally, but not site, specific;
- are focused on delivery mechanisms which make clear what is to be done by whom and when;
- should be well integrated with other regional strategies, including any regional tourism strategy;
- should address sub-regional issues where appropriate; and
- provide a spatial framework to inform the preparation of LDF documents, local transport plans and regional and sub-regional strategies and programmes that have a bearing on land use activities.

Local development frameworks should be:

- based on a clear understanding of the economic, social and environmental needs of the area;

- clear, succinct and easily understood by all;
- underpinned by a comprehensive and credible evidence base; and
- 'front-loaded', seeking consensus on issues and taking key decisions early in the process.

Development plans are expected to take a spatial planning approach which integrates land use policies with other policies and programmes. The aim should be to coordinate spatial plans with urban and rural regeneration strategies, regional economic and housing strategies, community strategies and local transport plans. Wherever possible, spatial plans should be consistent with these other strategies (including any strategies for or relating to tourism) and be drawn up in collaboration with those responsible for them.

Development plans should have a clear vision about the pattern of development they are seeking to achieve in the area and clear objectives for achieving it. These should reflect the needs and problems of the communities in that area.

They should be concerned not just with what can be built where and in what circumstances but also how the range of social, economic and environmental objectives will be achieved through plan policies. The plans should focus on outcomes, with specified indicators so that the progress made by the policies in meeting these desired outcomes can be measured.

Developing Tourism through Strategies and Plans

Regional Spatial Strategies (RSS)

At the regional level, regional planning bodies will need to decide how to deal with tourism in their RSS. Specifically they will have to decide whether:

- to treat tourism as an issue in itself;
- to subsume it within another issue such as economic development; or
- to deal with it as a consideration affecting a number of issues like the economy, the environment, regeneration and transport.

They should do this on the basis of the overall approach that they are taking in their RSS and in the light of the information they have gathered.

Whatever the chosen approach, the RSS should make clear:

- its vision and strategy for tourism in the region;
- how this contributes to broader regional objectives;
- what level of growth in tourism it is trying to achieve; and
- what the spatial characteristics of this will be.

Where the Regional Development Agencies (RDAs) have Produced Regional

Tourism or Visitor Economy Strategies, the RSS should draw on these as well as providing a context when such strategies are reviewed. They provide greater detail than the Regional Economic Strategies and may have specific spatial or locational dimensions. The West Midlands Visitor Economy Strategy contains the following vision for the future of tourism in the region, and an important context for RSS review.

The RSS should also make clear what the key tourism characteristics are and how these are expected to change during the period of the strategy. This should cover:

- what the scale and distribution of tourist activity within the area is and what it is likely to be. The strategy needs to be clear what degree of change it is seeking to oversee, what the nature of that change will be and where it will occur;
- likely future trends and change in volume, distribution and type of activity.

There needs to be an understanding of what the underlying trends are and how the strategy intends to respond to the opportunities which they present;

- what the implications of those trends are for land-use, traffic flows, and the transport system. It should explain the extent to which these trends are (i) dependent upon improvements to the transport network and (ii) where they are likely to increase the need for such improvements;

- identification of areas within the region where there are, or are likely to be, any problems associated with growth or decline in tourism. For example, it might be necessary to reconcile demand for tourist accommodation with the need for affordable housing within an area;
- how increased demand for tourism might be best accommodated. It might be that the provision of accommodation and attractions should be increased in towns adjoining existing resorts in order to spread the benefits and to diffuse pressures;
- environmental impacts of tourism and, where these have adverse effects, how they can be tackled;
- the need to protect key tourism assets. In addition to features that already have statutory protection (e.g. national parks), there will be other features such as the wider environment, the quality of beaches, choice of accommodation, availability of sports and leisure facilities and the presence of 'night life' that are important in sustaining the attractiveness of the area; and
- ways in which tourism can contribute positively to other objectives e.g. economic development, regeneration, rural diversification, conservation, and environmental improvements.

Local Development Frameworks (LDFS)

LDFs should comprise a number of development plan documents including the core strategy, site specific allocations of land and area action plans. Any need for further development plan documents, or supplementary planning documents, should be identified in the local development scheme, the purpose of which is to inform the public of the planning authority's programme for the production of local development documents.

In a similar way to regional planning bodies, those preparing LDFs will need to decide how to deal with tourism issues within the framework. Like RSS, the approach should seek to produce a plan which is integrated with other strategies that have been prepared for the area, including any that relate to the future of tourism.

In those locations where the future development of tourism is a key issue for the local authority, it will be appropriate for the core strategy to cover tourism issues together with any objectives relevant to tourism. In other local authorities it may be that the plan's broad approach to economic growth and regeneration sets the framework for the future development of tourism. In these cases this relationship should be acknowledged and taken into account in the development of the core strategy.

Those preparing LDFs should consider whether any policies for tourism are needed beyond what is set out in the core strategy. In determining the scope of the work required and what planning documents should be prepared, it will again be necessary first to decide whether tourism is to be addressed as a single issue or as part of a wider topic, such as economic growth. Where site allocations for tourism are made, these should follow from the objectives set out in the core strategy.

In some areas in which tourism and its growth are a key part of the spatial strategy, it may be appropriate to depict this in spatial terms in the core strategy such as in a key diagram. In specific locations where development for tourism is particularly crucial to meeting the plan's objectives, the core strategy could propose an area action plan to focus and programme the elements of that development.

In order to keep policies to a manageable number, authorities should aim to support the policies affecting tourism in the core strategy in the following ways:

- putting detail on matters such as mitigating the effects of development (e.g. by landscaping) into supplementary planning documents;
- putting good practice messages in other documents or in supporting text; and
- not repeating national or regional policies in LDFs, although LDFs should indicate how the objectives and any targets for tourism contribute to those set out in the RSS.

Where tourism is an important element of a LDF, the approach will need to be based upon a robust understanding of the characteristics of, and trends within, the tourism industry based on similar issues to those set out in RSS.

Bournemouth offers an example of where such an analysis of trends has occurred. This has provided the basis for the planned approach of diversifying tourism facilities at an important tourism destination whilst at the same time retaining the essential tourist accommodation. Although this was done through its preparation of its Local Plan and Supplementary Planning Guidance under the previous system of development plans, the approach in terms of analysis and response would be equally applicable to a LDF approach.

Devising Good Tourism Policies

General Principles

The strategy for tourism in the emerging development plan will provide the context for producing any specific policies for tourism. Whilst policies need to be developed to suit the particular circumstances of an area, there will be certain common features of a good tourism policy. Where specific tourism policies are included in a plan, they should aim to:

- maximise the benefits of tourism, in particular ensuring that the development is able to reach its potential to contribute to tourism in the area and for local communities to enjoy those benefits;
- identify optimal locations, for example to maximise synergies with other tourist attractions and to promote opportunities for access by public transport;
- integrate development with its surroundings both in terms of design and layout and in the way that the service or facility is able to function; and
- avoid adverse impacts, for example by disturbance to activities on adjacent land.

Planners will need to understand and often reconcile a number of important factors when preparing such policies, in particular:

- market demand – sometimes market demand will exist in a very precise location. This might be to do with prominence or accessibility. In other cases the demand will be of approximately the same level throughout a wide area;

- environmental impact – this can have a large number of facets, such as visual and noise impact, impacts on an historic setting, impact upon biodiversity and upon landscape quality. Impacts may be positive, negative or a mix of both;
- transport and accessibility – travel is an inherent element of tourism.

Whilst recognising that it is a principle of the planning system to seek to promote more sustainable transport choices, improve accessibility and reduce the need to travel, this may be particularly difficult for some types of tourism projects or for areas that are poorly served by public transport;

- functional links – whilst some forms of tourism may, in commercial terms, be able to be directed to a variety of locations (e.g. a hotel) others will be much more specific in their land use requirements (e.g. a visitor centre for a cathedral);
- regeneration benefits – tourism developments have the potential to bring jobs to an area, to improve physical appearance and to support local businesses and services. Plans to bring tourism into an area will often be developed in order to realise some of these advantages; and
- labour supply – the amount and quality of the labour supply will vary from place to place. Planning will often seek to locate new development where the need for jobs exist or where the population might benefit from a wider range and quality of employment.

The importance of these factors may vary for different developments and over time.

Tourists visit different areas for different reasons and to enjoy different experiences. It follows that the built infrastructure required for tourism will therefore vary from area to area. Tourism is certainly not a 'one-size fits all' product. In particular, different approaches may be needed in urban areas from those in rural areas.

Tourism in Urban Areas

Tourism can bring benefits to urban areas and help to deliver development that is sustainable. Amongst the particular advantages that tourism can bring to towns and cities is to:

- be the focus of regeneration, or help to underpin it;
- help to increase urban vitality and support linked trips;
- be a key ingredient of mixed-use schemes;
- support important services and facilities; and
- facilitate improved access by sustainable modes of transport.

There are many types of tourist and leisure activities that particularly lend themselves to urban locations and which exhibit these advantages. These include:

- hotel, guest house and bed & breakfast accommodation;
- cinemas, theatres and concert and bingo clubs;
- museums, galleries and conference facilities;
- restaurants, bars, pubs, casinos and night clubs; and
- indoor and ten-pin bowling and health & fitness centres.

Planning authorities need to ensure that they have assessed the need for these facilities and have allocated an appropriate range of sites which allow genuine choices to meet those needs.

Similarly, it is for developers and operators to ensure that they have anticipated what their need for such sites is likely to be and that they undertake active discussions with local planning authorities about these requirements.

Tourism in Rural Areas

The provision of essential facilities for visitors is vital for the development of the tourism in rural areas. Tourism can:

- be a key element in rural and farm diversification;
- help to revitalize market towns and villages;

- support important rural services and facilities; and
- underwrite environmental schemes and improvements to the built and natural environment. RSS and LDF policies should therefore engender a positive approach to rural tourism proposals, applying the following principles:
- Wherever possible, tourist and visitor facilities should be housed in existing or replacement buildings, particularly where they are located outside existing settlements.
- In statutorily designated areas they should seek to conserve and enhance the qualities and features that justified the designation.
- Large-scale tourist proposals must be assessed against the whole range of sustainable development objectives. This includes not only their transport implications but also other sustainability considerations such as how they assist rural regeneration and the well being of communities.

Planning Policy Statement 7 (PPS7) : Sustainable Development in Rural Areas sets out specific national planning policies on tourism and leisure in rural areas.

How to Plan for Tourism

To ensure that their development plans are effective for future development of tourism and thereby provide a framework to make sound planning decisions on tourism proposals, planning authorities should:

- develop and maintain a thorough dialogue with representatives of the tourism industry;
- ensure that this dialogue helps to support a sound data base on the characteristics and needs of tourism in the area; and
- use that data in applying effective techniques designed to ensure that those needs are met as fully as possible.

Involving Stakeholders

It is likely that a large number of groups and individuals will be affected by strategies and proposals for tourism in a particular area. Planners will need to ensure that they have:

- adequately canvassed and considered all of these views;
- in particular, received and understood the views of the community affected and those with a commercial interest in what is proposed; and
- done this at the earliest possible time, in accordance with the principle of 'front-loading' that is an element of the new development plan process.

The Government has issued advice about how the community and other stakeholders should be involved at all stages of the planning process. This is contained in its planning policy statements (PPS) and supporting guidance.

In meeting the requirement to consult business interests, the regional planning bodies will need to ensure that the tourism business interests that they engage are sufficiently wide-ranging and representative of this large and diverse sector. Annex D of PPS identifies potential participants in the RSS revision process. In addition to bodies in that annex that might be consulted to help develop the regional approach to tourism development, specialist tourism organisations such as the Tourism Alliance, the British Holiday and Homes Parks Association and the group of 'Tourism heads' of the Regional Development Agencies will also be potential consultees.

Key Inputs from the Tourism Industry

Plan-making and review is a continuous process, and this needs to be reflected in the way that stakeholders are consulted and involved. Plan-making bodies should develop constructive dialogues with key players in the tourism sector, and build partnerships with those who have a role in delivery of tourism schemes and programmes. Above all, there must be constructive and effective engagement with the tourism industry. This will help to ensure that plans are developed with the benefit of a realistic and sustainable commercial perspective, and that those plans relate well to the aspirations of the industry. In particular tourism operators and developers will be able to provide information and views upon:

- tourism markets, levels of demand and planned investment: those making plans for or affecting tourism will need to know what the principal tourism activities in the area are, whether these are growing or declining and if there are any specific types of tourism that the industry is expecting to expand;

- tourism revenues and broader economic impact: plans should be based upon a detailed understanding of the economic value of key tourism sectors and the impacts of these in terms of the number of jobs provided and the services and facilities which are assisted by that tourism activity;
- tourism labour markets: plans for tourism should be based upon information about the number of jobs currently in tourism, whether these are full-time, levels of skill and of pay. This information will be important to ensure that where plans may change the number or types of tourism jobs, these are realistic in terms of available labour and that they take opportunities to improve the quality and levels of pay for these jobs wherever possible; and
- costs and timings of types of tourism development: where plans propose new tourism development for an area, these should be based upon sound estimates of the cost and timing of this development. This will be necessary in order to ensure that development proposals are realistic and optimal in terms of the expected benefits. Whilst the commercial decision is distinct from the planning process, those responsible for plan-making and implementation are responsible for ensuring that those plans have a good chance of being realised.

Information of this sort will be important in terms of:

- the development of plans at both the regional and local level;
- determining what strategy for tourism is most realistic;
- ascertaining what level of benefits might be expected for local economies and communities; and
- helping support particular proposals, for example to help to demonstrate the benefits of a particular scheme.

Such information will often be complemented, particularly in the urban context, by planning authorities' work on needs assessments for leisure and other town centre uses. Good practice on this process is currently being prepared by Communities and Local Government. It will provide information for forward planning of a wide range of land uses of importance to tourism such as cinemas, restaurants, concert halls, health & fitness clubs, hotels and conference centres.

It is clearly in the interests of the tourism industry to ensure that their aspirations, and particularly their land use requirements, are known and understood by those responsible for drawing up plans. The particular advantages of early and active engagement by the industry and its representatives will be:

- to specify site requirements for inclusion in plans;
- to propose elements of tourism to be included in large scale proposals, such as mixed use and regeneration schemes;
- to comment upon how well the visions and objectives proposed for plans and strategies reflect the aspirations and expectations of the industry; and
- to provide an industry perspective on proposed policies so as to influence their final form.

There are a number of other tourism stakeholders who will similarly need to make an input to emerging plans. Their interests will be broad and include those who control a particular tourism resource (e.g. British Waterways), those seeking to protect the environment (e.g. conservation boards for Areas of Outstanding Natural Beauty) and those supplying a service (e.g. transport operators).

In addition to providing important views, these bodies will often be able to provide information on matters such as:

- the characteristics and attributes of the area which attract tourists, and how these might be protected, developed or enhanced;
- the nature of, and prospects for, transport infrastructure; and

- other existing and emerging plans and investment programmes that are likely to affect the area

Use of Data and Techniques

Data

It is important that strategies and plans for tourism are based upon the best information available. Annex C provides more information about the sources of data and techniques that may assist in planning for tourism. It is for those preparing plans to decide what information they need to gather, and the degree of detail that they will require. To plan effectively for tourism, the following types of information are likely to be required:

- demographic data – drawn from census and other Government sources such as the Labour Force Survey and General Household Survey. This information will be used to establish how many people are employed in different sectors, earnings and qualifications, commuting patterns, skill levels and unemployment levels;
- visitor data – drawn from surveys of tourism behaviour (e.g. Leisure Day Visits Survey, the UK Tourism Survey and the Attractions Survey), statistics from individual tourism attractions, transport operators, area organisations (e.g. National Parks) and hotel occupancy surveys. The information is likely to have already been gathered, but will not always be free to the user. It is useful for establishing seasonal variations and longer term trends in tourism behaviour, which in turn will be important for planning future provision;
- economic studies – these will be used to develop options for particular tourism strategies or to test the business case for a particular tourism development. They may be undertaken by the public or private sector, or a partnership of the two. Such studies are likely to examine how existing patterns of visiting or spending might be influenced by particular initiatives such as the introduction of a new facility, increased bedspaces or new transport links; and

- plans, proposals and programmes – a further reason for consulting a wide range of stakeholders is for the plan-maker to ensure that he has a comprehensive understanding of any relevant programme that may affect tourism in the area and therefore the strategy that he is developing. These initiatives will include the investment plans of tourism operators, statutory undertakers and public bodies, and documents that set out longer term aspirations.

Techniques

Planners will need to consider what methods they need both to access and handle data and in using it to make robust plans and decisions. A clear and methodical approach will be particularly required in respect of:

- community involvement and consultation – including with those who have a commercial interest and those likely to be affected by local changes arising from tourism. This could include:
    * formal written consultation at the outset to establish the nature and extent of local business interests in tourism;
    * focus groups, panels or one-to-one meetings to explore options and support for particular proposals;
    * public meetings and exhibitions to disseminate the plan's vision for tourism and establish the degree of support for those amongst the wider community; and
    * area forums, workshops and 'planning for real' exercises to develop detailed ideas and to promote ownership of the plan's proposals.
- visitor behaviour, including transport choices, use of attractions and accommodation usage. The technique adopted will depend upon why the particular information is being sought. For example, if the development plan is considering whether more overnight accommodation is required in an area, data on use of the current accommodation will be the key requirement. However, patterns of transport use and information about

what brings people into the area in the first place will also be important to understand what scope there is for further hotel development and where that could be best located.

When data and techniques are being sought and applied, it is important that those managing and contributing to the process recognise that the same information is likely to be required again at a later date, to assess the plan's progress and effectiveness. So the selection of data and techniques needs to recognise what the ongoing demand upon resources is likely to be. It also means that cooperative working and partnerships need to be nurtured and sustained to enable such monitoring to be readily undertaken.

Key Planning Considerations for Tourism Developments

This section examines some of the key planning issues which may arise in considering proposals for individual tourism developments. The enormous variety of tourism developments mean that the planning considerations will always vary on a case by case basis. However, the following will apply to most developments:

- where the development is located – developments need to be located where they are accessible to visitors (and for many, but not all developments, by means other than just by private car) and where they do not have an adverse impact upon sensitive environments;
- how they are designed – developments should be attractive to users, they need to work well in functional terms and they need to use natural resources in an efficient manner; and
- how they fit into their surroundings – developments need to respect their environs and complement them rather than detract from them. They should be designed to have a positive impact upon landscape, the historical setting and upon ecology.

Choosing the Best Location

In order to be commercially competitive and thus successful, tourism developers will choose sites that are accessible to visitors, and design their developments in such a way that visitors can readily and conveniently enjoy the attraction or facility. The planning authority will share this objective, but in particular will wish to maximise access by sustainable modes of transport, minimise any congestion that the development might give rise to, and ensure that particular sectors of the population are not discouraged from using the attraction when it is completed. Where the attraction or facility is one which lends itself to an urban location, the local planning authority will seek to ensure a town centre location wherever possible.

Planners and developers should work together in order to ensure that new tourism developments are as sustainable as possible in transport terms. At the same time, planners will need to recognise that the wide variety of developments that are inherent in the tourism industry means that there are some developments (e.g. touring sites for caravans) that are car dependent. Wherever possible and feasible for the development concerned, they should look to:

- locate the development close to public transport interchanges and bus routes which will not only help to reduce travel by car but also enable a wider range of people to visit the attraction;
- produce green transport plans – these are often appropriate for larger schemes where there may be scope to reduce private car travel by providing dedicated bus services or greater access by walking or cycling. Park-and-ride provision can be an element of this, as can schemes which provide discounts for those arriving by public transport; and
- establish a visitor management programme– this can be a particularly appropriate solution where an attraction or its surroundings are subject to or the cause of congestion. It may also be advisable where an attraction is fragile or sensitive to use by a large number of people. Visitor management may be achieved by regulating flow (e.g. timed ticket sales) or via development. An example of the latter would be by adding a visitor centre to an historic

abbey so that visitors spend less time in the 'fragile', historic part of the site, and more time in the modern, purpose built 'interpretation' building.

There will be some occasions where development for tourism is sought at a location where it will be difficult to meet the objective of access by sustainable modes of transport. The choice of location may have been determined by a functional need, such as in the above example of a visitor centre.

Developers and planners may find that in such cases there will be limited opportunities to make the development accessible by sustainable modes of transport or to reduce the number or proportion of visits made by car. For small-scale schemes, the traffic generated is likely to be fairly limited and additional traffic movements are therefore unlikely to be a reason for refusal for otherwise suitable tourism developments.

In all cases, planners will need to weigh up the other benefits of a tourism proposal against any disadvantages arising from its location. Some of the key considerations will be the extent to which the proposal:

- helps to protect or improve a specific site or general location. Many new proposals offer the opportunity for landscape enhancement, to re-use an historic building or to improve a derelict and unattractive site;
- contributes to tourism in the locality. New tourism developments will usually be beneficial to the local economy and complement the area's tourism function;
- provides a new facility for the local community as well as visitors;
- assists more generally with diversification of rural economies; and, where appropriate,
- impacts on the vitality and viability of town centres.

Design and Sustainability

Good design is important for tourism because:

- tourism is essentially a commercial activity and its success will depend upon how attractive it is to visitors;

- in areas with many tourist attractions, it is important that each attraction is perceived as contributing to the overall experience; and
- wherever tourist proposals are to be situated, it is important that they complement and improve the wider built and natural environment.

Good design is also a key element in achieving development which is sustainable and will contribute positively towards making places better for people. Developments that are well-designed will be more successful. They will last longer and be more liked. As such they will contribute more to the people who live near or visit them and to the surrounding area as a whole. Further material on design issues can be found in PPS.

Two important aspects of design will be layout and accessibility. Developments that are easy to reach, easy to get around and easy to use are likely to be successful in attracting visitors in the first place and in encouraging them to return. This in turn will assist their commercial success. The details of design are particularly important for tourism because, by definition, visitors are often unfamiliar with the building and its environs. In order to be accessible and used by a wide range of people, tourism developments should be designed to be:

- physically accessible, including to people with impaired mobility and to people with other disabilities such as impaired sight or hearing;
- socially inclusive, facilitating use by all sectors of the community;
- a positive contribution to the host community;
- safe and healthy; and ·attractive.

The careful design of buildings can also make them more sustainable by reducing carbon emissions resulting from their construction and operation. Good energy conservation and using renewable technologies such as wind power and solar gain can reduce the energy needs of buildings and operating costs, whilst improving their sustainability. An important contribution to sustainability can also be made by the selection and use of appropriate materials. Materials from local sources will have less 'embodied energy' (i.e. less fossil fuels will have been taken up transporting and perhaps processing them). Locally-sourced material will also provide local jobs, thus strengthening and diversifying the local economy, and making it more likely that the final development will fit well with the local environment.

The re-use of buildings that have become redundant further improves the overall sustainability of new developments. This also often has the advantage of maintaining important and historic buildings and providing continuity in the landscape and townscape. These sustainable attributes, which may be substantial, may offset certain planning objections to a proposal such as poor location or access.

So, for example, if a hotel was proposed in a redundant building outside of an existing town centre, the decision maker would need to consider and reflect the advantages of the refurbishment proposal against the disadvantage of the less central location.

Contributing to the Environment

Tourism developments may offer considerable opportunities to conserve and enhance the local environment and its inherent qualities. Such advantages will be important considerations in assessing the overall sustainability, and thus acceptability, of a particular proposal. Developers of tourism projects should therefore consider whether new developments can:

- protect and enhance the visual quality of the site and its surroundings, to ensure that the development fits in well with its environs;
- respect the historic interest of the surrounding buildings and areas and ensuring that proposals do not adversely affect the historic environment that people value;
- protect and improve biodiversity. New development should not only protect nature conservation interests (whether it is a statutory requirement or not), but can provide an opportunity to improve biodiversity in an area, for example through the creation of new features of wildlife interest. Such initiatives can complement the wider

objectives of tourism developments by increasing the attractiveness of the development to visitors; and

- achieve small-scale improvements to sustainability, for example by recycling waste, using renewable energy and sourcing produce and materials locally.

Determining Tourism Proposals

This section outlines some of the initiatives that developers and planning authorities can take to ensure that proposals for tourism development are processed in an effective and fair manner which will promote optimal outcomes.

Information

Developers can help their proposals to be determined quickly, and achieve a positive outcome, if they provide adequate and appropriate information in support of their applications. For their part local planning authorities need to make clear what information they will be seeking in support of applications for tourism developments.

The information required is likely to vary greatly depending on the nature of the proposal, its scale and its location. For larger proposals there may be a wide range of information needed by the planning authority, including:

- the nature of the visits expected to the development, how many they will be, how long and when they will occur;
- what seasonal fluctuation is likely and the extent to which there are expected to be joint trips with other activities in the locality;
- where visits are likely to originate from, and modal split of visitors; and
- the levels of spend and the amount of money expected to be drawn into the local economy.

Developers can help themselves and the local planning authority by seeking discussions with the authority in advance of submitting their planning applications. Such discussions will be an opportunity to identify what information may be required to be submitted in support of the planning application. They will also be helpful in identifying any planning issues and problems and how these might be resolved.

Consultation

Consultation is a statutory requirement and thus an integral part of the planning process. However, there are many potential advantages in going beyond the minimum requirements, particularly through getting the community involved at an early stage in the planning of future developments. Local people are likely to be affected in a number of ways by new tourism proposals. They may be users of a new facility, perhaps even the main users. They may stand to benefit because of jobs or because their businesses may be affected by the presence and operation of the new development.

So there can be distinct advantages in involving local people as their knowledge and opinions will allow adjustments to be made to proposals as they are being developed. This might help in overcoming later objections or help to identify ways of making the proposal more attractive and thus more profitable or successful. The level of consultation with the community should be in proportion to the nature, size and scale of the proposed development.

When undertaking such consultation, it is important that efforts are made to be as inclusive as possible and to understand the needs of groups who might otherwise find it difficult to engage with the planning system. This should include providing the opportunity to put forward ideas and suggestions and to participate in developing proposals and options.

Additional Guidance

One way that local authorities can help developers to draw up schemes that will meet the requirements for new development set out in development plan policies is to provide guidance in advance. This can take a number of forms and will depend upon the characteristics of the area and any particular aims for tourism development that the local plan documents have established.

Where the local planning authority is seeking or expecting considerable tourism development in a number of locations in its area, then it might even be appropriate to draw up a dedicated supplementary planning document on tourism developments to deal with such issues as preferred locations, access, transportation and design.

This document could explain the key objectives for tourism development and seek to ensure that new development supported the overall vision for tourism. Eastbourne has chosen to prepare a supplementary planning document specifically to provide planning advice to developers and others on how the Council will administer its financial viability test for tourist accommodation as set out in the Core Strategy.

Where tourism development is expected just at one or two particular sites within the area, it may be more appropriate to prepare supplementary documents providing design advice to support particular sites allocated in the relevant development plan document. This will help prospective developers to understand the type of development envisaged for the site and how it is expected to integrate physically and functionally with its surroundings.

Another approach might be for the planning authority to provide design guidance for particular types of development, such as for hotels, amusements premises or caravan sites. This will be appropriate where an area has high demand for a particular type of development or when a particular land use is subject to pressures for change or redevelopment.

Compliance with other Statutory Regimes

When planning applications for development are made, the proposals may be subject to other statutory regimes as well. Most planning applications also require approval under building regulations, but there are a range of other statutory requirements that certain developments may need to meet or that developers will need to consider when preparing a planning application for development.

Examples may include the need to obtain listed building or conservation area consent; the need to provide an Environmental Statement to comply with the requirements of the Environmental Impact Assessment (EIA) Regulations; and the need to have regard to the Habitats Regulations, for example in cases where there may be European protected species present on a proposed development site.

Further advice on such matters should be obtained, if necessary, from the local authority before planning applications are submitted.

Using Conditions and Obligations

The granting of planning permission will often be subject to certain conditions being met. These conditions may be used to improve the appearance or functioning of the development or to mitigate against adverse impacts. Conditions must be seen to be fair, reasonable and practicable. For example, typical planning conditions for a tourism or leisure development might:

- regulate the hours during which an attraction could open in order to avoid undue disturbance to people living nearby; or
- require that a caravan site or another type of holiday accommodation be used only for holidays and not as permanent accommodation or as a main residence.

Where it is not possible to include matters in a planning condition, for example where the planning authority wishes to secure on-going management or financial payments, they may seek to negotiate a planning obligation with the developer under section 106 of the Town and Country Planning Act 1990. Obligations must meet certain tests including being directly related to the proposed development and reasonably related in scale and kind to the proposed development.

One example of a tourism-related planning obligation is at the London Wetland Centre where a bus route and terminal have been created and alterations made to cycle lanes. New cycle racks and storage facilities have also been provided, creating a packet of measures that have substantially increased the overall sustainability of this visitor facility.

Tourist Accommodation

1. Tourism accommodation takes many different forms, including hotels, guest houses and bed and breakfast premises, self-catering, touring and static caravans and

camping, and caters for a variety of tastes and budgets. But all are capable of bringing economic benefits to the areas in which they are located. These benefits will need to be assessed alongside other issues such as suitability of the location in terms of its sustainability.

2. The issues that will need to be addressed in considering planning applications for tourist accommodation will vary according to the type, size, and nature of the accommodation being provided. These are considered further below.

Hotel and Serviced Accommodation

General Locational Principles

The process of identifying suitable locations for hotel and serviced accommodation, whatever its nature, should be an integral part of the plan making process. Local planning authorities and the tourist industry should therefore engage constructively to identify suitable locations in plans for hotel accommodation to meet identified current and future needs.

This is particularly important for major hotels – for example those with business, conference and banqueting facilities, or large hotels catering for tourists – where the preference should be to identify town centre sites wherever possible, in line with national policies set out in PPS.

Such sites are the most sustainable in planning terms, since they allow greater access by public transport, contribute to urban vitality and regeneration, and allow visitors to easily access other town centre facilities and attractions. Where proposals for major hotel facilities come forward outside the development plan process, their location should be assessed in line with the policies in PPS and the sequential approach to site selection.

Proposed locations for other types of hotel and serviced accommodation should also be considered through the plan process wherever possible. The emphasis, whatever the type of accommodation, should be on identifying the most sustainable locations, having regard to national planning policies. But in allocating sites in plans, or considering planning applications that come forward outside of the plan process, developers and planning authorities need to recognise that the particular market being met by the accommodation may influence the nature of the location chosen. So, for example, accommodation catering for those seeking to enjoy the natural environment through walking and outdoor recreation may be better located in a rural area, in or at the edge of the centre of a village or small town, rather than in a major town centre some distance away from the attractions it serves.

Whatever the type of hotel or serviced accommodation and whatever its location, it should:

- fit well with its surroundings, having regard to its siting, scale, design, materials and landscaping; and
- be in harmony with the local environment (taking account of, amongst other factors, residential amenity, noise, traffic and parking in the vicinity).

Hotel Accommodation in Rural Areas

National planning policies set out in PPS *Sustainable Development in Rural Areas* makes it clear that the expectation is that most tourism accommodation requiring new buildings should be located in, or adjacent to, existing towns and villages. PPS also recognises that proposals to convert existing rural buildings to provide hotel and other serviced accommodation should be acceptable, subject to any general criteria that may be set in development plans on the re-use of such buildings.

National Parks and Areas of Outstanding Natural Beauty attract visitors who wish to enjoy the special qualities of the landscapes and the countryside of these areas. It is important that sufficient accommodation of a suitable range of types is provided for these visitors. However, particular care needs to be taken over the number, scale and location of accommodation facilities in these designated areas to ensure that the particular qualities that justified the designation are conserved. These considerations are best addressed through the plan process wherever possible.

Historic Towns and Cities

Historic towns and cities are an attraction to tourists from home and overseas and there is pressure to increase hotel accommodation in them. Great importance is attached to the preservation of buildings of architectural or historic interest both for their intrinsic qualities and for the contribution they make to our towns and villages, and to tourism. It is therefore important that any proposals for new hotel accommodation in such towns and cities are sensitive to their surroundings.

Conversion into hotels is often a realistic proposition for ensuring the retention and maintenance of historic buildings provided it is sensitively handled, does not materially alter the character or historic features of the building, and provided the new use does not generate traffic movements which cannot be accommodated.

Many historic buildings in town and country are already in use as hotels. If carefully designed, additions can be achieved without adversely affecting the historic fabric or character and maintain the historic building in viable use. But large-scale buildings in a small-scale setting, buildings which adversely affect the existing skyline, and those which by their design, materials, illumination or building line are out of sympathy with neighbouring historic buildings will normally be unacceptable.

Modernisation and Extensions

Aside from historic buildings, there are many redundant or semi-obsolete buildings – such as closed mills, distilleries, warehouses, or railway stations – that can lend themselves well to adaptation and modernisation as hotels, other forms of serviced accommodation or restaurants. To convert such buildings to compatible use can bring life back to an otherwise wasted asset–thus conserving a useful and often attractive building, improving a neglected site and helping the local economy.

Similarly, moderate-sized extensions to an existing hotel or public house, including the addition of bedroom accommodation, can help to ensure the future viability of such businesses. This may satisfy a local need as well as a tourism one, by fully utilising the potential of the site but without any disproportionate increase in scale. In all cases, careful consideration should be given to ensure that the size of the extension proposed is not disproportionate for the location concerned.

Budget Hotels, Motels, and Travel Lodges

Where budget hotels are designed to cater for longer stays at a destination (for example, those catering for visitors to historic towns and cities), their location should be considered in light of policies in the development plan and national policies in PPS on town centres. Location of such hotels in town centres maximises the opportunities for visitors to easily access other town centre facilities and attractions.

Other types of budget hotels and similar types of development such as motels and travel lodges cater more for car-born travellers, often for a single overnight stay – e.g. business travellers en-route to a destination. In such cases, the preference of developers will be for sites on major traffic routes outside of the centre of large towns or tourist centres.

However the aim should be to make any development as sustainable as possible, and it will not normally be appropriate for such developments to be located in open countryside away from major settlements. Edge of town centre locations, for example on a ring road or on a major route out of the town centre, will usually be the most appropriate locations if a town centre location is not suitable, available or viable.

For out-of-centre locations, design and layout of the development is likely to be of considerable importance in deciding whether it is acceptable in planning terms. Depending on the setting, an open layout in which careful attention has been paid to achieving a high standard of design and landscaping is likely to be more acceptable than a dense concentration of buildings.

Where a proposal includes other new facilities, such as a petrol station or shop, these will have to be considered on their own merits. If they are objectionable in themselves, the fact that they are combined with a hotel will not remove the objections. Restaurants, fast food outlets, leisure, fitness and other facilities open to the general public as well as residents are also sometimes combined with hotel proposals, in which case the extra traffic they are likely to generate and its effect on the highway must also be taken into account.

Car Parking

Maximum car parking standards for hotel and serviced accommodation may be included in development plans. Where such standards are not included in plans, planning authorities will need to consider what are appropriate levels of parking, based on the market which the hotel serves, its location and availability of public transport facilities.

In addition, for those hotels where a substantial part of the parking needs are attributable to public rooms used mainly for functions which attract non-residents, then the availability of public parking in the vicinity of the hotel will also need to be taken into account.

Planning authorities should also take account of the proposed arrangements for service loading and unloading and setting down space for visitors. Organised tours demand adequate loading and unloading facilities for coaches. Access and waiting areas should be designed with this in mind. Access points should be sited so as to minimise turning movements across traffic and to avoid congestion of the highway caused by vehicles queuing to pick up or drop passengers. Developers should discuss proposed access arrangements with the highway authority at the earliest possible stage.

Holiday, Touring Caravan, and Chalet Parks

In the UK as a whole, the parks industry accounts for tourist spend of some £3.23 billion each year, accommodating some 22% of all holiday bed nights. The industry comprises holiday chalets, caravan holiday homes, pitches for touring caravans, motor-homes and tenting and all types of self-catering accommodation. Holiday parks are the largest provider of rural tourism bed spaces.

PPS. provides advice for planning policies and development proposals for static holiday and touring caravan parks and holiday chalet developments. Planners should carefully weigh the objective of providing adequate facilities and sites with the need to protect landscapes and environmentally sensitive sites.

They should examine the scope for relocating any existing visually or environmentally-intrusive parks away from sensitive areas, or for re-location away from sites prone to flooding or coastal erosion. However, the high land values associated with holiday parks, the cost of infrastructure and possible planning issues relating to a proposed site may make such proposals impractical and unviable.

This advice recognises that planning provides an opportunity to improve the attractiveness of such developments to those who visit them and as features in the landscape.

The *Environmental Code for Holiday parks, Caravan and Camping Sites, and Park Home Estates advises* park owners on fulfilling the industry's commitment to environmental protection. *Holiday Parks: Caring for the Environment – a guide to good practice* (1991), published by the Countryside Commission, remains an important reference document that includes many case studies directing holiday park operators toward best practice. Planners should work with owners and developers of sites to ensure that the most is made of these opportunities. Where there is an identified demand for new or expanded sites, planners should ensure that environmental impacts and impacts on visual amenity are minimised.

New sites that are close to existing settlements and other services will generally be more sustainable as some local services may be accessed by means other than by car. Similarly caravan storage facilities that are close to existing settlements may have less adverse impact and be more sustainable.

However, there may be valid reasons for extending or improving existing holiday parks that are not be located close to existing settlements by virtue of their support for successful local businesses and the provision of employment. Authorities should also consider how the proposal will affect tourism in the area, particularly in terms of its economic and environmental impacts.

Local planning authorities may attach conditions to planning permissions for holiday parks to ensure that they are used for holiday purposes only.

However, with better caravan standards and the trend towards tourism as a year round activity, authorities should give sympathetic consideration to applications to extend the opening period allowed under existing permissions. Annex B covers these matters in more detail.

Staff Accommodation

For many types of holiday parks, a residential managerial presence is often essential, to achieve quality service to the customer, security for the property, and to meet the obligations of health and safety regulations. Accommodation may sometimes also be needed for key members of staff.

As far as possible, suitably located existing dwellings should be used to meet these accommodation needs. But where this is not a feasible option, and particularly in locations where suitable housing is not available, or is unaffordable, it may be necessary to provide new, on-site accommodation for managerial and/or other staff. In such cases the conversion of any suitable available existing buildings should be considered first in preference to the construction of new and potentially intrusive housing development in the countryside.

PPS makes it clear that isolated new houses in the countryside require special justification for planning permission to be granted. PPS further states that one of the few circumstances in which isolated residential development may be justified is when accommodation is required to enable agricultural, forestry and certain other full-time workers to live at, or in the immediate vicinity of their place of work.

There will be some cases where the nature and demands of the work concerned make it essential for one or more people engaged in a tourism enterprise to live at, or very close to, the site of their work. Local planning authorities should give consideration to the essential needs of all businesses located in rural areas, including tourism and should apply the policies set out in PPS– in particular those in Annex A. Planning conditions can ensure that such accommodation is occupied for this purpose only.

Other Forms of Self-catering Accommodation

PPS advises that local planning authorities should support the provision of other forms of self-catering holiday accommodation in rural areas where this would accord with sustainable development objectives. The re-use and conversion of existing non-residential buildings for this purpose may have added benefits, e.g. as a farm diversification scheme.

Seasonal and Holiday Occupancy Conditions

1. The nature of holidays in this country has become increasingly diverse, in location, in season and in duration. Many people go away several times a year, often for short breaks and not exclusively in the summer months. Much of this demand is for self-catering accommodation – whether in new or converted buildings or in caravan holiday homes. This spread of demand improves the use that is made of this accommodation and so is advantageous to the businesses which provide it and to those host communities which are supported by the spending that it generates. It can help to reduce the disadvantages of seasonal employment, including the difficulties of retaining trained and experienced staff.
2. Whilst extension of the season has these advantages, the demand for this accommodation may occur in areas in which the provision of permanent housing would be contrary to national or local policies which seek to restrict development, for example in order to safeguard the countryside. The planning system can reconcile these two objectives through the use of occupancy conditions designed to ensure that holiday accommodation is used for its intended purpose. Planning authorities commonly impose such conditions when granting permission for self-catering holiday accommodation.
3. One type of condition frequently used for holiday accommodation, particularly in holiday areas, is known generically as a 'holiday occupancy condition'. The aim of such conditions is generally to ensure that the premises are only used by visitors and do not become part of the local housing stock. There are three principal reasons why a planning authority might seek to do this:
   - in order that national or local policies on development of the countryside are not compromised. Often the

conversion of redundant rural buildings to holiday accommodation provides a means to retain those buildings without introducing a level of activity that would occur with permanent households;

- to avoid occupation by permanent households which would in turn put pressure upon local services. Permanent households may place demands for local schools and social and health services that would not normally arise from visitors. Moreover, in remote locations the cost of providing these services is greater. It may therefore be reasonable for the planning authority to place an occupancy condition when properties are being built or converted for residential use; and
- to strengthen tourism in a particular area by ensuring that there is a wide range of properties available to encourage visitors to come there on holiday.

Planning authorities will frame these conditions according to local circumstances, and in accordance with general Government advice that conditions should be reasonable and fair. They will also need to frame them so that they can be readily enforced by the authority but in a way that is not unduly intrusive for either owners or occupants.

Another type of condition that may be appropriate for tourist areas is known as a 'seasonal occupancy' condition. This would seek to restrict use of holiday accommodation during particular times of year, perhaps to protect the local environment. This could be used if, for example, use of the premises or the site might affect an important species of bird during its breeding season or when it is winter feeding. Local planning authorities will need to balance the need to impose seasonal occupancy conditions with the wish to avoid exacerbating the seasonal nature of tourism in the locality and its possible adverse effects upon local businesses and jobs.

Data Sources and Techniques

Planners will need to consider relevant quantitative data, including data relating to the economics of tourism development, in both the plan making process and in respect of specific proposals.

Development plans (regional spatial strategies and local development frameworks) must be based upon a sound evidence base which has been subject to a rational appraisal. This will need to include an explicit rationale for the vision and strategy for tourism which is being proposed, based in part upon the economic benefits that have been used to justify it.

Local Surveys and Methodologies

Planners may identify a need for local surveys to establish the need for a specific tourist related development. So planners considering hotel accommodation need to have a detailed understanding of the level and demand for accommodation within their area.

Tourism Planning in India

Tourism planning in India started quite late with the first tourism policy being announced by the Government of India in November, 1982 after tourism was recognized as an industry by the Planning Commission of India in June, 1982.

In July, 1986 the Planning Commission of India set up the National Committee on Tourism in order to formulate plans for this sector. The government's initiatives of incorporating a planned tourism sector in India went a long way in boosting Indian tourism.

In May, 1992 the National Action Plan for tourism was announced. The objectives of this landmark plan for tourism planning in India were:

- To improve the economy category domestic tourism
- To develop the tourist areas socially and economically
- To preserve the environment and the national heritage
- To encourage international tourism
- To improve in world tourism India's share
- To increase opportunities for employment in this sector

India tourism planning increased with the seventh five year plan India (1985-1989). The various policcs advocated by the seventh plan for tourism planning in India are:

- To promote aggressively domestic tourism

- It laid stress on creating more beach resorts
- To conduct conferences, trekking, conventions, and winter sports so that various options are available to the foreign tourists

These polices of the seventh five year plan gave a boost to the tourism planning India. To further encourage tourism planning in India, the eighth five year plan (1992- 1997) mentioned that the private sector should increase its participation in the sector. The various polices advocated by the eighth plan for tourism planning in India are:

- To develop the tourists places
- To develop winter sports, beach resort, and wildlife tourism
- To restore the projects of national heritage
- To provide in tourists centres economy class accommodation

Tourism planning in India has increased by leaps and bounds in the last few years and the government and Department of Tourism needs to make continuous efforts to ensure that tourism planning in India takes the tourism sector of the country to greater heights on a sustainable basis.

Ecotourism and the Tourism Industry

Ecotourism

'Ecotourism' (also known as ecological tourism) is responsible travel to fragile, pristine, and usually protected areas that strives to be low impact and (often) small scale. It purports to educate the traveller; provide funds for conservation; directly benefit the economic development and political empowerment of local communities; and foster respect for different cultures and for human rights.

Eco tourism is held as important by those who participate in it so that future generations may experience aspects of the environment relatively untouched by human intervention. Most serious studies of ecotourism including several university programs now use this as the working definition.

Ecotourism appeals to ecologically and socially conscious individuals. Generally speaking, it focuses on volunteering, personal growth and environmental responsibility. It typically involves travel to destinations where flora, fauna, and cultural heritage are the primary attractions. One of the goals of ecotourism is to offer tourists insight into the impact of human beings on the environment, and to foster a greater appreciation of our natural habitats.

Responsible ecotourism includes programs that minimize the negative aspects of conventional tourism on the environment and enhance the cultural integrity of local people. Therefore, in addition to evaluating environmental and cultural factors, an integral part of ecotourism is the promotion of recycling, energy efficiency, water conservation, and creation of economic opportunities for local communities.

Criteria

Ecotourism is a form of tourism that involves travelling to tranquil and unpolluted natural areas. According to the definition and principles of ecotourism established by The International Ecotourism Society (TIES) in 1990, ecotourism is "Responsible travel to natural areas that conserves the environment and improves the well-being of local people." (TIES, 1990). Martha Honey, expands on the TIES definition by describing the seven characteristics of ecotourism, which are:

- Involves travel to natural destinations.
- Minimizes impact.
- Builds environmental awareness.
- Provides direct financial benefits for conservation.
- Provides financial benefits and empowerment for local people.
- Respects local culture.
- Supports human rights and democratic movements.

Ideally, ecotourism should satisfy several criteria, such as:

- conservation of biological diversity and cultural diversity through ecosystem protection

- promotion of sustainable use of biodiversity, by providing jobs to local populations
- sharing of socioeconomic benefits with local communities and indigenous peoples by having their informed consent and participation in the management of ecotourism enterprises
- tourism to unspoiled natural resources, with minimal impact on the environment being a primary concern.
- minimization of tourism's own environmental impact
- affordability and lack of waste in the form of luxury
- local culture, flora and fauna being the main attractions.

For many countries, ecotourism is not simply a marginal activity to finance protection of the environment, but is a major industry of the national economy. For example, in Costa Rica, Ecuador, Nepal, Kenya, Madagascar and Antarctica, ecotourism represents a significant portion of the gross domestic product and economic activity.

The concept of ecotourism is widely misunderstood and in practice is often used as a marketing tool to promote tourism that is related to nature. This is an especially frequent malpractice in the realm of Jungle tourism. Critics claim that these greenwashing practices, carried out in the name of ecotourism, often consist of placing a hotel in a splendid landscape, to the detriment of the ecosystem. According to them, ecotourism must above all sensitize people to the beauty and the fragility of nature. They condemn some operators as greenwashing their operations: using the labels of "green" and "eco-friendly", while behaving in environmentally irresponsible ways. Although academics disagree about who can be classified as an ecotourist and there is little statistical data, some estimate that more than five million ecotourists - the majority of the ecotourist population - come from the United States, with many others from Western Europe, Canada and Australia. Currently, there are various moves to create national and international ecotourism accreditation programs, although the process is also controversial. National ecotourism certification programs have been put in place in countries such as Costa Rica, Australia, Kenya and Sweden.

History

Ecotourism, responsible tourism, jungle tourism, and sustainable development have become prevalent concepts since the late 1980s, and ecotourism has experienced arguably the fastest growth of all sub-sectors in the tourism industry.

The popularity represents a change in tourist perceptions, increased environmental awareness, and a desire to explore natural environments. At times, such changes become as much a statement affirming one's social identity, educational sophistication, and disposable income as it has about preserving the Amazon rainforest or the Caribbean reef for posterity.

Criticisms

Definitional Problems and Greenwashing

To approach an understanding of the problem, a clear definition must delineate what is, and is not, ecotourism. Ideally, ecotourism satisfies several general criteria, including the conservation of biological diversity and cultural diversity through ecosystem protection, promotion of sustainable use of biodiversity, share of social-economic benefits with local communities through informed consent and participation, increase in environmental and cultural knowledge, affordability and reduced waste, and minimization of its own environmental impact. In such ways, it contributes to the long term benefits to both the environment and local communities.

However, in the continuum of tourism activities that stretch from conventional tourism to ecotourism proper, there has been a lot of contention to the limit at which biodiversity preservation, local social-economic benefits, and environmental impact can be considered "ecotourism".

For this reason, environmentalists, special interest groups, and governments define ecotourism differently. Environmental organizations have generally insisted that ecotourism is nature-based, sustainably managed, conservation supporting, and environmentally educated.

The tourist industry and governments, however, focus more on the product aspect, treating ecotourism as equivalent to any sort of tourism based in nature. As a further complication, many terms are used under the rubric of ecotourism. Nature tourism, low impact tourism, green tourism, bio-tourism, ecologically responsible tourism, and others have been used in literature and marketing, although they are not necessary synonymous with ecotourism.

The problems associated with defining ecotourism have led to confusion among tourists and academics alike. Definitional problems are also subject of considerable public controversy and concern because of green washing, a trend towards the commercialization of tourism schemes disguised as sustainable, nature based, and environmentally friendly ecotourism.

According to McLaren, these schemes are environmentally destructive, economically exploitative, and culturally insensitive at its worst. They are also morally disconcerting because they mislead tourists and manipulate their concerns for the environment. Despite objections, green washing continues to grow unabated.

The Nature's Sacred Paradise, a theme park in Quintana Roo, Mexico, is responsible for displacing local Mayan communities and illegally keeping endangered species in captivity to attract visitors. The development and success of such large scale, energy intensive, and ecologically unsustainable schemes are a testament to the tremendous profits associated with being labeled as ecotourism.

Negative Impact of Tourism

Ecotourism has become one of the fastest-growing sectors of the tourism industry, growing annually by 10-15% worldwide (Miller, 2007). One definition of ecotourism is "the practice of low-impact, educational, ecologically and culturally sensitive travel that benefits local communities and host countries" (Honey, 1999). Many of the ecotourism projects are not meeting these standards.

Even if some of the guidelines are being executed, the local communities are still facing other negative impacts. South Africa is one of the countries that are reaping significant economic benefits from ecotourism, but negative effects - including forcing people to leave their homes, gross violations of fundamental rights, and environmental hazards - far outweigh the medium-term economic benefits (Miller, 2007). A tremendous amount of money is being spent and human resources continue to be used for ecotourism despite unsuccessful outcomes, and even more money is put into public relation campaigns to dilute the effects of criticism. Ecotourism channels resources away from other projects that could contribute more sustainable and realistic solutions to pressing social and environmental problems.

"The money tourism can generate often ties parks and managements to ecotourism" (Walpole et al. 2001). But there is a tension in this relationship because ecotourism often causes conflict and changes in land-use rights, fails to deliver promises of community-level benefits, damages environments, and has plenty of other social impacts.

Indeed many argue repeatedly that ecotourism is neither ecologically nor socially beneficial, yet it persists as a strategy for conservation and development (West, 2006). While several studies are being done on ways to improve the ecotourism structure, some argue that these examples provide rationale for stopping it altogether.

The ecotourism system exercises tremendous financial and political influence. The evidence above shows that a strong case exists for restraining such activities in certain locations. Funding could be used for field studies aimed at finding alternative solutions to tourism and the diverse problems Africa faces in result of urbanization, industrialization, and the over exploitation of agriculture (Kamuaro, 2007). At the local level, ecotourism has become a source of conflict over control of land, resources, and tourism profits. In this case, ecotourism has harmed the environment and local people, and has led to conflicts over profit distribution.

In a perfect world more efforts would be made towards educating tourists of the environmental and social effects of their travels. Very few regulations or laws stand in place as boundaries for the investors in ecotourism. These should be implemented to prohibit the promotion of unsustainable ecotourism projects and materials which project false images of destinations, demeaning local and indigenous cultures.

Direct Environmental Impacts

Ecotourism operations occasionally fail to live up to conservation ideals. It is sometimes overlooked that ecotourism is a highly consumer-centred activity, and that environmental conservation is a means to further economic growth.

Although ecotourism is intended for small groups, even a modest increase in population, however temporary, puts extra pressure on the local environment and necessitates the development of additional infrastructure and amenities.

The construction of water treatment plants, sanitation facilities, and lodges come with the exploitation of non-renewable energy sources and the utilization of already limited local resources. The conversion of natural land to such tourist infrastructure is implicated in deforestation and habitat deterioration of butterflies in Mexico and squirrel monkeys in Costa Rica. In other cases, the environment suffers because local communities are unable to meet the infrastructure demands of ecotourism. The lack of adequate sanitation facilities in many East African parks results in the disposal of campsite sewage in rivers, contaminating the wildlife, livestock, and people who draw drinking water from it.

Aside from environmental degradation with tourist infrastructure, population pressures from ecotourism also leaves behind garbage and pollution associated with the Western lifestyle. Although ecotourists claim to be educationally sophisticated and environmentally concerned, they rarely understand the ecological consequences of their visits and how their day-to-day activities append physical impacts on the environment.

As one scientist observes, they "rarely acknowledge how the meals they eat, the toilets they flush, the water they drink, and so on, are all part of broader regional economic and ecological systems they are helping to reconfigure with their very activities."

Nor do ecotourists recognize the great consumption of non-renewable energy required to arrive at their destination, which is typically more remote than conventional tourism destinations. For instance, an exotic journey to a place 10,000 kilometres away consumes about 700 litres of fuel per person.

Ecotourism activities are, in of itself, issues in environmental impact because they disturb fauna and flora. Ecotourists believe that because they are only taking pictures and leaving footprints, they keep ecotourism sites pristine, but even harmless sounding activities such as a nature hike can be ecologically destructive.

In the Annapurna Circuit in Nepal, ecotourists have worn down the marked trails and created alternate routes, contributing to soil impaction, erosion, and plant damage. Where the ecotourism activity involves wildlife viewing, it can scare away animals, disrupt their feeding and nesting sites, or acclimate them to the presence of people. In Kenya, wildlife-observer disruption drives cheetahs off their reserves, increasing the risk of inbreeding and further endangering the species.

Environmental Hazards

Unfortunately, industrialization, urbanization, and unsustainable agriculture practices have all had serious effects on the environment. Ecotourism is now also playing a role in this depletion. While the term ecotourism may sound relatively benign, one of its most serious impacts is its consumption of virgin territories (Kamuaro, 2007).

These invasions often include deforestation, disruption of ecological life systems and various forms of pollution, all of which contribute to environmental degradation. The number of motor vehicles crossing the park increases as tour drivers search for rare species. The number of roads has disrupted the grass cover which has serious effects on plant and animal species. These areas also have a higher rate of disturbances and invasive species because of all the traffic moving off the beaten path into new undiscovered areas (Kamuaro, 2007). Ecotourism also has an effect on species through the value placed on them. "Certain species have gone from being little known or valued by local people to being highly valued commodities. The commodification of plants may erase their social value and lead to overproduction within protected areas. Local people and their images can also be turned into commodities" (West, 2006). Kamuaro brings up a relatively obvious contradiction, any commercial venture into unspoiled, pristine land with or without the "eco" prefix as a contradiction in terms.

To generate revenue you have to have a high number of traffic, tourists, which inevitably means a higher pressure on the environment.

Local People

Most forms of ecotourism are owned by foreign investors and corporations that provide few benefits to local communities. An overwhelming majority of profits are put into the pockets of investors instead of reinvestment into the local economy or environmental protection. The limited numbers of local people who are employed in the economy enter at its lowest level, and are unable to live in tourist areas because of meager wages and a two market system.

In some cases, the resentment by local people results in environmental degradation. As a highly publicized case, the Masai nomads in Kenya killed wildlife in national parks to show aversion to unfair compensation terms and displacement from traditional lands. The lack of economic opportunities for local people also constrains them to degrade the environment as a means of sustenance. The presence of affluent ecotourists encourage the development of destructive markets in wildlife souvenirs, such as the sale of coral trinkets on tropical islands and animal products in Asia, contributing to illegal harvesting and poaching from the environment. In Suriname, sea turtle reserves use a large portion of their budget to guard against these destructive activities.

Displacement of People

One of the most powerful examples of communities being moved in order to create a park is the story of the Masai. About 70% of national parks and game reserves in East Africa are on Masai land (Kamuaro, 2007). The first undesirable impact of tourism was that of the extent of land lost from the Masai culture. Local and national governments took advantage of the Masai's ignorance on the situation and robbed them of huge chunks of grazing land, putting to risk their only socioeconomic livelihood. In Kenya the Masai also have not gained any economic benefits. Despite the loss of their land, employment favours better educated workers. Furthermore the investors in this area are not local and have not put profits back into local economy. In some cases game reserves can be created without informing or consulting local people, who come to find out about the situation when an eviction notice is delivered (Kamuaro, 2007).

Another source of resentment is the manipulation of the local people by their government. "Ecotourism works to create simplistic images of local people and their uses and understandings of their surroundings.

Through the lens of these simplified images, officials direct policies and projects towards the local people and the local people are blamed if the projects fail" (West, 2006). Clearly tourism as a trade is not empowering the local people who make it rich and satisfying. Instead.ecotourism exploits and depletes, particularly in African Masai tribes. It has to be reoriented if it is to be useful to local communities and to become sustainable (Kamuaro, 2007).

Threats to Indigenous Cultures

Ecotourism often claims that it preserves and "enhances" local cultures. However, evidence shows that with the establishment of protected areas local people have illegally lost their homes, and most often with no compensation (Kamuaro, 2007). Pushing people onto marginal lands with harsh climates, poor soils, lack of water, and infested with livestock and disease does little to enhance livelihoods even when a proportion of ecotourism profits are directed back into the community.

The establishment of parks can create harsh survival realities and deprive the people of their traditional use of land and natural resources. Ethnic groups are increasingly being seen as a "backdrop" to the scenery and wildlife.

The local people struggle for cultural survival and freedom of cultural expression while being "observed" by tourists. Local indigenous people also have strong resentment towards the change, "Tourism has been allowed to develop with virtually no controls. Too many lodges have been built, too much firewood is being used and no limits are being placed on tourism vehicles. They regularly drive off-track and harass the wildlife. Their vehicle tracks criss-cross the entire Masai Mara. Inevitably the bush is becoming eroded and degraded" (Kamuaro, 2007).

Mismanagement

While governments are typically entrusted with the administration and enforcement of environmental protection, they often lack the commitment or capability to manage ecotourism sites effectively. The regulations for environmental protection may be vaguely defined, costly to implement, hard to enforce, and uncertain in effectiveness.

Government regulatory agencies, as political bodies, are susceptible to making decisions that spend budget on politically beneficial but environmentally unproductive projects. Because of prestige and conspicuousness, the construction of an attractive visitor's center at an ecotourism site may take precedence over more pressing environmental concerns like acquiring habitat, protecting endemic species, and removing invasive ones. Finally, influential groups can pressure and sway the interests of the government to their favour. The government and its regulators can become vested in the benefits of the ecotourism industry which they are supposed to regulate, causing restrictive environmental regulations and enforcement to become more lenient.

Management of ecotourism sites by private ecotourism companies offers an alternative to the cost of regulation and deficiency of government agencies. It is believed that these companies have a self interest in limited environmental degradation, because tourists will pay more for pristine environments, which translates to higher profit. However, theory indicates that this practice is not economically feasible and will fail to manage the environment. The model of monopolistic competition states that distinctiveness will entail profits, but profits will promote imitation. A company that protects its ecotourism sites is able to charge a premium for the novel experience and pristine environment. But when other companies view the success of this approach, they also enter the market with similar practices, increasing competition and reducing demand. Eventually, the demand will be reduced until the economic profit is zero. A cost-benefit analysis shows that the company bears the cost of environmental protection without receiving the gains. Without economic incentive, the whole premise of self interest through environmental protection is quashed; instead, ecotourism companies will minimize environment related expenses and maximize tourism demand.

The tragedy of the commons offers another model for economic unsustainability from environmental protection, in ecotourism sites utilized by many companies. Although there is a communal incentive to protect the environment, maximizing the benefits in the long run, a company will conclude that it is in their best interest to utilize the ecotourism site beyond its sustainable level. By increasing the number of ecotourists, for instance, a company gains all the economic benefit while paying only a part of the environmental cost. In the same way, a company recognizes that there is no incentive to actively protect the environment; they bear all the costs, while the benefits are shared by all other companies. The result, again, is mismanagement.

Taken together, the mobility of foreign investment and lack of economic incentive for environmental protection means that ecotourism companies are disposed to establishing themselves in new sites once their existing one is sufficiently degraded.

World Tourism Statistics and Rankings

Most Visited Countries by International Tourist Arrivals

The World Tourism Organization reports the following ten countries as the most visited in between 2006 and 2008 by number of international travellers. When compared to 2006, Ukraine entered the top ten list, surpassing Russia, Austria and Mexico, and in 2008 surpassed Germany. In 2008 the U.S. displaced Spain from the second place. Most of the top visited countries continue to be on the European continent.

International Tourism Receipts

In 2008, there were over 922 million international tourist arrivals, with a growth of 1.9% as compared to 2007. International tourism receipts grew to US$944 billion (euro 642 billion) in 2008, corresponding to an increase in real terms of 1.8% on 2007. When the export value of international passenger transport receipts is accounted for, total receipts in 2008 reached a record of US$1.1 trillion, or over US$3 billion a day.

International Tourism Expenditures

The World Tourism Organization reports the following countries as the top ten biggest spenders on international tourism for the year 2008. For the fifth year in a row, German tourists continue as the top spenders.

History

Wealthy people have always travelled to distant parts of the world, to see great buildings, works of art, learn new languages, experience new cultures and to taste different cuisines. Long ago, at the time of the Roman Republic, places such as Baiae were popular coastal resorts for the rich. The word *tourism* was used by 1811 and *tourist* by 1840. In 1936, the League of Nations defined *foreign tourist* as "someone travelling abroad for at least twenty-four hours". Its successor, the United Nations, amended this definition in 1945, by including a maximum stay of six months.

Leisure Travel

Leisure travel was associated with the Industrial Revolution in the United Kingdom – the first European country to promote leisure time to the increasing industrial population. Initially, this applied to the owners of the machinery of production, the economic oligarchy, the factory owners and the traders. These comprised the new middle class. Cox & Kings was the first official travel company to be formed in 1758. The British origin of this new industry is reflected in many place names. In Nice, France, one of the first and best-established holiday resorts on the French Riviera, the long esplanade along the seafront is known to this day as the *Promenade des Anglais*; in many other historic resorts in continental Europe, old, well-established palace hotels have names like the *Hotel Bristol*, the *Hotel Carlton* or the *Hotel Majestic* – reflecting the dominance of English customers. Many leisure-oriented tourists travel to the tropics, both in the summer and winter. Places often visited are: Cuba, the Dominican Republic, Thailand, North Queensland in Australia and Florida in the United States.

Winter Tourism

Major ski resorts are located in the various European countries (e.g. Austria, Bulgaria, Czech Republic, France, Germany, Iceland,

Italy, Norway, Poland, Sweden, Slovakia, Spain, Switzerland), Canada, the United States, Australia, New Zealand, Japan, South Korea, Chile and Argentina.

Mass Tourism

Mass tourism could only have developed with the improvements in technology, allowing the transport of large numbers of people in a short space of time to places of leisure interest, so that greater numbers of people could begin to enjoy the benefits of leisure time. In the United States, the first seaside resorts in the European style were at Atlantic City, New Jersey and Long Island, New York. In Continental Europe, early resorts included: Ostend, popularized by the people of Brussels; Boulogne-sur-Mer (Pas-de-Calais) and Deauville (Calvados) for the Parisians; and Heiligendamm, founded in 1797, as the first seaside resort on the Baltic Sea.

Mountainous Regions of Central Asia and in the Himalayas

Tourism is coming to the previously isolated but spectacular mountainous regions of Central Asia, the Hindu Kush and the Himalayas. Closed for so many years to visitors from abroad, it now attracts a growing number of foreign tourists by its unique culture and splendid natural beauty. However, while this influx of tourists is bringing economic opportunities and employment to local populations, helping to promote these little-known regions of the world, it has also brought challenges along with it: to ensure that it is well-managed and that its benefits are shared by all.

As a response to this concern, the Norwegian Government, as well as the UNESCO, organized an interdisciplinary project called the Development of Cultural and Ecotourism in the Mountainous Regions of Central Asia and the Himalayas project. It aims to establish links and promote cooperation between local communities, national and international NGOs, and tour agencies in order to heighten the role of the local community and involve them fully in the employment opportunities and income-generating activities that tourism can bring. Project activities include training local tour guides, producing high-quality craft items and promoting home-stays and bed-and-breakfast type accommodation.

As of now, the project is drawing on the expertise of international NGOs and tourism professionals in the seven participating countries, making a practical and positive contribution to alleviating poverty by helping local communities to draw the maximum benefit from their region's tourism potential, while protecting the environmental and cultural heritage of the region concerned.

The University of TRAVELHOST, Dallas, Texas has an extensive travel library continually gathering travel related research and tourism economic impact studies nationwide.

Space Tourism

Space tourism is the phenomenon of tourists paying for flights into space. As of 2009, orbital space tourism opportunities are limited and expensive, with only the Russian Space Agency providing transport. The price for a flight brokered by Space Adventures to the International Space Station aboard a Soyuz spacecraft is US$20–35 million. The space tourists usually sign contracts with third parties to conduct certain research while in orbit. This helps to minimize their own expenses.

Infrastructure for a suborbital space tourism industry is being developed through the construction of spaceports in numerous locations, including California, Oklahoma, New Mexico, Florida, Virginia, Alaska, Wisconsin, Esrange in Sweden as well as the United Arab Emirates. Some use the term "personal spaceflight" as in the case of the Personal Spaceflight Federation.

A number of startup companies have sprung up in recent years, hoping to create a space tourism industry. For a list of such companies, and the spacecraft they are currently building, see list of space tourism companies.

Russia announced on 3 March 2010 that they would be ending their space tourism program, at least for the next several years.

Dark Tourism

Dark tourism (also black tourism or grief tourism) is tourism involving travel to sites associated with death and suffering. Thanatourism, derived from the Ancient Greek word *thanatos* for the personification of death, is associated with dark tourism but refers more specifically to violent death; it is used in fewer contexts than the terms dark tourism, grief tourism, and quite tourism.

This includes castles and battlefields such as Culloden near Inverness, Scotland, Chernobyl in ex USSR, or Bran Castle, Poienari Castle in Romania; sites of disaster, either natural or man made such as Ground Zero in New York; prisons now open to the public such as Beaumaris Prison in Anglesey, Wales; and purpose built centers such as the London Dungeon. A notable example is how tourism to Detroit is sometimes geared towards looking at the fall of the former glamor instead of what it has managed to retain.

The best-known destination for dark tourism is the German extermination camp at Auschwitz in Poland.

3

Future of Hospitality Industry

No hotel company operating today can be unaware of the swift pace of global change and its impact on every facet of the hospitality industry. With just five years left in this century, we can expect change to be the only constant. New business practices are evolving virtually as fast as our technologies, while resistance to change has become one of the primary causes of business failure. The specter of constant change raises fundamental questions as to the creation of shareholder wealth in a capital-constrained, highly competitive environment.

How will hotel organizations build shareholder wealth, and what key drivers will result in success? What future products and services will be essential in a technology-driven, global environment marked by rising customer expectations? Moreover, what alternative approaches and skills must organizations develop to ensure market success?

The future success of hotel organizations will be driven in large part by the ability to foresee — and capitalize — on change. Beyond this truism, however, there is an urgent need to identify what will be required in the competitive environment of the future with its intense focus on serving customer needs. The hospitality industry — as is the case with business generally — is subject to deep currents of change set in motion as economic and social systems shaped in the industrial era evolve to a knowledge-based era driven by technology advances.

In this period of global transition, it behooves hotel organizations to examine the key factors that will not only define success, but the ability to survive in coming years. Many of these issues were spotlighted in a global study undertaken by the Economist Intelligence Unit and co-sponsored by Arthur Andersen. The Successful Corporation of the Year 2000 surveyed more than 600 senior executives around the world. Its mission was to identify the characteristics needed to lead successful businesses in the next century. These executives offer a number of compelling messages regarding the key success factors of the future.

Customers will have the strongest influence on the corporation in the year 2000. Indeed, these executives believe that the customer will be "king" in the new century. Exceptional leadership was by far the attribute most frequently cited by CEOs and senior executives; the consensus appears to be that successful companies in the year 2000 will be led by corporate visionaries. A strategic planning focus is not only essential, but must embody a concept of planning for the future that anticipates change, rather than being based exclusively on historical models. In structuring organizations for the future, companies must build management capabilities to deal with one of the most critical challenges — diversity in the marketplace. Employing information technology to drive business success in this information-driven era is not only the path of least resistance, but vital to virtually every aspect of operations.

The study's top-line results create an excellent backdrop to address key issues confronting the hotel industry, and what factors will lead to membership — rather than rejection — in the elite club of the world's corporate success stories in the year 2000.

From an Asset to Customer Focus

Recognizing that the hotel industry has a somewhat split personality reflecting the inherent conflicts between its real estate and operational aspects, it is important to understand the industry's real estate origins and how they are shaping the challenges ahead.

The origins of the industry's real estate persona are embodied in the classic theory of location-"if we build it, they will come." As a result of this "building" complex, the industry has tended to have a real estate and asset orientation, rather than a customer focus. From the hotel company perspective — especially that of the brand-oriented "chain" – the varied interests of a diffused property ownership group can be quite different than the singular interest of the chain that operates and markets the properties.

Even when the ownership of geographically dispersed hotel properties is controlled by a single hotel organization, the financial structuring tends to be property-specific. Corporate financial strategies are frequently subjugated to the needs of the last property deal brought into the company's fold. Each property in a so-called "chain," is frequently the subject of a unique and distinctive ownership and financial structure. This phenomenon – quite common in the real estate sector, but unusual for business enterprises generally – makes for elusive economies of scale in the structuring and financing of property-driven expansion.

Collectively, these factors have produced low comparative returns in real estate, although criticism leveled at commercial real estate returns is somewhat less germane to the hotel industry, where management and franchise fees can produce high returns for those companies where property ownership is held by third parties. Nevertheless, average returns in the real estate industry in the United States, for example, are just over 10 percent, compared to small company stock returns at almost 20 percent and large company stocks at an average of about 15 percent.

While hotel chains have adopted traditional corporate frameworks, there are a number of predominantly real estate-driven, family-owned businesses in the hotel sector that continue to operate as relatively unstructured organizations. In meeting the future, these businesses will need plans, people and processes in order to establish viable corporate forms that can compete in tomorrow's marketplace and capitalize upon its opportunities.

In today's changed environment, the hotel organization must deal with a number of new realities. Investors in our industry are no longer satisfied with long-term capital appreciation and psychic income that heretofore were often the justification for otherwise seemingly uneconomic investments in hotel property or, indeed, hotel chains. The first reality is that there is a very specific and identifiable relationship between bottom line performance and value. Improvements in business operations raises values. It is not surprising, therefore, that the new owners attracted to this industry in recent years have new sets of demands. This transformation from an old-guard group of investors and owners to income and return-driven newcomers has meant that the once "quiet enjoyment" of operators in their management of hotels for third parties is being disturbed, interrupted and overturned.

These challenges all take place in an environment where capital has become extremely selective in markets that have little stability. A global shortage of capital will not remain a short-term problem, and future hotel organizations must have a stronger alignment to capital providers — a critical "customer" group. Hotel companies will need to compete by offering better returns and performance than in the past. Hotel chains have found their development timetables quashed in recent years, making it difficult to achieve goals of critical mass often required to improve performance. These factors are driving consolidation in the brand "sweepstakes." Capital markets, therefore, continue to favour well-established companies, a reality that must drive entrepreneurial organizations to meet the future now by planning for an evolving corporate context in which to operate.

Key Success Factors-The Future

Within this broad context, hotel developers, owners and management companies will all need to develop new strategies, skills and processes that look forward to the competitive demands of the future. These ultimately must address issues related to vision and planning, as well as organizational skill sets and processes to attract and retain customers. To stake a claim in the future, current business practices should be examined in light of what can be expected to be the key success factors in the year 2000. Embrace a global change orientation. As the information age produces greater worldwide integration of business activities, a global knowledge base will become invaluable. Success in local and regional hotel markets will be shaped decisively by a global business environment that defines capital movement, customer expectations and applications of new technologies.

Focus on the Customer. If the customer is "king" in the 21st century, hotel organizations will be best served by focusing less on their hotel assets as measures of success, and more on their customers. This involves a fundamental shift in viewing the real estate asset as the wealth creator — to the customer as the key to building shareholder wealth. A customer focus must imbue business decisions at all levels of developing and operating a hotel organization. Pursuing such a course will inevitably impact shareholder wealth. To accomplish this, however, customers need to participate in the product development process.

Fully realizing a customer focus in the industry poses a significant challenge. The hotel industry must confront problems due to conflicts between operational needs and real estate goals. Quite simply, an operator must remain customer-focused, but the short-term strategies to meet these needs may be inconsistent with the long-term objectives of property owners. Balancing those goals will be essential. A customer. focus implies a significant shift in what drives hotel development — placing primary emphasis on the customer with the locations to follow. Nevertheless, a hotel organization with its large investment in fixed assets — the real estate — can never be as nimble as a consumer products company in adjusting products and services to match rapid shifts in the marketplace.

The Japanese taught us that the concept of "zero defects" in products and services can yield tremendous benefits. But today an even more rigorous standard dominates — quality that surprises. In practical terms, the hotel industry finds it extremely difficult to meet the standard of zero defects in service. Hotel services are based primarily on people, not computers or other equipment. Quality that surprises takes the concept of zero defects a step further. Yesterday's surprising product or service is today's status quo. Twenty years ago, a business executive did not expect a consistent and predictable level of service wherever he or she travelled in the world. Today that is a standard — not the exception — as is the expectation for sophisticated technology in hotel rooms to support business needs. With customer discrimination so acute, it is not surprising that brand loyalty is a diminishing "commodity" in the hotel industry.

Find the ingredients for visionary leadership. Today's hotel organizations need to recognize the need for visionary leadership. The ability to forecast the future — to anticipate change rather than react to it – will be one of the single greatest determinants of market dominance in the years ahead. The old "command and control" model of leadership is giving way to a focus on leadership in ideas, information, inspiration, vision and teamwork. Warren Bennis, an authority on leadership in the U.S., puts it this way – "For the most part, failing organizations tend to be over-managed and under-led. The leader sets the tone for the moral character, the vision, the corporate culture and the fiber of the institution."

While visionary leadership is essential, it must be linked to business operations and foster a risk bias, rather than a procedural bias. This will allow the organization to stretch and, in turn, change. And it must be shared by empowered professionals and staff throughout the organization, including those who meet the customer.

Overcoming the resistance to change can be a daunting task, particularly in large hotel organizations in which diversions from the status quo may threaten established management lines. It suggests that a culture based on conformance may need to be replaced by an emphasis on flexibility, learning and cooperation. Management competencies will need to be aligned in order to achieve the desired result. For many organizations, this may mean a shift from traditional hierarchies typical of companies in an industrial era to a flatter organization with a more transparent interface between leadership, organizational functions and employees.

Create a defensible position through corporate strategy. For many of the industry's leaders, vision is driven by the strategic planning process, a function which has become critical for success.

Strategic planning, however, has at times been a step-child in the hotel industry, and it is often the first to be cut when organizations are downsized. It is clearly in transition. There also has been a tendency to decentralize and simplify this function – both actions of potential benefit. Strategic planning must be led by the top people in the organization – the CEO and COO. On the other hand, it should be close enough to the customer to ensure that planners can "listen" to and be influenced by customer needs.

Empower Management. Beyond the ability to envision the future, core management capabilities will make the difference – they are essential. A clear vision without the management skills to support it cannot be a recipe for success. First and foremost, hotel management must have strategic development skills and the ability to integrate complex factors affecting success. Market volatility has become the norm, in part caused by the rapidly changing tastes of customers. Customers are increasingly approaching the hotel industry with widely different social, economic and political backgrounds, to say nothing of employees. Being able to deal with these diversities in a positive and constructive fashion that capitalizes on the differences, rather than working to find ways to mitigate them, is the clear path for successful management in the future.

The organization will also need to be imbued with a sense of entrepreneurship that reacts proactively to the market's diversity. Traditional organizations that follow well-documented rules must give way to leaders who can balance a sense of discipline with that of flexibility. Talent and resources must be marshaled and leveraged. In an industry with high fixed costs and labour intensity, the concept of leverage in the hotel business is an all-important one. Improving labour productivity through technology must be a goal for today's forward-looking hotel organization. Management must also be able to narrow the gap between the employer and the employee, forcing a flatter organization in the process. This will put management closer to the customer and speed the two-way communication process up and down the organization.

Be in the information fast lane. The traditional role of information technology (IT) as a back office support for accounting and bookkeeping has clearly moved front and centre stage. IT today influences all aspects of business from corporate strategies to organizational structure – and from the very business processes it is designed to support to performance measurement. In a world where the customer is "king," IT must also deliver in two critical areas: sales and marketing and customer service.

Technology was once viewed as a way to reduce costs by replacing people. That attitude has been firmly supplanted by one that seeks IT support for the creative work that all organizations must pursue. IT must allow organizations to react more speedily to market needs and, of course, produce the fulfilment of customer demands both quickly and accurately. To do this IT must operate on a decentralized basis. IT delivers, but it has to be the right information to the right people, and it needs to be done on a timely basis.

Human Resource Development

The traditional constraints of the hotel, catering and tourism industry – long, antisocial working hours, low pay, unstable, seasonal employment, low job status, etc. – make employment within the industry appear unattractive to many. A study carried out in 1996 in Germany found that employment in the hotel and catering trade was not the first choice for nine out of ten employees, while only one employee in seven was satisfied with the trade as a choice of career. Nevertheless, the industry does attract some people either on a short-term basis or for a long-term career.

The immediate and most obvious consequences of such a situation are the difficulty of recruiting suitable staff and high staff turnover; both these effects are costly to the industry. There is therefore a perceived need for human resource development, to raise the profile of the industry, increase productivity and provide decent, sustainable employment within the sector.

Estimating Labour Productivity

A wide range of technological developments in service in hotels may be affecting productivity. Integrated management systems are enabling hotel companies to computerize day-to-day reception operations. Clients are thus able to make their own reservations via the Internet, while electronic in-room installations make it possible to settle accounts from the hotel room. This technology will also make it possible to monitor the productivity of personnel, while new techniques in food preparation and storage are reducing the skills needed in the kitchen and the time required for food preparation. Hotels are therefore seeking new ways to measure service delivery that take into account customer satisfaction and return visits, rather than sticking to a narrow "input/output" system. In Europe, tourist-related activities account on average for 5.5 per cent of GDP in all European Union Member States and for a total of 9 million employees, representing 6 per cent of the total workforce. The precise percentages vary from country to country. According to WTTC simulated figures, the tourism industry's labour force represents about 3 per cent of the world's total labour force and produces about 4 per cent of total world GDP. The industry can therefore not be regarded as labour intensive throughout.

New Forms of Work Organization

Flexible Work

The First World Travel and Tourism Summit, held in 1977 in Vilamoura, Portugal, recognized that travel and tourism create an unparalleled number of entry-level jobs for young people and women and provides part-time or seasonal employment for people seeking flexible working arrangements. The Summit called for the reduction of rigid practices in labour markets to encourage greater staff mobility, productivity and innovation in a progressive employment environment, with emphasis on a flexible market economy, avoiding protectionist regulation. The Conclusions and Recommendations of the European Union's High Level Group on Tourism and Employment drew attention to the fact that notable adjustments were taking place in European tourism, that these were critical to its competitiveness, and that they would lead to important changes in the tourism labour market.

Those are: a refocusingof core competencies; a deskilling of operational tasks in some sub-branches; upgrading of skills and specializations, in particular in large enterprises and tourist organizations and in complementary services; and the creation of new professional profiles to meet tourists' needs and preferences. The document draws attention to a tendency within the industry to transfer work operations from traditional core sectors to ancillary service suppliers.

A positive example of flexibility is provided by the Sheraton-Denver West Hotel in the United States, where two experienced sales managers share one full-time job, thus enabling the company to benefit from the energy and experience of two persons for the price of one. In this instance, both managers wanted to work part time to accommodate their personal and family needs. The arrangement was particularly effective, since both managers were in continual contact. Job-sharing opportunities of this kind will be even more viable in the future, as information becomes more comprehensively shared and more easily transmitted.

Seasonal Employment

One opportunity which has been insufficiently investigated is the possibility of using the inter-season period as a time for training to impart new skills, guaranteeing re-employment of qualified staff in successive seasons so as to retain their services. A hotel located in Savonlinna (South-Savo, Finland), a city famous for its summer opera festivals, has adopted this approach.

To deal with the multicultural and demanding clientele drawn by the summer festival, the hotel pays its core staff to attend off-season training courses in language skills, knowledge of food and wine and leadership skills. Employee development is seen not as a cost but as an investment which pays good returns during the summer season.

Multiskilling

The employers argue that one way to create sustainable, realistic employment in the industry is to implement a policy of "multiskilling". This is also viewed as a means of reducing the problems of recruitment. Multiskilling has always been practised in small enterprises, but it is only recently that particular attention has been paid to it. As demand for general competencies in small enterprises as well as in major hotel and restaurant chains has grown, and as appropriate means of training for these competencies have been developed, awareness has grown of the importance of multiskilling in that segment. One person fulfilling several roles at different times of the day combines the tasks of several (part-time) jobs into one job.

Multiskilling is also seen as a way to create or preserve a number of full-time jobs, as opposed to part-time jobs, since the tasks may be performed at any time of the day. Instead of employing specialists on a less than full-time basis, employees are trained to perform the tasks of several specialists, often supported by facilitating technology. In Finland, a relatively small hotel has adopted a "multitask" policy. All its employees must be willing to perform any of the tasks that are necessary to operate the hotel. When hiring staff, the hotel manager gives precedence to "right personality" over all other criteria. Some workers left when this decision was taken which suggests that the approach is not universally appealing to employees. According to the CBI, "... skills flexibility is indispensable for functional flexibility. It requires a strong basic education system and a commitment on the part of employers and employees to the acquisition of new and transferable skills.

It helps maintain high employability and reduces frictional unemployment associated with skills mismatch". The IUF, on the other hand, considers that such multiskilling may have the effect of devaluing specific skills, since the flexible worker, as viewed by the employer, has no specialized skills or job qualifications, and performing a variety of tasks requires a lower level of knowledge for each of them. The highly skilled, and consequently better remunerated, specialist worker may become a thing of the past. However, the unions also concede that an employee able to perform a variety of tasks is more valuable to an employer and should be remunerated accordingly.

New Mnagement Methods

Corporate organizations are downsizing and restructuring, which means that they are cutting back on layers of management. This means that less direction is being imparted to employees, who are more frequently required to accept a greater degree of responsibility and accountability. Increased use of technology in the workplace also means an added responsibility for individual workers. It is estimated that the "knowledge revolution", by providing clear information via the Internet on all the industry's tangible elements (illustrations of accommodation and hotel facilities) will make the intangible elements (those imparted by personal contact and service) all the more important.

Lower levels of staff will be empowered to act autonomously. Command and control structures are thus largely giving way to a participatory teamwork approach. Human resources trained to fit in with new working methods will have to be regarded as an asset in which investment must be made, rather than merely as a cost, or employees will seek employment elsewhere. Management is developing ways in which to attract and retain employees.

The advent of new technology will not stop the industry from being a supplier of entry-level jobs; clearly, a large number of routine jobs will continue to exist. However, the question of staff retention will remain a management problem. Information technology will make potential entrants to the industry more aware of the possibilities available, compounding the problem for the industry. In order to retain staff, certain companies have already set up an incentive system. McDonalds introduced a broad-based stock ownership programme in 1995 to improve staff morale and productivity, while in Europe, one major hotel chain has established the CHAMPS reward programme, in which employees earn points for cleanliness, hospitality, accuracy, product quality and speed. These points can be used to buy catalogue merchandise.

Career Development

Truly structured careers, in which workers have genuine prospects of career development, are not numerous in the hotel, tourism and catering sector, and efforts to retain employees through incentives or promotion are the exception rather than the rule. Not only do people tend to "pass through" the sector, but research has shown that it is often the most talented who leave, since they are the most confident of finding other employment, while the less confident stay for fear of becoming unemployed. However, for many young people the industry is an entry point to the world of work. It brings workers into direct contact with the public and can provide opportunities for travel. Moreover, for young people, the provision of food and lodging – a common practice in the industry – facilitates entry into active adult life. These factors combine to make tourism a major motor for the social and professional integration of the young.

New and Changing Occupational Profiles

With the advent of new technologies and an increasingly discerning public able to keep informed through the Internet, the hotel sector is being forced to widen its sphere of action beyond the traditional provision of food and accommodation. In the pursuit of improving the intangibles, major hotel chains are seeking to provide more services, both in response to customers' needs and in an effort to provide an "experience" rather than simple lodging. For example, the French Accor Group has expanded into travel agency services, car hire, casinos and on-board train services, while other groups have established connections with sectors that are indirectly linked to tourism, such as insurance, travel articles and health and beauty services. The range of services now expected by customers naturally requires an upgrading of skills among front-desk staff, who will for the most part be required to administer these services. This will call for motivated personnel with excellent social skills and an understanding of what people want.

Advances in computer technology allow far more rapid and detailed generation of information on quality and economic performance. Hotel managers will thus be called on to react more quickly, to analyse situations and take appropriate decisions. The wider range of services on offer will also call for greater marketing skills than were previously necessary. In large hotels and hotel chains this is resulting in the creation of posts which are new to the industry, but which already exist in other fields, such as budget analysis and management accounting expert, quality manager, yield manager, technical and computer services manager. With greater emphasis being placed on environmental protection, there is also an increasing need for experts on the environmental impact and planning of tourism development. Similarly, greater concern over food safety is creating a growing need for food safety and health experts. As the hotel sphere increasingly includes services catering for customers' entertainment needs, sports and games specialists as well as specialized tour guides are opening up as careers in the tourism sector.

Women's Careers

Women traditionally play an important role in the hotel, restaurant and tourism sector. However, their access to the higher levels of the corporate structure remains problematic. Moreover, they represented only 4 per cent of the industry's highest ranking officers, and 4 per cent of its top earners. To an extent this is the result of friction between family and work responsibilities, especially given the prevailing long working hours in the food-service business. The lower wages paid to women make it more feasible for them to take time off from work to look after family needs than for their husbands to do so. To help resolve this problem, enterprises are starting to introduce family-friendly programmes involving flexi-time, tele-commuting and childcare schemes.

At the level of line employees, a United Kingdom hotel has found an innovative solution to problems it had been encountering in recruiting and retaining room service staff. The hotel decided to target its recruitment efforts on mothers of school-age children and agreed to provide a play leader to look after the children during school holidays. The cost of the play leaderwas made up by saved advertising and recruitment costs previously incurred as a result of high staff turnover. Nonetheless, it remains generally true that there is a gender-based income disparity across all segments of the hotel, catering and tourism industry.

Measures to Promote Career Building in the Enterprise

New divisions of labour and changes in the nature of jobs within the tourism sector mean that the industry is employing an increasingly varied range of employees. However, although tourism is a diverse sector which can provide many working opportunities for a wide range of skills, there is a shift within Europe away from specific skills towards broader, more generic competencies. Good practice in training is largely limited to large hotel chains, and small, individual enterprises tend to rely on training given "on the job". According to research in Spain, managers of three-star hotels recognized that older workers rarely had any of the formal training required to deal with a more sophisticated clientele, and younger workers lacked industry-specific practical skills. However, they were generally reluctant or unable to invest in training, on the grounds that the cost could not be sustained by their operations. The key training needs established by employers and trade unions are food safety, IT, environmental awareness and foreign language skills. The industry provides few post-experience training or retraining opportunities, and, indeed, commitment by the private sector to human resource development appears slight, especially where such development lies beyond their immediate operational needs: "European companies, especially smaller businesses, provide little by way of financial and practical support for human resource development within the wider educational and training framework."

Within the multinational hotel industry, however, there is a trend towards investment in education, training and development, to meet the need for a higher level of customer-oriented service. The Radisson Hotel Group acknowledges that the success of the company depends on the knowledge, skills, abilities, motivation and dedication of its employees, and consequently has a well-developed internal training system, with links to outside training establishments as well, to which 0.4 percent of each hotel's total revenue is dedicated. Through the Radisson SAS climate analysis system, outstanding efforts and exceptional results, both individual and on a team basis, are rewarded through local incentive schemes. The training emphasis is shifting towards continuous learning and increasing the potential of individual employees. A total of 515 employees were trained in different areas in the Radisson SAS Management School in 1999, with specific training in business finance, revenue management, euro handling and business planning. Efforts have been made by the enterprise to establish relations with European and American hotel schools, so that a steady flow of students takes up internships at a Radisson hotel. The Per-Axel Brommesson Scholarship enables four talented employees a year to develop management skills through professional development programmes at institutions such as Cornell University, and other business schools.

In order to bring the training provided by formal education institutions into harmony with the requirements of the everyday operation of the trade, the industry has entered into partnership with teaching establishments, to ensure that the content of their courses is relevant to work in the sector, and to offer students, through that linkage, practical experience in all fields. In the United States in 1996, the Hospitality Business Alliance (HBA) was formed between the National Restaurant Association and the American Hotel and Motel Association to create a school-to-career programme. Worksite experience is an integral element of the training. During the school year, students work between 15 and

20 hours a week in the enterprise, gaining experience in front-desk operations, housekeeping, room service, safety and health, reservations, sales and marketing and convention services. The system has grown from involving three high schools in 1997 to 600 high schools in 1999, covering 25 States and 11,000 students.

One hotel group in the United Kingdom noted a training gap which was preventing the company's (multi-)unit managers, whose role is a largely implementational one, from progressing to a more strategic role within the enterprise. The company's human resource department has organized strategic management development schemes at a number of leading business schools in the United Kingdom and the United States. The courses are designed to expose area managers to the strategic concepts of operational management, including corporate governance, finance, marketing and human resource strategy. This move to supply appropriate training is appreciated by unit managers aspiring to strategic, policy-creative posts.

A number of hotel chains have introduced schemes to enhance careers within their structures, with a view to reducing staff turnover. Choice Hotels International in the United States analysed the requirements for its senior executives on the basis of suitable existing competency models, then assessed the competencies of current top executives and compared these with the competencies needed for the future. This enables the company to carry out annual readiness assessments and to establish a genuine career structure within the group, thus avoiding the disruption and expense of replacing executive staff. A further example is provided by Motel 6, which has established an HRD approach whereby every employee is eligible to become a manager, via a three-tier training scheme. By early 1998 this system had allowed around 300 Motel 6 employees to reach the grade of general managers, thereby helping to fill a need for qualified managers by providing employee training and the basis of a career structure.

Developing Language Skills

An increasingly culturally diverse clientele has necessitated specialist training in the field of knowledge building for staff. ITT Sheraton operates a number of resort hotels in the Hawaiian islands, where the presence of Japanese clients has encouraged the creation of Japanese language and culture courses. This initiative has resulted in a significant increase in the number of Japanese guests frequenting the hotels, while the courses themselves have become problem-solving sessions with staff. In 1992, the Four Seasons Hotel and Resort developed the Self-Access Learning Centre in Indonesia, where the company was opening a new resort, to teach English to locally recruited staff. The courses were designed to take account of the fact that around 80 per cent of the staff had no more than primary-school education. The centre now teaches French and Japanese as well as Bahasa Indonesia. Employees are rewarded as they complete each of the five levels of the course with bonuses ranging from Rps.100,000 to Rps.250,000 (about $8-20), and a certificate of achievement. Turnover at the resort is low, at 4-6 per cent.

Career Enhancement through Increased Employee Responsibility

The Ritz-Carlton Company has identified the empowerment of individual staff members as a way to retain staff through increased job satisfaction. Employees were invited to take on certain management duties: the front-office employees, for example, were invited to take over the role of the front-office manager. As an incentive, the hotel proposed dividing half of the savings obtained through the elimination of the post among the employees who had taken on the duties (about $1.00 each an hour). The replaced staff members were not sacked, but redistributed elsewhere in the company. At another hotel, a system of self-directed housekeeping teams was established and responsibility given to the teams for choosing their own work areas, evaluating room quality and conducting room inspections; this has increased the staff retention rate and morale among room attendants. In 1993, Accor launched a three-year programme to "re-engineer" the structure of Sofitel North America. The programme was designed to empower employees to make decisions to benefit guests, and called for volunteers eager to make improvements in services provided by the hotels. Since suggestions for improvements and alterations were now originating from the employees, peer resistance within each department was minimal: a culture of trust and communication was established. The result has been an increase not only in customer satisfaction, but in employee satisfaction as well. Staff turnover fell from 58 per cent in 1993 to 39 per cent in 1998, below the industry average.

Among the reasons frequently cited for reluctance to taking up employment in the hotel, tourism and catering trade, lack of promotion possibilities features prominently. The broad pyramid of the hierarchy within the industry renders interpretation of the word "career" difficult.

While careers are possible in the sector, and it is theoretically possible to progress from waiter to managing director of a major hotel chain, the increasingly flat management structures can only make this increasingly difficult. On the other hand, systems designed to reward staff financially for their performance, with the aim of reducing staff turnover and encouraging a feeling of "belonging" to the enterprise, are not yet accepted by all staff, and vertical career aspirations are still widespread. Modern-minded employers trust that job satisfaction is tending to shift away from hierarchical feelings. Bonuses to enhance job satisfaction can be awarded (and sometimes withdrawn) at any time, according to individual or collective performance.

Tourism Education and Training

Recognizing the Need for Tourism Education and Training

Employers maintain that many enterprises, especially SMEs, cannot pay wages commensurate with formal training and recognized qualifications. Others argue that the greater productivity made possible by training will make higher wages possible. In general, many of the operational activities in the industry require learning on the job, rather than formal training, and managers frequently state their preference for recruitment on the basis of personality rather than formal qualifications. More than 60 per cent of operational staff in Germany and more than half the labour force in Austria have had no formal training. The industry displays a reluctance to give formal recognition to acquired skills, and this may reflect a wish to avoid claims for higher wages and prevent undesired mobility.

On the other hand, a recent study also suggests that practical training and experience is more highly valued in the countries covered than formal, accredited training qualifications. Moreover, high staff turnover in the industry makes returns on training investment hard to evaluate. Employees, who may not wish to develop a career in the industry or may be discouraged by poor scholastic performance, also avoid measurement by public standards. At middle management level and higher, however, tourism education is a formal requirement. In Canada, it is estimated that more than one-third of jobs in hotels require post-secondary education, including language proficiency, but a Brazilian study shows that only 12 per cent of hotel and restaurant staff have completed secondary school.

Tourism-related degree programmes have been slow to acquire recognition as a truly academic discipline although, given the increasing social and economic importance of tourism, a sound knowledge of its economic, social, cultural, environmental and political dimensions is essential. This is particularly the case in countries, including developing countries, where tourism is growing rapidly. In Europe, tourism training is seen as a means of boosting employment and recouping Europe's dwindling market share in the industry.

New Skill Requirements

In the Rhone-Alpes region of France, 7,000 new hotel and restaurant workers are required. Half the posts do not match formal training schemes. The bipartite committee on vocational training is therefore proposing that graduates acquire additional certificates to become waiters or wine-cellar specialists, as well as cooks, and is considering replacing the certification system with a system listing a variety of competencies. Given the higher customer expectations of quality in a one-to-one relationship with the service personnel, an important part of the required skills concerns personal behaviour and communication, as opposed to specialized operational skills.

The new skill requirements have an undeniable vertical element. The joint vocational training committee in Rhone-Alpes therefore recommends recruiting waiters with higher school qualifications (baccalaureate). However, workers with that level of education rarely seek employment as waiters.

More complex workplaces have brought about a shift in training concerns from operational or vocational skills to personal and social skills. Operational skills are still required, but are increasingly focused on technological innovation. A capacity to learn and develop activities, and to assimilate all elements of a complex process, and effective communication skills, including negotiation in cases of conflict, are among the skills needed to enable today's worker to attain the necessary autonomy at work. This presents a challenge for training institutions geared towards operational skills, rather than "soft" skills.

New technical skills which need to be acquired by line-level employees include: deeper and more up-to-date knowledge of materials and production processes; knowledge of computer programs and other new technologies employed in kitchens and the concomitant new working methods; awareness of safety and health issues, an understanding of the house "business culture"; and an ability to impart an increasingly broad range of information to customers. Language knowledge and a developed inter-cultural sensitivity are key skills for tourism personnel who have direct contact with customers.

Management-level requirements mirror the qualities listed above, but also embrace a new approach to human resource management and development. Enterprises are espousing a philosophy by which workers receiving "good service" from their superiors are more likely to provide "good service" to customers. Another important area of innovation and emphasis for management training is quicker response to – or anticipation of – market developments.

This requirement is nothing new for top chain hotel managers, but it is new for many managers of smaller units and for department chiefs or supervisory-level managers. Adjusting in an autonomous way and developing innovative strategies require a capacity to generate the necessary flux of market information, and consequently also the ability to manipulate computer programmes. This marks a significant departure from the traditional picture of the independent hotel manager as "a jack of all trades" who does not work within budgets or performance targets.

The Importance of Continuous Training

Formally structured initial or primary training, including apprenticeships with practical and technical schooling, seems less adapted to the new "soft" skill requirements of today's industry than continuous training, and current thinking holds that it might be restricted to a minimal, multisector learning platform to raise the employability of young people and their mobility between different sectors. Continuous training, which has the advantage that it may be used to react quickly to changing circumstances, is being directed towards imparting the new skills.

Learning for Competencies

Exchanging the concepts of skills, capacities and qualification for that of competencies is consonant with the idea of the enterprise as a learning organization in which personnel have enhanced strategic and problem-solving capacities at all levels. Competencies are described in terms of the results to be achieved, whereas earlier methodologies prescribed tasks, abilities and desired attitudes, leaving the responsibility for the result to the hierarchy. To promote the new concept, the European Working Group on improving training in the tourism industry" convened by the European Commission recommends that research should be undertaken into ways to develop individuals' capacity to make full use of general, technical and personal skills as well as the "soft skills" needed to make use of the other skills, and into how the enterprise can engage and combine the competencies of individuals in an organic manner. The concept of competencies and their standardization and certification can more easily be introduced where training schemes are flexible. Modular training has always been the basis of training systems in countries where no neat distinction was made between initial training and continuous training. Courses of varying duration, institutional backing, and funding modalities were extended to students of all ages. The new concept of competencies can therefore be introduced speedily to satisfy an increasing need for certification arising from more flexible employment relationships. Training systems in Costa Rica, the

Dominican Republic and Mexico now provide standards for competencies in the hotel, restaurant and tourism sector. Whilst employers offer "earning with learning" to encourage multiskilling, i.e. each acquired competency leads to an increment in salary, trade unions observe that the acquisition of various competencies by workers who occupy jobs outside conventional job classifications tends not to be remunerated appropriately. Bargaining for appropriate remuneration is more difficult where qualifications are diffuse and do not fit into any pre-established scheme. Moreover, bargaining collectively can hardly take account of all possible individual skill combinations. Indeed continuous training has been far less subject to social dialogue than has initial training. Where training for competencies has been introduced, standardization and certification of acquired skills are therefore essential.

Certification

Globalization of the travel and tourism industry and the increased use of e-commerce require a common international understanding and certification of core skills in order to facilitate distance business transactions and assure buyers and sellers that the services they deal with meet certain standards anchored in the qualifications of the labour force. The competitiveness of small tourism enterprises will increasingly depend on the credibility and reliability of the services they can offer. Hotel and restaurant management training provided by colleges and universities is quite transparent even across national borders, but for operational level workers it is often developed by industry associations of the different sectors involved, and it is difficult to avoid overlapping even at the national level.

In recent years, the certification of skills has also been debated as a means of improving the functioning, transparency and permeability of local and national labour markets. Greater workers' mobility between different employers, seasonal locations and ultimately across borders would enhance human resources allocation and create benefits for all players in the sector. On the other hand, there could be immediate disadvantages for some. Increased mobility of workers would counteract efforts made by employers to promote in-house human resources development, as the training and incentives provided would not necessarily pay off within the enterprise. Where elaborate initial training systems exist, they are regarded by trade unions as an acquired right. Certification of skills is therefore not endorsed as a substitute for formal initial training (where it exists), but only as a new way of presenting its results. Greater international recognition of certification is needed where economic integration creates greater mobility within the labour market. In Latin America, an ILO project in the 1990s assisted nine countries on an inventory of qualifications with a view to agreeing on a common classification at a later stage.

The European sectoral social partners are considering a proposal to make the description of acquired skills compatible between the European Union countries. The ECF-IUF and HOTREC are examining the possibility of implementing a "European qualifications passport" for the hotel and restaurant sector. Objections have been voiced on the grounds that certified skills for migrant workers might lead to higher wage claims; however, a qualifications passport could also help employers to find and recruit the right personnel much more easily.

Providers of Continuous Education and Training

There is a very wide range of private, public and semi-public institutions offering continuous education and training in the HCT sector. In some countries, such as Austria, entrepreneurs are required to obtain an entry certificate to the industry from the public authorities. In Switzerland, this practice has been abolished by most local governments. In these countries, and in others with a strong tradition of public training, the social partners run institutions to deliver continuous training, especially at a higher or middle level. Although continuous training features frequently in public debate in Austria, only 5 per cent of the workforce had recourse to it in 1996. This may be explained by the reluctance of employers to give workers time for training or to pay for the courses, or it may be caused by the workers' own disinclination to undergo training.

Private and Semi-private Institutions

Private hotel and restaurant training facilities are many and varied and employers as well as students tend to criticize the weakness or absence of public or joint (employer/government) control of private training establishments unless they have the authority to issue government-guaranteed certificates. In Switzerland, tight public control is exercised over the six establishments that issue government certificates. Their owners include government, employers' organizations, a workers' organization, a mixed foundation, and a fully private institution. The remaining 31 private hotel and restaurant schools in Switzerland are not publicly monitored: the Swiss Association of Hotel and Restaurant Schools performs this function. These establishments tend to recruit students from abroad and charge annual fees of up to Sw.frs.20,000. The training provided by the Swiss schools has already assimilated the requirements of the new skills and concentrates on continued general education, languages, and personality skills for managers. On the technical side, the emphasis is on marketing and product development, while more basic skills are dealt with in training blocks.

In the 1960s and 1970s, universities and colleges in the United States were the first to offer hotel and tourism degrees at the tertiary level. Since then, hotel and tourism curricula have been established at college and university level in Germany, Austria and Switzerland. In Spain, tourism schools used to have agreements with British universities to issue college certificates,.but they have now linked up with local universities and their work has been integrated into the official Spanish education system. The training at universities, colleges and generally private specialized schools focuses on management of tourism enterprises or developing tourism destinations and also provides a grounding in both conceptual and practical skills geared to a sector dominated by small and medium-sized enterprises. The schools are responding to criticism, heard mainly in developing countries, regarding a lack of practical skills in their graduates. In recently industrialized countries, such as Brazil and China, local centres are upgrading their curricula through cooperation with renowned American and European hotel and restaurant schools.

Tourism education and training provided by trade associations is widely available in many industrialized countries. This in general consists of non-degree programmes of a more practical nature. In the United States, as an outstanding example, the Educational Institute of the American Hotel and Motel Association has provided educational services to almost 300,000 persons within the country and elsewhere. The institute offers its own diplomas and certificates in six areas of specialization using textbooks and distance learning materials produced by leading educators from various universities. Distance training systems with interactive Internet technology and worldwide outreach are starting to operate in all sectors, to the benefit of employees unable to leave work.

New work structures require more direct customer contact. Training institutions will accord greater attention to this area which is critical to improvement in productivity. However, there is little information available about changes in the area of traditional apprenticeships, through which (in Austria, for example) apprentices continue to be trained for the classical occupations of cook or waiter. It is probable, in view of the emphasis on personality and social skills, that training will become less formalized. These changes pose a considerable challenge as regards certification of skills for career purposes.

Training Provided by the Employer

Elaborate human resource development strategies are usually linked to long-term business development plans, and these are more frequently associated with large enterprises. They are based on a budget set aside for training and providing for trainers to be contracted from outside the hotel. Training budgets can account for up to 3 per cent of a hotel's financial turnover although 1 per cent of payroll is considered substantial. A system of assessing training requirements through frequent staff appraisal is found at establishments where staff development is taken seriously. Where training is less formalized, on the other hand, it is done by managers or supervisors who are not training specialists; there may be no budget set aside for it in spite of a declared willingness to offer training to staff. In such cases, training is often reactive rather than proactive, i.e. restricted to induction training for newly recruited staff and statutory (compulsory) safety and health training. It is also common for scheduled training sessions to be cancelled when employees are not replaced at their workplaces and therefore fail to turn up.

Major hotel chains rely largely on their own internal training systems. The Accor Group employs about 140,000 people in 132 countries. Five per cent of staff-related expenditure goes on training in three main areas: initial training for basic qualifications or as an introduction for new employees (delivered in-house); continuous training for director-level employees (department chiefs and others), covering areas such as sales, leadership, customer contacts and so on; and inter-cultural education.

Accor's training is delivered by the group's own Paris-based academy which has training centres in various locations and countries. The Accor academy receives 14,000 trainees each year. In addition, the group has concluded agreements with a number of schools to accept Accor personnel for certain courses and to run fellowship programmes for Accor.

In spite of notable efforts by employers, the HCT industry comes bottom of a table of 16 industries in Germany in terms of the percentage of its enterprises that provide training for their employees (24.4 per cent, the median being about 70 per cent). On the other hand, continuous training for employees of hotel chains is quite common at management level. The Hyatt Group, to give one example of many, runs a "corporate management training programme". In-house training at management level generates a strong commitment to the company culture among beneficiaries and yields very high dividends in terms of competitive advantage. In the United Kingdom, a recent survey showed that 60 per cent of all hotels, 53 per cent of restaurants and 70 per cent of pubs and caterers arranged some form of continuous training. Enterprises employing 11 or more workers provided significantly more continuous training than smaller establishments, as did hotel chains, as opposed to individual, private hotels. This was also the case in Brazil, where research shows that it is generally large or medium-sized hotels that provide training, and that courses are short (21 hours on average). Since the larger hotels also tend to offer better employment conditions in other respects too, they can lure workers away from smaller hotels, to the detriment of any staff development policy in the independent hotels.

An example of the way in which some independent hotels address the problem of skills deficiencies is provided by one group of United Kingdom hotels. The group in question has formed a training consortium which works with a regional college to run an employee training and development programme, thus allowing economies of scale. All the hotels in the group can send one or two staff members to attend the courses as required.

Defining the Training Gap

The hotel and restaurant industry suffers from a discrepancy between training supply and demand. The specialized training institutions tend to lag behind developments in the industry, and these developments are particularly radical at present. The current skills gap is felt to be at the operational level, whereas training institutions, especially private institutions, are largely geared towards management training. This situation is seen in Brazil, where a study shows that training institutions are relevant only for the higher qualification levels and the majority of staff recruited by enterprises have not undergone any formal.

New Techniques of Training Delivery

Education and training are benefiting from developments in information and communication technologies and are increasingly being delivered through multimedia devices such as interactive on-line connections and CD-ROM. Investments in competitive training packages can be immense: the cost of a recent training CD-ROM for the hotel and restaurant sector was US$1 million. Large chains of hotels are also making use of this technology to fulfil their training needs: Holiday Inn spent US$2.5 million in 1995 to create online training multimedia for its employees. In 1998, Cendant's Days Inn launched an interactive web-based training programme to maximize the efficiency of the training budget and employee time.

Traditional schools are finding themselves in competition with "cyberschools", and where multimedia training devices are used within traditional schools, teachers are moving away from their traditional role as sources of knowledge towards a new role as "coaches" who help students to tap into much better (electronic) sources of knowledge. Hotel and restaurant firms are already developing and using multimedia components to guide employees through everything from making a pizza to providing a help desk for night auditors. Students will be able to chose when and where to undergo their training, and to adapt it to their individual learning speed. Education and training will shift from being teacher-centred to being learner-centred.

In the Netherlands, the Hotel School of The Hague has developed an innovative teaching method. There are no traditional classes. Students are set problems individually or in groups and then seek the information they need to solve them, coached by former teachers. In order to do this they have to develop technical and behavioural skills of various kinds and in different areas which hitherto were taught separately. Students are expected to return to the school throughout their professional life for recycling and "lifelong learning", supported by more or less permanent on-line learning. Increased motivation has been noted both among staff and students. However, performance measurement was harder, and prospective employers will have to adjust their selection criteria in order to assess the new type of training.

Conditions for electronically supported learning are almost ripe for a further "quantum leap". The interconnection of individuals and the formation of virtual learning groups, as well as the ability to call up from a local workstation all the knowledge accumulated by a company or made available through leasing contracts, will change lifelong learning into a continuous updating of personnel. Expert support will be made available on line and in real time, and there will be virtually no limits, other than those of cost, to the instant accessibility of the multimedia training material needed for individual learning plans.

Social Dialogue on Training

Tripartite or bipartite cooperation on training policies is common in many countries, at central or local levels. In many countries, developed or developing, staff training is guided by tripartite bodies, some of them sectoral. In Canada, the Hotel Employees and Restaurant Employees International Union (HERE), the Canadian Auto Workers (CAW) and the United Food and Commercial Workers sit beside management on the board of the Canadian Tourism Human Resource Council (CTHRC) which provides labour-oriented input to new certification and training programmes. The dual system of initial training common in a number of European countries has long been based on a firm consensus between employers' and workers' organizations and on detailed legislation. Proposals for changes in pertinent legislation go through solid consultation procedures before they can be adopted by the competent authorities. Quicker action and intensive consultation is required in the sphere of continuous training, particularly where the improvement of workers' skills is part of a broader strategy for the development of the hotel, catering and tourism sector on a national or regional basis.

Spain provides an example of an effort to rapidly improve the quality of the tourism product in the face of increased international competition. Joint sectoral committees composed of delegates from representative workers' and employers' organizations, technically supported by the Foundation for Continuous Training (FORCEM), appraise training plans with a view to submitting recommendations for public funding to a central (inter-sectoral) joint committee. The sectoral committees propose certification criteria for continuous training courses in accordance with a national qualification system. Women's training heads the list amongst the target group criteria of the Spanish joint committee on hotels and restaurants.

In a number of Latin American countries, tripartite committees on vocational training have been in existence for decades and have influenced some vocational training policies. However, as most efficient vocational training systems were run by sectoral employers' organizations using payroll-based funding modalities (Brazil, Colombia), unions felt that their participation in steering committees did not always have the desired effect. Designing standards for competencies is a new area in which tripartite cooperation is developing at a rather technical level.

In the European Union, an important step was taken by the ECF-IUF and the European Federation of Contract Catering Organizations (FERCO). In 1999 they concluded an "Agreement on vocational training in the European contract catering sector," which provides for joint initiatives in the area of continuous vocational training. In particular, it refers to non-discrimination between men and women, full-time and part-time employees and professional categories, in respect of access to continuous training measures. Before the agreement, the ECF-IUF prepared a survey on continuous training in the European contract catering industry based on a questionnaire. It produced a very heterogeneous picture across the countries in terms of regulations (none at all, legislation or collective agreements), volume (in terms of percentage of payroll spent on continuous training), distribution (between blue-collar and white-collar workers), participation of workers' representatives in planning, certification, and other areas. The survey concluded that continuous training was provided by enterprises, and that the skills required were not recognized officially. It noted that such training still helped workers to advance in their careers or to find alternative employment. However, such training did not fully meet workers' expectations, and there was inadequate trade union involvement.

Social Dialogue

The social dialogue relationship between the social partners in the hotel, catering and tourism sector in general seems to need more development. Both workers and employers agree that much remains to be done. There are differences, however. Trade unions' concerns are centred on being recognized as partners for social dialogue everywhere, as pointed out below. Employers generally favour greater social responsibility of the enterprise, but not all employers actively promote partnership with trade unions as a means of achieving their social goals. Whatever the current and future shape of partnerships, the understanding of the International Hotel and Restaurant Association (IH&RA) is that the social role of enterprises will be determined by a general trend towards democratization. Employers also see better partnership between management and labour arising from a common response to the challenges of global competition. They anticipate that workers' organizations will adjust to the discipline that capital markets impose on business, while trade unions are worried by practices such as subcontracting and franchising which they feel create divisions among those working at the same location. They also favour the ratification by ILO member States of the Working Conditions (Hotels and Restaurants) Convention, 1991 (No. 172), and the promotion of equality between women and men at the workplace.

A trend towards improving social partnership can be observed in the Caribbean, where the tourism industry is by far the most important economic sector and where employers' "increasing recognition of the need to engage the cooperation of labour is matched by an increasing recognition on the part of labour that the transformation of business into more productive and competitive operations could mean higher levels of employment and income security".

Organizations

The coverage by workers' and employers' organizations of the hotel, catering and tourism sector can vary from country to country and from region to region. In general, workers' organizations are more diverse than employers' associations. For historical reasons, trade unions either: (a) cover a number of sectors, of which the hotel, catering and tourism sector is only one; such is the case of those trade unions that represent the entire food production chain from farms to restaurants or groceries; or (b) cover a proportion of workers in the hotel, catering and tourism sector as a result of overlapping with their main sectors, such as office workers (travel agencies), transport workers, workers in services in general (France) or in personal services in particular (Austria).

On the other hand, employers' organizations in the HCT sector are more uniform, as hotels and restaurants form a clear majority amongst their membership. As far as the restaurant subsector is concerned, however, representation of employers in a number of countries is subdivided into three different types of specialized organizations covering conventional restaurants, collective or institutional catering, and, more recently, fast-food restaurants, as in Germany. At the European level, there are two federations of employers' organizations: the Confederation of National Associations of Hotels, Restaurants, Cafes and Similar Establishments in the European Union and European Economic Area (HOTREC), for conventional hotels and restaurants; and the European Federation of Contract Catering organizations (FERCO), for collective or institutional restaurants.

The International Hotel and Restaurant Association (IH&RA) is the largest organization of hotel and restaurant employers at the international level, representing over 750,000 establishments in more than 150 countries. Among its affiliates are some 50 national and international hotel and restaurant chains, many independent hotel operators and restaurateurs, over 110 national hotel and restaurant associations, a number of industry suppliers, and 130 educational institutions in the hotel and restaurant industry.

The largest workers' organization at the international level, the International Union of Food, Agricultural, Hotel, Restaurant, Catering, Tobacco and Allied Workers' Associations (IUF), has 326 affiliated organizations representing 10million workers in 118 countries.

Other international trade secretariats, the International Transport Workers' Federation (ITF), and Union Network International (UNI), which represents workers in travel agencies, coordinate their action with the IUF. At the European level, this coordination has resulted in a special European Trade Union Liaison Committee on Tourism (ETLC).

Obstacles to Workers' Organizing

Workers in the hospitality sector are in general organized in trade unions to a lesser degree than workers in other sectors. This is due to a number of circumstances including the following:

- *The small size of enterprises:* Owing to the prevalence of small enterprises, trade union affiliation in the HCT sector may be as little as 10 per cent on average in industrialized countries. However, major hotels in large cities are often unionized, even in countries where smaller units or hotels located outside the centres of large cities are not. For example, in Canada (Vancouver, Toronto and Montreal), an estimated 80 per cent of large full-service down-town and airport hotels were unionized in the mid-1990s. In the United Kingdom, the role of trade unions is stronger in institutional catering, mainly in the public sector, and in a minority of large hotel groups.
- *The mainly young workforce:* Most workers in the HCT sector lack experience with labour issues as they are in their first formal employment, which in most cases is still of a transient nature.

- *High staff turnover:* Even those workers who stay in the sector will change employers frequently or leave work altogether during certain periods of their life; this is notably the case with women when their children are small.
- *Prevalence of part-time and casual work, irregular hours:* Part-time or on-call arrangements, as well as irregular working hours, keep communication between workers at a low level. In particular, the increasing number of students working in the sector are not necessarily inclined to join trade unions.
- *Varying employment contracts:* Subcontracting, fixed-term employment, and internships in many modern hotel and restaurant enterprises split workers up into several segments with different employment conditions, even when they perform the same tasks. This results in individualization of workers and competition between them.
- *Gender:* Weak affiliation to workers' organizations is more common among women workers since they are disproportionately represented among part-time, casual and young workers and in small enterprises. As they form the less qualified and less well-remunerated segment of the labour force, they also tend to have less access to information and are less able to contribute to workers' collective bargaining power.
- *Attitude factors:* Low self-esteem among the workforce as a collectivity is specific to the hotel and restaurant sector. This is due, firstly, to its generally poor image from which only modern enterprises are immune. The sector is still associated with service in the traditional sense, which involves a "submissive" relationship. Secondly, success in hotel and restaurant services is hard to measure objectively, as it depends on the subjective feelings of customers. The modern customer relationship is built on individual capacities, skills and style, and there is little collective kudos to be had from excellent service.

These factors are reflected in the attitudes of many employers who do not favour the organization of workers in independent bodies with roots outside the enterprise. This is particularly marked in small and medium-sized enterprises and in multinational enterprises whose central management is not used to a trade union culture. Some observers stress the paternalistic management style prevalent in small hotels and restaurants as a factor working against any collective workers' representation.

Subcontracting and Franchising

Trade unions in the hotel and restaurant sector take the view that subcontracting is a method increasingly used to divide workers and thereby weaken collective bargaining power. Moreover, subcontractor enterprises are normally less unionized or belong to a different sector from that of the contracting enterprise. As a result, they tend to pay lower wages and provide less stable employment conditions. Increasingly, subcontracted services relate to security and surveillance, maintenance, cleaning, catering for hotel personnel and restaurant services for guests. As profit margins are considerably lower for restaurants than for hotel operations, subcontracting of restaurants is being increasingly used in large and medium-sized hotels.The Hotel Employees and Restaurant Employees International Union in the United States and Canada acknowledges that leasing out a hotel restaurant is economically attractive where the hotel is unionized and the leasing enterprise is not. The phenomenon is "exacerbated [for the unions] because in most major North American cities the restaurant industry is largely non-union". At the "New York-New York" Casino in Las Vegas, for example, where virtually all food and beverage services have been subcontracted, HERE represents 900 workers; it would represent 2,700 workers in the hotel if food and beverages were not leased out. Safeguarding workers' interests in the context of subcontracting has become one of the main objectives of collective bargaining in the hospitality sector. Trade unions are not opposed to subcontracting in principle but want to negotiate the modalities in order to protect workers against dismissal or deterioration of employment and working conditions. The IUF regards subcontracting as a priority area.

Some of here's local affiliates bargain to establish joint liability of the employer and the subcontractor. Agreements include a commitment on the part of the (old) employer, e.g. "to require such contractor to offer employment to existing personnel, to recognize their length of service, and to recognize the union as the collective bargaining agent".

The franchising system creates similar difficulties with regard to worker representation as subcontracting, especially where legislation provides for company-wide workers' representative bodies based on minimum numbers of employees per unit. Franchised units have the legal status of independent employers, although in terms of their workplace activities they are an integrated part of a larger company. Trade unions therefore believe that there is an imbalance between the actual size of a company and the legal status of its smaller units. Franchised units benefit from the support of central management in areas such as labour relations, marketing, technological innovation and standardization of procedures. However, agreements concluded between trade unions and companies such as Accor or McDonald's apply only to those units that are owned centrally, not to other franchised units which may well represent the majority of all units, as is the case with McDonald's. The IUF therefore proposes to its affiliates a strategy aimed at creating the same social conditions for workers in franchised units as for the workers in units fully owned by the multinational company in question, in accordance with the principle "same brand-same rights".

Workers' Representation at the Enterprise Level

It has been pointed out in previous sections of this report that the hospitality sector, with its subdivision into relatively small units, its service industry character and its flexible orientation towards the customer, has been guided by teamwork for a long time. Bodies that organize workers within the enterprise on the basis of teamwork structures, such as quality circles, are therefore more common than formalized works councils.

Workers' representation at the employer's initiative rarely addresses fundamental interests such as pay or working time. It is intended more to improve communication between staff and management and among staff members, and to deal with questions concerning the improvement of day-to-day business operations and staff training. For example, the British Hospitality Association (representing 25,000 establishments in the United Kingdom) advises that the issues dealt with in consultation with the workers should be selected at the discretion of the employer and as required by legislation.

The actual presence and activity of employees in non-elected workers' participation structures seems to vary considerably depending on the subject dealt with, whether the meeting takes place during working hours, at what time of day, and other factors. Participation is therefore largely on an ad hoc basis. An Accor hotel manager in Paris, referring to meetings with staff on hotel refurbishing options, stated that as a rule one-third of the staff had participated actively, another third remained rather passive but were present at the meetings, and the rest did not attend.

Collective Bargaining

Collective bargaining in the hotel, catering and tourism sector varies according to the social dialogue culture of a country or region. Collective agreements often differ from each other according to local conditions or enterprise cultures. Trade unionists say that the great variety of collective agreements in the sector may reflect a low level of coordination across geographic and enterprise borders and ultimately follows from low trade union density. Collective agreements are not yet fully applied to ensure decent working conditions for all and competitive human resource development, even where appropriate clauses are contained in the text. They normally cover mainly remuneration and working conditions, as well as non-discrimination and, more recently, the prohibition of child labour. Training provided by the employer is mentioned only in a minority of collective agreements. Among the working conditions reflected in most agreements, working time predominates owing to the prevailing irregular working hours and the difficulty of assessing overtime and guaranteeing rest periods. Works councils, where they exist, are often given ad hoc power to agree to changes at short notice.

Remuneration is determined in collective agreements according to occupational group, hierarchical level and personal criteria such as age and seniority. The definition of these criteria often creates difficulties, as classifications of occupations are not generally agreed by the social partners in all countries. Especially in the HCT sector, the definition of occupations is becoming increasingly fluid as phenomena such as multiskilling and flexible distribution of tasks in the enterprise prevail as a result of restructuring and new management methods imposed by competition. Trade unions are concerned with providing, through collective bargaining, minimum definitions in order to prevent salaries from deteriorating as a result of unclear notions of new work patterns. The classifications of occupations reflected in collective agreements are generally established by bipartite or tripartite bodies, often within the framework of vocational training policies.

The structure and scope of collective bargaining in the HCT sector varies according to legislation and national practice. In North America, Asia and Africa, the workforce of an enterprise tends to be the representative group for the purposes of bargaining. In European countries, on the other hand, negotiations are frequently undertaken on behalf of all workers in the sector or of a subsector on a geographical basis, i.e. at national or regional level. In Germany, collective agreements with geographical coverage at the regional (Lander) level stipulate minimum regulations and are complemented by collective agreements at the enterprise level. Recently, there has been a tendency to negotiate more issues at the enterprise level than was done in the past in order to take account of sharper differences between the economic performance of individual enterprises.Collective bargaining in the HCT sector is based on the subsectors covered by employers' organizations, so that separate negotiations are often held for hotels and restaurants, catering and the tour operating and travel agency subsector. Chain enterprises may engage in collective bargaining, leaving small and medium-sized enterprises behind; this has been the case in France, where collective agreements were concluded for a number of years for hotel and restaurant chains, while the independent hotels and restaurants adopted the procedure only recently. As many as 80 per cent of independent (predominantly small) enterprises are covered by the collective agreements, although their workers are normally not unionized. In addition, the collective agreement is regularly extended by Government decree to cover all enterprises and all workers in the sector. Collective bargaining and collective agreements have been useful in mitigating the negative effects on workers of increased competition between enterprises resulting from globalization, and in preventing an unbalanced distribution between employers and workers of the burden resulting from rapid changes. A common challenge arises when ownership of an enterprise changes. In such cases, a general clause is sometimes introduced in collective agreements to guarantee the preservation of employment contracts and other arrangements for a certain period.

One example of this is an agreement between the Italian-based company, Autogrill and the Dutch trade union federation, Horecabond in 1998. Following Autogrill's purchase of the Dutch company AC Holding, the agreement guaranteed that no worker would be dismissed within a period of two-and-a-half years and that existing employment conditions and workers' rights would remain in force during that period. Collective agreements addressing similar situations have been concluded in other European countries.

Trade unions have had difficulties in bargaining on the continuity of working and employment conditions in cases where they are faced with a weak local interlocutor and the acting party behind the change is a multinational enterprise based outside the country. This situation may arise in cases of franchising or in cases of management contracts with strict decentralization of power with regard to labour relations. It is generally the policy of transnational companies to leave labour relations to the local level to ensure that local conditions are taken fully into account. Trade unions object to this policy, however, where it puts workers in a subsidiary of a multinational enterprise in a less favourable position than other workers of the same chain, or where the mother enterprise's absence from labour relations leaves the local employer in a weak position or unwilling to assume contractual responsibility.

Social Dialogue Plus: Community Involvement

Organizations involved in campaigning for changes in the hotel, catering and tourism sector can find partners and supporters in different segments of the community because the sector overlaps with many others. This is more likely in countries where tourism is the most dynamic sector or where it is the major source of foreign exchange income, as is the case in many small island States, such as those of the Caribbean. An interesting example is the "living wage campaign" conducted in the 1990s in the hospitality sector in Los Angeles.

Regional Social Dialogue: The Case of Europe

At the level of the European Union and the European Economic Area (EEA), employers and workers of the hotel, restaurants and cafes sector engage in social dialogue at the sectoral level within a framework provided by the European Commission. A formal social dialogue committee at sectoral level was set up in 1999 after social dialogue activities had been launched by the social partners (ECF-IUF and HOTREC) in the early 1990s. The group meets four times a year for sessions conducted by the European Commission.

The results of sectoral social dialogue at European level include various joint declarations adopted by the social partners since 1995. The most recent one, dated 3 May 1999, is the Joint Declaration for the promotion of employment in the European hotel and restaurant sector. It reflects the major social issues concerning this sector at present. In order to achieve improved competitiveness and efficiency of European enterprises, provide better qualified and motivated staff and create new job opportunities, the social partners propose to adopt certain measures concerning, in particular, the reduction of taxes and non-wage costs, and improved training and certification to enhance workers' employability and mobility. Issues of part-time employment and flexible working hours are also addressed. The creation of full-time jobs remains a priority; the intention is that flexible working hours should be applied within the framework of agreements between the social partners and adapted to the respective needs of companies and employees.

An Agreement on vocational training in the European contract catering sector was reached by FERCO and ECF- in October 1999. The Agreement covers joint initiatives in the area of continuous vocational training, commitments to equal treatment for men and women and for full-time and part-time workers, and commitments to non-discrimination against workers involved in training. It also stimulates joint action at the company level to identify training needs, elaborate programmes and evaluate their effectiveness.

Employers' and workers' representatives also participated, through individually named experts or the European Trade Union Liaison Committee on Tourism (ETLC), in the High Level Group on Tourism and Employment convened by the European Commission in 1998. The resulting recommendations have reportedly been useful in many bipartite or tripartite debates on the development of tourism as an employment-creating activity. They cover issues such as: negotiation of flexible employability systems and a dynamic approach to social protection; promotion of vocational training for career development; mutual recognition of qualifications between European countries to enhance workers' mobility; and structured, sectoral social dialogue.

European Works Councils

Social dialogue within multinational companies at European level is provided for by the EU Directive on European Works Councils (EWCs), which has initiated cross-border meetings between workers' representatives and managers of companies having business in more than one country within the European Economic Area (including the United Kingdom since the 1997 Amsterdam Treaty).

The essential requirement of the Directive is the creation of a European Works Council in every active enterprise with at least 150 employees in each of at least two countries and a total of at least 1,000 employees within the EEA. A procedure for consultation and information sharing must be established if at least 150 employees from at least two countries request it. Those meetings are not so much collective bargaining sessions as information and consultation procedures, and employee representatives cannot block management decisions.

Most of the European Works Councils in the hotel, catering and tourism sector were created by multinational companies that established "voluntary agreements" for a transitional period before full implementation of the Directive in September 1996. Those agreements could be concluded with appointed employee representatives instead of those determined in accordance with national law or practice, as required by the Directive. At present, there are 14 EWCs of which only two were established after the deadline for voluntary agreements (by Sodexho, the world's largest institutional caterer, and in American Express)., The achievements of the EWCs so far have only partially lived up to the expectations of the trade unions involved. This seems to be mainly due to the infrequency of (annual) meetings.

Internationalization of Information on Labour Issues

Communication technology makes it possible to post information for an international audience without delay. Labour disputes in hotels or restaurants are increasingly drawn to the attention of the public through trade unions websites. Those sites also contain recommendations on hotels to avoid and those that should be patronized in the light of management attitudes to trade union activities and workers' interests. Detailed accounts of labour disputes are given in cases of non-recommendation by the IUF. Employers' associations object to the practice, which they maintain does not adequately distinguish between labour relations disputes which do not necessarily involve any illegal actions and acts which are "illegal and socially reprehensible".

In response to the limited success of collective bargaining, trade unions have also resorted to international solidarity campaigns. A major labour dispute in the Lotte Hotel in Seoul came to an end on 21 August 2000 after several trade unions posted information on the dispute and the workers' claims on their website and representations were made by trade unions in different countries to Korean diplomatic missions. The agreement provides for an automatic mechanism to stabilize precarious employment of staff.

Information and communication technologies also increase the potential for pressure on tourism destinations that fail to comply with minimum standards. An example of this is the tourism boycott against the military regime in Myanmar pursued by the IUF through the Internet. A number of companies involved in tourism activities in that country and engaged in social dialogue with trade unions affiliated to the IUF have responded by discontinuing their engagement until the social and political situation in the country is stabilized and pending civil rights issues are resolved.

Social Dialogue on Tourism Development Policies

Workers' and employers' organizations are involved in tourism development policies in many countries where tourism boards include workers' and employers' representatives. In a number of cases, the structure was established following ILO technical cooperation.

At the international level, workers' and employers' organizations are represented at the annual meetings organized by the United Nations Commission for Sustainable Development (CSD) as a follow-up to the 1992 United Nations Conference on Environment and Development (UNCED), which identified tourism as one of the key economic sectors which could make a positive contribution to achieving sustainable development.

At the Seventh Session of the Commission for Sustainable Development (CSD-7, 1999), which dealt with sustainable tourism development among other topics, business and industry was represented by the International Hotel and Restaurant Association (IH&RA) and the World Travel and Tourism Council (WTTC). Workers were represented by the International Confederation of Free Trade Unions (ICFTU) and the Trade Union Advisory Committee to the OECD (TUAC). During the discussions, the social dimension of sustainable tourism development was widely recognized. Both groups called for training of hotel and tourism personnel in environmental protection, and emphasized the importance of making tourism sustainable so as to maximize its potential for job creation.

The workers and trade union representatives noted a deterioration of working conditions and labour rights in tourism arising from globalization and from competition among countries for foreign investment. The business group presented its environmental initiatives – WTTC's "Green Globe" label and the annual environmental award "Green Hotelier" given by IH&RA and UNEP – and set out its views on the criteria for sustainable growth in the industry and many voluntary initiatives undertaken by it.

Summary and Suggested Points for Discussion

The hotel, catering and tourism sector, as defined by the ILO in 1980 within the framework of its sectoral activities, includes enterprises most of which fall under sections 55 (Hotels and restaurants) and 6304 (Travel agencies and tour operators, etc.) of the International Standard Industrial Classification of All Economic Activities (ISIC), Revision 3, 1990. However, owing to the strong development of the tourism economy in the last decades both in developed and in developing countries, many other organizations focus their activities on the United Nations definition of tourism as all economic activities providing products and services to travellers or tourists. The ILO definition of the HCT sector differs from this in including not only services provided to travellers but also those used by residents. Although in national accounting the tourism ratio of hotels and restaurants, i.e. the proportion of their services provided to travellers, may range from one-quarter to three-quarters, it is normal practice to subsume the sector under "tourism". On the basis of a United Nations recommendation of 1993, national statistical offices are starting to prepare Tourism Satellite Accounts in accordance with a methodology worked out jointly by the World Tourism Organization, OECD and EUROSTAT. An extension for tourism labour statistics is being contributed by the ILO. The private World Travel and Tourism Council (WTTC) has been issuing simulated Tourism Satellite Accounts based on input-output analysis of a number of countries.

The economic concept of tourism includes personal travel (for leisure and other purposes) as well as business trips, international as well as domestic travelling. The industry's direct or "face-to-face" services to tourists represent between 3 and 4 per cent of GDP in most of the world economy and employ about 3 per cent of the world's total labour force, although in some countries tourism employs up to 10 per cent of the workforce. Currently, the industry is growing worldwide by about 3 per cent annually, with Europe showing a lower than average growth rate of 2.3 per cent, and the Asia-Pacific region having the lowest, at 1.4 per cent in the aftermath of the Asian crisis. The highest annual growth rates have recently been seen in South Asia (9.1 per cent) the Caribbean (6.8 per cent) and Central and Eastern Europe (5.2 per cent). However, the travel and tourism industry's share in the world's GDP has been fairly constant because the largest tourism volumes are still in the regions where growth is in line with economic growth in general (according to the WTTC in 2000).

If we include the industries that serve tourists indirectly, i.e. those that do not involve face-to-face contact with tourists but provide infrastructure or inputs to the direct tourism industry, the total tourism-related economy has been estimated to produce as much as 11 per cent of GDP and to employ 8 per cent of the labour force worldwide (WTTC, 2000). Worldwide, one job in the direct tourism industry induces roughly one-and-a-half additional (indirect) jobs in the tourism-related economy. The figure has been estimated to vary from 1.2 (in North America and Latin America) to about 2 (in the Caribbean and Europe), while falling somewhere between those values in Asia and Africa (WTTC, 2000).

Border-crossing tourism has grown faster than tourism overall. According to statistics published by the World Tourism Organization, international tourist arrivals have grown at an average annual rate of 7 per cent since 1950 and will grow at an average annual rate of 4.5 per cent over the next 20 years. In recent years, however, the growth of international tourism has been no more rapid than the growth of the world economy as a whole, i.e. about 3 per cent. During the year 2000, almost 700 million tourists crossed a border and spent over US$500 billion while abroad. Border-crossing tourism adds about 25 per cent to domestic tourism GDP worldwide, with certain regions depending more markedly on international tourism than others. In the Caribbean, a fifth of GDP is produced for tourists, directly or indirectly, by one out of every seven workers. Latin America and Africa have increased their market shares recently, while that of Asia has declined but is recovering rapidly.

The demand for tourism services is also changing qualitatively. Travelling is increasingly becoming part of the lifestyle of a substantial proportion of some nations' populations, including the better-off in developing countries. Trips have become shorter but more frequent. New market niches are being exploited, such as nature tourism, ecotourism and adventure tourism. Tourists are becoming more knowledgeable and aware of issues such as the protection of the environment. The spread of information technologies enables tourism providers to cater more efficiently for a more diversified clientele.

Globalized tourism has been strongly supported by the deregulation of air transport. In developing countries, no less than 80 per cent of international tourists arrive by air. Air fares are falling drastically as a result of increased competition and the abolition of national monopolies. The General Agreement on Trade in Services (GATS) has had an impact on the liberalization of the international tourism economy. Most countries have made tourism-related commitments under GATS concerning issues such as commercial presence or access to technology. The liberalization of the "presence of natural persons", however, is not far advanced.

Economic blocs also promote the increase of tourism activities among their member countries and support their development as global tourism destinations. In particular, the European Union (EU) and the Association of South-East Asian Nations (ASEAN) are known for having specific tourism promotion policies, whereas in the Caribbean, regionally coordinated tourism is developing.

Concerns have been raised about the relatively low participation of developing countries in electronic distribution and reservation systems run by large air carriers, which do not sufficiently take into account the needs of small and medium-sized enterprises. However, the Internet is increasingly being used to market destinations worldwide, including by associations of independent enterprises. Tourism is among the most important application domains in the World Wide Web. It is estimated that up to half of all online transactions are tourism-oriented, but these still represent only a tiny proportion of total travel business (as yet not more than 1 or 2 per cent). However, this amount is increasing rapidly as Internet sales of travel products reduce costs and present low entrance barriers in terms of financial investment and know-how. E-commerce therefore clearly increases the opportunities for developing countries to reap the benefits of their competitive advantage as tourism destinations.

Large hotel chains are constantly increasing their business through mergers, as well as franchising and management contracts.

The largest hotel chain, Cendant, operates 6,000 hotels with a total of 500,000 rooms. The four next largest chains operate half as many hotels each, but still offer between 300,000 and 460,000 rooms. The 20 largest chains together operate as many as 27,000 hotels with 3.26 million hotel rooms out of an estimated world total of 15 million. Some operate in almost 100 countries (Bass Hotels and Resorts in 98 countries; Best Western in 84; Accor in 81; Starwood in 80). The value of the capital involved in a single merger or acquisition can amount to US$14 billion. The last five years have witnessed nine major hotel merger and acquisition transactions involving a total of US$40 billion. In Europe, only about 30 per cent of all hotels are affiliated to chains in some way, whereas the proportion in the United States is as high as 79 per cent. A large majority of five-star hotels in developing countries are managed by international chains. Some of the largest international hotel chains run all their affiliated hotels through management or franchising contracts. Most large hotel chains, however, own a majority of their hotels. Management contracts and franchising often raise questions regarding the identity of an employer in labour relations, as chain companies may be composed of large numbers of legally independent enterprises.

Tour operators are consolidating their operations through vertical integration as well as horizontal takeovers in order to have better control over their forward and backward linkages such as air companies, hotels, travel agencies and retail distributors. As the tour operating business generates only small profit margins, economies of scale represent only a few (if relatively important) percentage points of revenue.

Capital consolidation is also important in the institutional catering subsector, where the largest companies employ respectively 212,000 workers (Compass) and 125,000 workers (Sodexho). The institutional catering subsector has good expansion prospects, as its market is far from saturated. Catering is also growing in the restaurant subsector through the sale of pre-prepared meals.

Whilst large chain enterprises are growing dynamically, independent enterprises tend to be left behind. Small and medium-sized enterprises (SMEs) employ at least half of the sector's workers and represent a majority of its enterprises; in Europe, the figure is more than 90 per cent. Almost all of them are micro-enterprises with up to ten workers, often family members drawing little or no remuneration for unmeasured working time. They are hardly able to compete in global markets, as they suffer from low productivity, poor product quality and a lack of access to credit and training. Their strongest comparative advantage comes from low labour costs. In order to benefit from other advantages, such as presence in niche markets and adaptability to customer demands, they need to boost their technology and training. This is being undertaken by special schemes or through associations of entrepreneurs. Legal deregulation and lower taxation also make their survival easier.

Most HCT enterprises, large or small, employ only a core of permanent and full-time staff. Other staff are employed under atypical contracts including part-time, seasonal and casual labour arrangements. Flexible employment is convenient for many young workers who are studying or aim eventually to move to other sectors, and for female workers with children, but these workers are often unable to make a living as head of a family. Up to half the workers in the industry are under 25 years old and up to 70 per cent are women. However, women are much less represented at management levels, where they occupy just over 40 per cent of posts. The higher up in the hierarchy one goes, the fewer women are present, and women occupy a low percentage of the top earning posts in the industry.

The HCT sector pays its workers on average at least 20 per cent less than other economic sectors, as it employs a higher proportion of unskilled workers. Tips increase the income of workers with customer contact. However, little is known about overtime payments and remuneration for irregular work. Performance-dependent remuneration is not yet common in the HCT sector, although it has been introduced in some restaurant chains. Payment is in general less attractive in small enterprises and in enterprises performing subcontracted services. Large enterprises in general pay their core staff better.

Staff turnover is costly to employers, who have to find new staff for up to half or more of their posts every year, and is estimated to cost several thousand US dollars per employee. It is tempting to presume a correlation between unattractive working conditions and high turnover, a correlation frequently cited by employees. There are in fact a variety of reasons for employee turnover, of which poor career prospects, low pay, unsocial working hours and physical stress appear to play a part. Working hours are irregular for half of all employees in the HCT sector, most of whom perform work on Sundays and in the evenings, and almost half of whom also work at night. However, employees now also have a greater say in the choice of hours and can thus adjust them better to their needs. Chain employers have started to implement personnel development strategies, including training and career development plans, in order to improve staff retention.

Part-time and fixed-term work is increasing. However, the social partners stress that the creation of full-time jobs should be a priority, that workers in part-time and fixed-term jobs should not be subjected to discrimination and should receive all available benefits on a pro rata temporis basis. Casual workers are included in this category. In Australia, they account for over half of all employees in the sector. Atypical employment relationships, however, entail a weaker link between the partners, and trade union affiliation is rare.

Certain forms of tourism, such as nature tourism, rural, agri- or ecotourism and adventure tourism, have grown over the past decade. Populations living in remote areas, or peasant farmers with diminishing incomes, benefit considerably from employment opportunities and income generated by tourism. However, ensuring that the benefits exceed the potential damage is a delicate task. Indigenous populations need training to resist cultural destruction, natural parks need the proper involvement of local populations to guarantee their preservation, and agritourism needs regulation in order to reduce or prevent unfair competition with professional lodging. The sustainable exploitation of these "soft" forms of tourism therefore requires participatory institutions and social dialogue in the communities concerned.

Very young children work in all kinds of HCT occupations, particularly in family-based enterprises, but also on their own as vendors or helpers. Probably the worst form of child labour in tourism is seen in the sex trade. The international community has expressed its concern at this phenomenon at a number of meetings. A task force against the commercial sexual exploitation of children, involving the participation of international employers' and workers' organizations and the World Tourism Organization, is promoting appropriate counter-measures. The industry is also engaging in innovative programmes to prevent and combat child prostitution in tourism. Migrant workers are another vulnerable group over-proportionately employed in the HCT sector, mostly in the lower paid, less stable segment of the sectoral labour market. This is often due to language problems or inadequate knowledge of the host culture.

The hotel and restaurant industry is very conscious of the fact that human resources are becoming more valuable to the sector, given the new customer demands, new technologies, intense competition and continuing shortage of job applicants. Additional efforts are needed to make working conditions more attractive to a range of age groups, not just young workers, to increase worker responsibility and to make employment in the sector a prestigious lifetime engagement. The need to value labour is also reflected in the fact that output per worker has increased dramatically in recent years, as employment in the sector continues to grow more slowly (about 2 per cent a year worldwide) than its value added (about 3 per cent).

The best performers, as far as hotels are concerned, are in the European Economic Area and the Caribbean. New forms of work organization are certainly an important factor boosting productivity. They include multiskilling, flat hierarchies and subcontracting of ancillary or specialist tasks. At the same time, a growing number of occupational profiles demand higher skills, especially among managers and staff in direct contact with customers. Some managers need to carry out planning exercises in order to identify and exploit market trends more rapidly, while others need to improve their knowledge, including ICT skills, in order to satisfy customers' demands for more meaningful experiences when travelling. All employees need enhanced social skills in order to play a full part in organizational teamwork, as more customer contact and more teamwork have brought about a shift away from operational or vocational skills towards personal and social skills. Within the hotel chain industry, there is a trend towards greater investment in staff training, up to 1 per cent of revenue being earmarked for this purpose. In general, however, both employers and workers often fail to recognize the need for training. Employers often prefer to select staff on the basis of personality rather than formal qualifications, although, at management level, post-secondary education is generally required. Tourism-related degree programmes have proliferated all over the world and are on their way to recognition as an academic discipline.

Continuous training beyond initial vocational training is becoming increasingly important for workers at all levels, in response to rapidly changing skill requirements. There are proposals that initial training should be reduced to a multisectoral learning platform. However, continuous training schemes are still very limited and benefit only a tiny percentage of workers, even in the most advanced countries. Policies on continuous training have been the subject of social dialogue far less than initial training policies. Standardization and certification of competencies is essential if continuous training policies are to make full use of workers' efforts and capacities in a context of flat hierarchies, teamwork and labour mobility. The new paradigm of competencies is replacing traditional occupational qualifications. Competencies are described in terms of the results to be achieved by a worker instead of tasks, reflecting the underlying concept of problem-solving responsibilities of workers at all levels. Their international recognition and certification will also help in the global marketing of quality services.

Tourism education and training is provided by a wide range of institutions, public, semi-public, such as trade associations, or privately owned. Distance training systems with worldwide outreach, based on CD-ROM and interactive Internet technology, are starting to operate and are changing the training business profoundly, raising quality and lowering costs despite the huge investments made in the new training instruments.

New training technologies will also be accessible to small and medium-sized enterprises. This will allow more training to be extended to lower skill groups which at present are largely restricted to spontaneous on-the-job training. Social dialogue in the HCT sector still needs to be developed further. The primary concern of trade unions is to be recognized as genuine partners in social dialogue throughout the world, whereas many employers, while favouring greater social responsibility of enterprises, also expect trade unions to understand the pressures arising from increased competition. Trade unions are concerned with the anti-union attitudes shown by some multinational companies in countries where trade unions are traditionally strong and with the adverse impact on workers' representation arising from subcontracting, franchising and management contracts which split large enterprises into small units that are too weak to be effective partners in social dialogue. Among the positive developments from a trade union perspective is a collective agreement concluded with the Accor Group which guarantees recognition of free trade unions in all units carrying the group's brands around the world.

The largest international organizations of social partners represent, either directly or through their affiliates, some 750,000 establishments and 10 million workers in most of the world's countries. The SME subsector is under-represented in employers' associations and trade unions, but employs as much as half of the labour force. Among other factors limiting the trade union density in the HCT sector are the young workforce and the low level of education and training, the high proportion of women, high staff turnover, frequent atypical employment and working patterns, employment by different employers acting in the same unit through subcontracting, and the generally low degree of identification of workers with the sector owing to the poor image of personal services. Trade union density is generally not greater than ten per cent, although it is higher in a few European countries and in large enterprises located in urban areas, where it can reach as much as 90 per cent of the workforce.

Some workers' representation is initiated by employers at the enterprise level in various forms, including quality or safety circles or communication groups to comply with legal requirements or to promote improvements in day-to-day life in the enterprise. Where freely elected bodies exist, however, trade union presence is the rule. Works councils generally do not exist in small enterprises, whose workers are therefore largely left out of social dialogue, although they may be covered by any agreements that may be concluded.

Collective agreements in the HCT sector vary considerably even within countries and from enterprise to enterprise. They mainly concern remuneration and working time. Detailed matrices of occupations and hierarchies are used to reflect the value of the labour force, and these are challenged by flexibility requirements such as multiskilling, new forms of work and new "soft" skills. Ad hoc collective agreements have been important instruments for mitigating the negative effects on workers of increased competition and frequent changes of ownership in the context of globalization. They have provided workers with a certain minimum continuity of employment and working conditions. Collective bargaining is not conducted at the international level, but other forms of international social dialogue are being developed. European Works Councils derived from EU legislation provide for yearly communication between the multinational companies and local trade unions from different countries.

The meetings are considered an important means of dealing with questions of principle concerning possible redundancies or workers' training.

Sectoral social dialogue between regional employers' and workers' organizations in the European Union has resulted in common statements on flexibility or the promotion of employment in the HCT sector. The sectoral social partners also engage in international forums not directly concerned with labour issues, such as those provided by the United Nations to promote sustainable tourism development or by the European Union to promote employment in tourism.

Information technology is starting to open up a new dimension of internationalization in the form of workers' solidarity campaigns and calls to boycott destinations or hotels that do not comply with established or perceived rights. In view of the dangers of biased or distorted information through the Internet and the possible economic losses involved, industry representatives have voiced concern at boycott appeals in general.

Suggested Points for Discussion

1. Globalization;
    a. What strategies should be pursued in the HCT sector to reap the benefits of globalization?
    b. What measures should be adopted to help developing countries to enhance their capacity building in relation to market access and to the promotion of human resource development and employment in tourism?
2. *Employment creation and working conditions;*
    a. What are the barriers to employment creation in small and medium-sized enterprises and what role can the tripartite partners play in removing those barriers?
    b. In view of the increasing importance of subcontracting, what measures should be taken to ensure that minimum working and employment standards are applied?
    c. What are the reasons for the existence of seasonal, casual and on-call employment in the HCT sector and what measures should be taken to improve the conditions of such employment?
    d. What measures should be taken to enhance the employment of women in the HCT sector?
    e. What are the obstacles to the ratification and implementation of the Working Conditions (Hotels and Restaurants) Convention, 1991 (No. 172), and what measures should be taken to address them and to promote the ratification of the Convention?
3. Human resources development.
    a. What strategies should be adopted for human resources development to ensure that workers are attracted to and retained in the HCT sector?
    b. What should be the role of the tripartite partners and the ILO in the provision of training in the HCT sector? What measures should be taken to increase training opportunities for workers in small and medium-sized enterprises? How can vocational training be enhanced particularly in developing countries?

4. Social dialogue.
   a. What measures should be taken to promote social dialogue, including collective bargaining, in the HCT sector?
   b. How can the tripartite partners and the ILO contribute to sustainable tourism and employment?

The Hospitality Executive's Guide to Reducing Labour Costs & To Improving Customer Service

1. Forecast major volume indicators seven days out by day and by shift to anticipate employee workloads for the next weekly work schedule. Establish a weekly "Forecast" meeting with department heads that lasts a maximum of 20 minutes, to specifically discuss upcoming business.
2. Identify and analyse hourly customer traffic patterns by day on an annual basis.
3. Develop employee-staffing guidelines that identify "fixed" (non-volume related) and "variable" (volume related) labour requirements by job.
4. Make sure that all employee staffing guidelines/labour standards are related to a realistic frame of time for completion. Quantify the work.
5. Report and analyse actual daily employee hours worked, versus scheduled daily employee labour hours, versus target daily employee labour hours.
6. Measure current employee productivity levels weekly versus historical productivity levels to see if improvement occurs or gets worse.
7. Observe and rate customer service and quality levels for all departments.
8. Experience what your customer goes through in all aspects of your operation on all shifts.
9. Get to know all of your employees on all shifts. Let them see you.
10. Stay out of your office and be "on the floor" as much as possible.

4

Markets and Services in Hospitality Sector

Concepts of Service Quality Measurement in Hotel Industry

The domination of the service sector today is confirmed by the fact that 70% of the world GDP is realized in the service sector. The same sector sees the concentration of 70% of workforce. In order to ensure and keep the quality expected by today's customer/tourist, we need to differentiate two aspects of quality in general with particular attention to tourism, namely: design quality and the quality of conformity with design. The design quality is a concept implying the presentation of products/services directed to the needs of the clients.

The hotel company can satisfy the demands of the client (tourist) only if they are included in its design, i.e. in order to do that, his demands need to be included or "built into" the product/service of the hotel. The hotels do market research in order to determine who their customers are and which of their demands require special attention. The quality of conformity with the design completes the first aspect because it represents the level to which the product/service meets the demands of the market.

The quality represents the satisfaction of the client's needs and in order to achieve it and keep it in time, we not only need a continuous research into the demands of the clients but also of our own capabilities. Such an approach would ensure the pursuing of constant improvements according to the demands of the clients. The harsh competition on tourist market requires the development of a new approach to management known as TQM– Total Quality Management. When introducing the quality management system, hotel companies use various approaches adapted to their business conditions. The following part of the paper describes the most common service quality measurement criteria, in particular the model of internal service quality and the Servqual model.

Review of the Literature

Service quality is a way to manage business processes in order to ensure total satisfaction to the customer on all levels (internal and external). It is an approach that leads to an increase of competitiveness, effectiveness and flexibility of the entire company.

Benefits arising from a high quality are reflected in a more competitive positioning on the market, but also in a better business result. This statement can be proved by measuring the increase of profitability and market share. The results of a research carried out in the USA on a sample of 2600 companies in the period between 1987 and 2002, show a direct connection between the level of quality of goods and services and their financial performances. As a matter of fact, it was observed that all indicators of success of a company, like market share, return on investments, property turnover coefficient, show significantly more value in companies with a higher level of goods and services.

The efficiency of the whole system is possible only if we monitor and analyse the demands of the customers, as well as define and control the process and implement constant improvements.Quality is a complex term, made up of several elements and criteria. All quality elements or criteria are equally important in order to obtain one hundred percent quality. If only one element of quality is missing, the complete quality of product or service is impossible to obtain.

Besides the mentioned general elements of quality, the product or service have to satisfy specific elements of quality, according to the demands of the profession in their pertaining activity. Today quality is the result of growing and increasingly diverse needs of the consumers, along with a highly increasing competition, market globalization and the development of modern technology.

Problems in service quality measurement arise from a lack of clear and measurable parameters for the determination of quality. It is not the case with product quality since products have specific and measurable indicators like durability, number of defective products and similar, which make it relatively easy to determine the level of quality.

The most important characteristics of services, separating them neatly from products, are the impossibility to separate production from consumption; the impossibility to store services; their non material quality; transience and heterogeneity.

The impossibility to separate production from consumption and the impossibility to store services implicitly includes a simultaneous production and consumption, which is characteristic for most services. Since the services are performances, ideas or concepts rather than objects, they cannot be seen in the same way as products and are, therefore, characterized by their being immaterial.

Furthermore, it is impossible to preserve services, which raises the issue of harmonizing offer and demand for services. The same service can be provided by different persons in an institution, and each of them might provide it in their own way so that heterogeneity also counts among characteristics of services that differentiate them from products.

The quality system is based on principles such as commitment of the management, focus on the customers, employees and facts, constant improvement and co-operation of all the participants to the process. Research carried out in 101 companies in the service provision field (Zemke, Schaff, 1989) show the following results:

- Managers are "obsessed" with listening to the changeable wishes, needs and expectations of their customers, and the wish to respond to them.
- A solidly defined strategy of servicing "inspired by consumers" is created by managers in their companies, and transferred to the staff.
- Managers develop and maintain a *customer-friendly* system of providing services.

- Managers look for, and then inspire and develop staff that is in direct contact with consumers.

Two basic approaches to service quality have been identified in the early nineties of the twentieth century. The first approach is "technical" and product oriented, while the second approach is customer related. These two approaches have been recognized as results of managerial efforts to consider the aspect of quality when providing services from two angles: on one hand, the manager tends to abide by the set standards, while on the other, he wishes to satisfy the customer. The first approach is production oriented and tends to the consistency of service by impeding or minimizing the influence of the personnel directly involved in providing a service.

The service providing process is defined as a standard performance. The role of the staff providing services is reduced to the realization of the defined performance and the staff's discretion, i.e. its influence on the performance itself is minimized. In that way we can achieve maximum efficiency. Such a "product based" approach to the process of service provision is the result of the managerial view on this process as a series of elements that require a trained coordination and control, while the service itself is strictly standardized. The "product based" approach is contradictory to the aspirations of the consumers to be treated as individual people with marked personal tendencies and expectations. Besides, such an approach, "industrial" and cliche, is in contrast with the wish of the consumer to find warm and friendly manners when *consuming* the service. The second approach is consumer oriented. Expectations are the basis for satisfaction. After consuming the service, they compare their earlier expectations with experience. Results can range from satisfaction to dissatisfaction. The consumer anticipates the service standards in his expectations. Wilkie claims: "The seed of the consumer's dissatisfaction is sown in the pre-purchase stage, before reaching the decision to purchase." According to this, the consumer creates his own, individual *benchmark*, and the rating of his satisfaction is the result of his after purchase state.

Normann, the creator of the concept "moment of truth", points out that the first generation of researchers in the field of service sector management, had the task to determine the specificities of the services as opposed to other sectors, which paved the way for the second generation of researchers who focused on the relations in the service industry, the behaviour when providing service and service design, with the aim to optimize the "moment of truth". On the basis of the above exposed thesis, the understanding of service quality is based on the *paradigm of service*. In that sense, the service sector company manager looks for a "balance between the human factor and technology, between expenses and profit and, after all, between quality and productivity" (Gummesson, 1993).

The organization has to strive for success. When the set goals are achieved, we set other goals, striving for higher levels of product, processes and service efficiency. Accepting the concept of constant improvement means changing the management style. A total quality cannot be a program of changes with a set duration, it is a continuous, constant process. The questions set before the organization are the following: How do you keep up the constant striving for new improvement? What kind of measures and revisions of the business process do you have to use? How do you convince the employees that the business success and survival of the organizations can only occur if all employees accept constant actions to improve all their activities in the organizations? A successful organization constantly identifies and tackles the causes of problems or potential problems that employees have in doing their jobs. For that reason every employee has to be trained to identify such problems. The management and the employees must work together on implementing suitable corrective and preventive measures.

Each business process is subject to variability. Process variability is considered a normal phenomenon that is usually counted on. Parameter variability in the field of transformation of incoming values into outcoming values of the process affects the variability of the entire business process. For example, a lack of a specific product on the supplies market may require a substitution with another product of similar characteristics. Departure from the usual process (*variability*) can affect the quality of meals as results of a process, the timing of a process cycle, expenses of process quality, the level of satisfaction of the consumer/user with the process result.

Each episode of variability and a departure from the optimal process does not necessarily have a negative impact on the quality level of the process results. However, if the process is moving away from its optimal course so much as to get close to the acceptable limit or it has surpassed the limit, cost incur due to poor quality. The process becomes too expensive, jeopardizing the quality of the results and thus seriously risking dissatisfaction on the part of the client/consumer, in other words, it becomes irrational.

Service Quality Measurement in Hotel Industry

In order to achieve rationality the models of business excellence also, in a way, determine whether the criteria have been met, but the evaluation of business excellence is based not only on the fulfilment of the set criteria but also on the determination of the level up to which the criteria have been fulfilled (systems of points).

When analyzing the quality of service it is desirable to analyse the largest possible number of companies supplying the same type of service. As we already mentioned, if a company carries out a research and finds that the results are negative, it can interpret this information in the wrong way and conclude that it provides services in a totally wrong way. On the other hand, when analyzing a large number of companies, it is possible to compare data and obtain a realistic picture of the position of an individual company compared to others regarding quality.

The upper part of the model includes phenomena tied to the consumer, while the lower part shows phenomena tied to the supplier of services. The expected service is the function of earlier experiences of the consumer, their personal needs and oral communication. Communication with the market also influences the expected service. Experienced service, here called perceived service, is the result of a series of internal decisions and activities.

The management's perceptions of the consumer's expectations is the guiding principle when deciding on the specifications of the quality of service that the company should follow in providing service. If there are differences or discrepancies in the expectations or perceptions between people involved in providing and consuming services, a "service quality gap" can occur, as shown in image 1. Since there is a direct connection between the quality of service and the satisfaction of clients in hotel industry, it is important for the company to spot a gap in the quality of service.

The first possible gap is the knowledge gap. It is the result of the differences in managing knowledge and their real expectations. This gap can lead to other gaps in the process of service quality and is, among other things, caused by:

- incorrect information in market researches and demand analysis;
- incorrect interpretations of information regarding expectations;
- lack of information about any feedback between the company and the consumers directed to the management;
- too many organizational layers that hinder or modify parts of information in their upward movement from those involved in contact with the consumers.

The second possible gap is that of standard. It is the result of differences in managing knowledge of the client's expectations and the process of service provision (delivery).

This gap is the result of:

- mistakes in planning or insufficient planning procedures;
- bad management planning;
- lack of clearly set goals in the organization; and
- insufficient support of the top management to service quality planning.

The management can be right in evaluating the client's expectations and develop business methods to satisfy these expectations, without the employees being correct in providing service. For example, a restaurant can order the waiters to serve the customers in two minutes after they sit at the table. Nevertheless, the waiters can ignore that specification and talk between them on the side.

The fourth possible gap is the communication gap arising when there is a difference between the delivered service and the service that the company promised to the clients via external communications.

The reasons are:

- the planning of communication with the market is not integrated with the services;
- lack or insufficient coordination between traditional marketing and procedures;
- organizational performance not in keeping with the specifications, while the policy of communication with the market abides by the given specifications; and
- tendency to exaggerate in accordance with exaggerated promises.

Should any of the mentioned gaps arise, the "service gap" will also appear because the real service will not satisfy the client's expectations. Hotel companies try to detect the "service gap" with survey questionnaires. Gap analysis is the file conducteur for the management to find the causes of problems regarding quality and to find suitable ways to remove such gaps. For this reason the first four gaps are also called organizational or internal gaps.

Although there are several models (scales) for the measurement of service quality and the satisfaction of customers, they are often too generalized or ad hoc, and as such hard to apply in the hotel industry. As opposed to TQM, which began before all in companies that dealt with products, due to the specificities of services (the basic are: impalpability, inseparability from provider

and receiver of service, impossibility of storage), a specific concept called Servqual (SERVices QUALity Model) was created. 8 The Servqual model offers a suitable conceptual frame for the research and service quality measurement in the service sector. The model has been developed, tested and adapted during various researches in cooperation with the Marketing Science Institute from Texas and numerous companies operating in the service sector. The model is based on the definition of quality as a comparison of the expected and the obtained as well as a consideration of gaps in the process of service provision. Servqual is based on the client's evaluation of service quality. The described concept is based on the gap between expectations and perception of the clients. Service quality represents a multidimensional construction. The choice of the most important characteristics was an issue dealt with in various ways. One of these is a logical attempt to work out a list of desirable attributes from the basic needs of the clients. A variant of a scale containing desirable characteristics of services, known as Servqual scale, is currently quite popular in literature. It was developed in marketing circles with the aim to measure service quality (Bakoviæ, Lazibat). In the original Servqual instrument, Parasuraman et al. (1985) define service quality through ten dimensions which they sum up in five in 1988:

1) Reliability,
2) Assurance,
3) Tangibles,
4) Empathy,
5) Responsiveness.

Each of the listed dimensions has different features. Just like dimensions have different influence on the final service quality, so do these features have different influence on the grading of success of a single dimension. Despite its popularity and wide application, Servqual is exposed to numerous criticisms, from both the conceptual and the operational aspect.

Theoretical Criticism

- pattern objections: Servqual is based rather on an affirmation pattern than on the pattern of understanding; it does not manage to tie in with proved economical, statistical and psychological theories.
- Gap model: there is little evidence that the consumer evaluates service quality in the sense of perception – expectation gaps.
- Direction to the process: Servqual is directed to the process of service delivery and not to the result of service experience.

- Dimensionality: the five dimensions of Servqual are not universal; the number of dimensions that encompass service quality is connected to the context; there is a high degree of inter-correlation between RATER dimensions. RATER is a mnemonic acronym where R = reliability, A = assurance, T = tangibles, E = empathy and R = responsiveness. Operative criticism:
- Expectations: the term of expectations has multiple meanings; in evaluating services consumers use standards instead of expectations; Servqual cannot measure the absolute expectations of service quality.
- Content of the elements: four out of five elements cannot encompass the variability inside each dimension of service quality.
- Moment of truth: the consumer's rating of the service can vary from one to the next moment of truth.
- Polarity: the reverse polarity of the scale elements causes wrong reactions.
- Scale grading: Likert's scale with 7 ratings is inadequate.
- Dual administration: dual administration of instruments causes boredom and confusion.

The most important criticism of Servqual was the usage of gap analysis results (difference between expectations and perception of the received service) in measuring service quality. Comparing the expectation-perception gaps with perception only, called Servperf, Cronin and Taylor concluded that measurement of service quality based only on perception was enough.

Servqual Model in Croatian Hotel Industry

The Faculty for Tourist and Hospitality Management in Opatija constructed an empirical model for the measurement of service quality in hotel industry on the model of hospitality on the Opatijska Riviera. Its use shall be simple and effective in hotel practice.

The aims of the research were:

a) Evaluate expectations and perceptions of hotel guests on the studied sample,

b) Evaluate and calculate the Servqual gap,

c) Test the reliability of the Servqual model in hotel industry,

d) Determine the dimensions of service quality in hotel industry by applying the method of factor analysis.

From a practical point of view, the research intended to test the adapted Servqual model for the measurement of service quality of hotel guests (Markoviæ: 2005). It represents the difference between the average ratings of perceptions and the average expectations ratings. The wider the gap, the greater the difference between expectations and perception.

The results of the quantitative application of the Servqual model in Croatian hotel industry show that the expectations of hotel guests are higher than their perception. This proves the existence of a negative Servqual gap. It is visible that tourists from Great Britain have the highest total expectations, followed by guests from Australia and USA, while the Japanese tourists have the least expectations. Compared to clients in other services, "reliability" and an "impeccable" service is important to all hotel guests, regardless of their country of origin. Hotel guests prioritize this dimension, and so should hotel managers and personnel.

Dimensions of Countries

The need for the application of Servqual model in hotel industry is confirmed by the fact that, in the observed sample, hotel managers do not know the expectations of their guests because the dimensions of service quality they consider most important, do not match those that are most important for the clients, which is confirmed by the total Servqual gap.

Conclusion

Servqual can be widely applied, not only in science but also in practice in various services. The aim of the scientists is to work out and test useful instruments for managers in order to help them determine those organizational variables (policy, staff, structure, technology, processes) that will guarantee the best service quality with minimal costs. This methodology can assist hotel managers in assessing the position of the hotel regarding its competition and strategic and operative decision-making.

In hotel industry, service quality, as an extremely subjective category, is crucial to the satisfaction of the client. It is therefore imperative for managers in hotel industry to apply the Servqual model for the measurement of service quality in their own hotel company, in order to satisfy the guest's expectations and ensure a position on the growing global tourist market.

The results of the quantitative application of Servqual instrument show that this model can provide managers with useful information for the assessment of expectations and perception of hotel guests, with the aim of learning about gaps in individual service quality dimensions. To sum up, this article tend to clarify the Servqual model as not only provider to the managers with a clear picture of the quality of the provided service, but also helping in discovering the needs, wishes and expectations of the guests. The same is analyzed by determining thecharacteristics of service quality that are most important for guests. We can say that it helps managers in setting the standards for the provision of services in the hospitality industry.

Marketing Strategies in Hotel Industry

Strategic or institutional management is the conduct of drafting, implementing and evaluating cross-functional decisions that will enable an organization to achieve its long-term objectives. It is the process of specifying the organization's mission, vision and objectives, developing policies and plans, often in terms of projects and programs, which are designed to achieve these objectives, and then allocating resources to implement the policies and plans, projects and programs. A balanced scorecard is often used to evaluate the overall performance of the business and its progress towards objectives.

Strategic management is a level of managerial activity under setting goals and over Tactics. Strategic management provides overall direction to the enterprise and is closely related to the field of Organization Studies. In the field of business administration it is useful to talk about "strategic alignment" between the organization and its environment or "strategic consistency". According to Arieu (2007), "there is strategic consistency when the actions of an organization are consistent with the expectations of management, and these in turn are with the market and the context." "Strategic management is an ongoing process that evaluates and controls the business and the industries in which the company is involved; assesses its competitors and sets goals and strategies to meet all existing and potential competitors; and then reassesses each strategy annually or quarterly [i.e. regularly] to determine how it has been implemented and whether it has succeeded or needs replacement by a new strategy to meet changed circumstances, new technology, new competitors, a new economic environment., or a new social, financial, or political environment."

Strategy Formulation

Strategic formulation is a combination of three main processes which are as follows:

- Performing a situation analysis, self-evaluation and competitor analysis: both internal and external; both micro-environmental and macro-environmental.
- Concurrent with this assessment, objectives are set. These objectives should be parallel to a time-line; some are in the short-term and others on the long-term. This involves crafting vision statements (long term view of a possible future), mission statements (the role that the organization gives itself in society), overall corporate objectives (both financial and strategic), strategic business unit objectives (both financial and strategic), and tactical objectives.
- These objectives should, in the light of the situation analysis, suggest a strategic plan. The plan provides the details of how to achieve these objectives.

Marketing Action Plan

- Placement and execution of required resources are financial, manpower, operational support, time, technology support
- Operating with a change in methods or with alteration in structure
- Distributing the specific tasks with responsibility or moulding specific jobs to individuals or teams.

- The process should be managed by a responsible team. This is to keep direct watch on result, comparison for betterment and best practices, cultivating the effectiveness of processes, calibrating and reducing the variations and setting the process as required.
- Introducing certain programs involves acquiring the requisition of resources: a necessity for developing the process, training documentation, process testing, and imalgation with (and/or conversion from) difficult processes.

As and when the strategy implementation processes, there have been so many problems arising such as human relations, the employee-communication. Such a time, marketing strategy is the biggest implementation problem usually involves, with emphasis on the appropriate timing of new products. An organization, with an effective management, should try to implement its plans without signaling this fact to its competitors. In order for a policy to work, there must be a level of consistency from every person in an organization, specially management. This is what needs to occur on both the tactical and strategic levels of management.

Strategy Evaluation

- Measuring the effectiveness of the organizational strategy, it's extremely important to conduct a SWOT analysis to figure out the strengths, weaknesses, opportunities and threats (both internal and external) of the entity in question. This may require to take certain precautionary measures or even to change the entire strategy.

In corporate strategy, Johnson and Scholes present a model in which strategic options are evaluated against three key success criteria:

- Suitability (would it work?)
- Feasibility (can it be made to work?)
- Acceptability (will they work it?).

Suitability

Suitability deals with the overall rationale of the strategy. The key point to consider is whether the strategy would address the key strategic issues underlined by the organisation's strategic position.

- Does it make economic sense?
- Would the organization obtain economies of scale, economies of scope or experience economy?
- Would it be suitable in terms of environment and capabilities?

Tools that can be used to evaluate suitability include:

- Ranking strategic options
- Decision trees.

Feasibility

Feasibility is concerned with whether the resources required to implement the strategy are available, can be developed or obtained. Resources include funding, people, time and information.

Tools that can be used to evaluate feasibility include:

- cash flow analysis and forecasting
- break-even analysis
- resource deployment analysis.

Acceptability

Acceptability is concerned with the expectations of the identified stakeholders (mainly shareholders, employees and customers) with the expected performance outcomes, which can be return, risk and stakeholder reactions.

- Return deals with the benefits expected by the stakeholders (financial and non-financial). For example, shareholders would expect the increase of their wealth, employees would expect improvement in their careers and customers would expect better value for money.
- Risk deals with the probability and consequences of failure of a strategy (financial and non-financial).
- Stakeholder reactions deals with anticipating the likely reaction of stakeholders. Shareholders could oppose the

issuing of new shares, employees and unions could oppose outsourcing for fear of losing their jobs, customers could have concerns over a merger with regards to quality and support.

Tools that can be used to evaluate acceptability include:

- what-if analysis
- stakeholder mapping.

General Approaches

In general terms, there are two main approaches, which are opposite but complement each other in some ways, to strategic management:

- The Industrial Organizational Approach:
  - o based on economic theory – deals with issues like competitive rivalry, resource allocation, economies of scale
  - o assumptions – rationality, self discipline behaviour, profit maximization.
- The Sociological Approach:
  - o deals primarily with human interactions
  - o assumptions – bounded rationality, satisfying behaviour, profit sub-optimality. An example of a company that currently operates this way is Google.

Strategic management techniques can be viewed as bottom-up, top-down, or collaborative processes. In the bottom-up approach, employees submit proposals to their managers who, in turn, funnel the best ideas further up the organization. This is often accomplished by a capital budgeting process. Proposals are assessed using financial criteria such as return on investment or cost-benefit analysis. Cost underestimation and benefit overestimation are major sources of error. The proposals that are approved form the substance of a new strategy, all of which is done without a grand strategic design or a strategic architect. The top-down approach is the most common by far. In it, the CEO, possibly with the assistance of a strategic planning team, decides on the overall direction the company should take. Some organizations are starting to experiment with collaborative strategic planning techniques that recognize the emergent nature of strategic decisions.

The Strategy Hierarchy

In most (large) corporations there are several levels of management. Strategic management is the highest of these levels in the sense that it is the broadest-applying to all parts of the firm-while also incorporating the longest time horizon. It gives direction to corporate values, corporate culture, corporate goals, and corporate missions. Under this broad corporate strategy there are typically business-level competitive strategies and functional unit strategies. Corporate strategy refers to the overarching strategy of the diversified firm. Such a corporate strategy answers the questions of "which businesses should we be in?" and "how does being in these businesses create synergy and/or add to the competitive advantage of the corporation as a whole?"

Business strategy refers to the aggregated strategies of single business firm or a strategic business unit (SBU) in a diversified corporation. According to Michael Porter, a firm must formulate a business strategy that incorporates either cost leadership, differentiation or focus in order to achieve a sustainable competitive advantage and long-term success in its chosen areas or industries. Alternatively, according to W. Chan Kim and Renée Mauborgne, an organization can achieve high growth and profits by creating a Blue Ocean Strategy that breaks the previous value-cost tradeoff by simultaneously pursuing both differentiation and low cost.

Functional strategies include marketing strategies, new product development strategies, human resource strategies, financial strategies, legal strategies, supply-chain strategies, and information technology management strategies. The emphasis is on short and medium term plans and is limited to the domain of each department's functional responsibility. Each functional department attempts to do its part in meeting overall corporate objectives, and hence to some extent their strategies are derived from broader corporate strategies.

Many companies feel that a functional organizational structure is not an efficient way to organize activities so they have reengineered according to processes or SBUs. A strategic business unit is a semi-autonomous unit that is usually responsible for its own budgeting, new product decisions, hiring decisions, and price setting. An SBU is treated as an internal profit centre by corporate headquarters. A technology strategy, for example, although it is focused on technology as a means of achieving an organization's overall objective(s), may include dimensions that are beyond the scope of a single business unit, engineering organization or IT department.

An additional level of strategy called operational strategy was encouraged by Peter Drucker in his theory of management by objectives (MBO). It is very narrow in focus and deals with day-to-day operational activities such as scheduling criteria. It must operate within a budget but is not at liberty to adjust or create that budget. Operational level strategies are informed by business level strategies which, in turn, are informed by corporate level strategies.

Since the turn of the millennium, some firms have reverted to a simpler strategic structure driven by advances in information technology. It is felt that knowledge management systems should be used to share information and create common goals. Strategic divisions are thought to hamper this process. This notion of strategy has been captured under the rubric of dynamic strategy, popularized by Carpenter and Sanders's textbook. This work builds on that of Brown and Eisenhart as well as Christensen and portrays firm strategy, both business and corporate, as necessarily embracing ongoing strategic change, and the seamless integration of strategy formulation and implementation. Such change and implementation are usually built into the strategy through the staging and pacing facets.

Historical Development of Strategic Management

Birth of Strategic Management

Strategic management as a discipline originated in the 1950s and 60s. Although there were numerous early contributors to the literature, the most influential pioneers were Alfred D. Chandler, Philip Selznick, Igor Ansoff, and Peter Drucker. Alfred Chandler recognized the importance of coordinating the various aspects of management under one all-encompassing strategy. Prior to this time the various functions of management were separate with little overall coordination or strategy. Interactions between functions or between departments were typically handled by a boundary position, that is, there were one or two managers that relayed information back and forth between two departments.

Chandler also stressed the importance of taking a long term perspective when looking to the future. In his 1962 groundbreaking work *Strategy and Structure,* Chandler showed that a long-term coordinated strategy was necessary to give a company structure, direction, and focus. He says it concisely, "structure follows strategy."

In 1957, Philip Selznick introduced the idea of matching the organization's internal factors with external environmental circumstances. This core idea was developed into what we now call SWOT analysis by Learned, Andrews, and others at the Harvard Business School General Management Group. Strengths and weaknesses of the firm are assessed in light of the opportunities and threats from the business environment.

Igor Ansoff built on Chandler's work by adding a range of strategic concepts and inventing a whole new vocabulary. He developed a strategy grid that compared market penetration strategies, product development strategies, market development strategies and horizontal and vertical integration and diversification strategies. He felt that management could use these strategies to systematically prepare for future opportunities and challenges. In his 1965 classic *Corporate Strategy,* he developed the gap analysis still used today in which we must understand the gap between where we are currently and where we would like to be, then develop what he called "gap reducing actions".

Peter Drucker was a prolific strategy theorist, author of dozens of management books, with a career spanning five decades. His contributions to strategic management were many but two are most important.

Firstly, he stressed the importance of objectives. An organization without clear objectives is like a ship without a rudder. As early as 1954 he was developing a theory of management based on objectives. This evolved into his theory of management by objectives (MBO). According to Drucker, the procedure of setting objectives and monitoring your progress towards them should permeate the entire organization, top to bottom. His other seminal contribution was in predicting the importance of what today we would call intellectual capital. He predicted the rise of what he called the "knowledge worker" and explained the consequences of this for management. He said that knowledge work is non-hierarchical. Work would be carried out in teams with the person most knowledgeable in the task at hand being the temporary leader.

In 1985, Ellen-Earle Chaffee summarized what she thought were the main elements of strategic management theory by the 1970s:

- Strategic management involves adapting the organization to its business environment.
- Strategic management is fluid and complex. Change creates novel combinations of circumstances requiring unstructured non-repetitive responses.
- Strategic management affects the entire organization by providing direction.
- Strategic management involves both strategy formation (she called it content) and also strategy implementation (she called it process).
- Strategic management is partially planned and partially unplanned.
- Strategic management is done at several levels: overall corporate strategy, and individual business strategies.
- Strategic management involves both conceptual and analytical thought processes.

Growth and Portfolio Theory

In the 1970s much of strategic management dealt with size, growth, and portfolio theory.

The PIMS study was a long term study, started in the 1960s and lasted for 19 years, that attempted to understand the Profit

Impact of Marketing Strategies (PIMS), particularly the effect of market share. Started at General Electric, moved to Harvard in the early 1970s, and then moved to the Strategic Planning Institute in the late 1970s, it now contains decades of information on the relationship between profitability and strategy.

Their initial conclusion was unambiguous: The greater a company's market share, the greater will be their rate of profit. The high market share provides volume and economies of scale. It also provides experience and learning curve advantages. The combined effect is increased profits. The studies conclusions continue to be drawn on by academics and companies today: "PIMS provides compelling quantitative evidence as to which business strategies work and don't work"-Tom Peters.

The benefits of high market share naturally lead to an interest in growth strategies. The relative advantages of horizontal integration, vertical integration, diversification, franchises, mergers and acquisitions, joint ventures, and organic growth were discussed. The most appropriate market dominance strategies were assessed given the competitive and regulatory environment.

There was also research that indicated that a low market share strategy could also be very profitable. Schumacher (1973), Woo and Cooper (1982), Levenson (1984), and later Traverso (2002) showed how smaller niche players obtained very high returns.

By the early 1980s the paradoxical conclusion was that high market share and low market share companies were often very profitable but most of the companies in between were not. This was sometimes called the "hole in the middle" problem. This anomaly would be explained by Michael Porter in the 1980s.

The management of diversified organizations required new techniques and new ways of thinking. The first CEO to address the problem of a multi-divisional company was Alfred Sloan at General Motors. GM was decentralized into semi-autonomous "strategic business units" (SBU's), but with centralized support functions.

One of the most valuable concepts in the strategic management of multi-divisional companies was portfolio theory. In the previous decade Harry Markowitz and other financial theorists developed the theory of portfolio analysis. It was concluded that a broad portfolio of financial assets could reduce specific risk. In the 1970s marketers extended the theory to product portfolio decisions and managerial strategists extended it to operating division portfolios. Each of a company's operating divisions were seen as an element in the corporate portfolio. Each operating division (also called strategic business units) was treated as a semi-independent profit centre with its own revenues, costs, objectives, and strategies. Several techniques were developed to analyse the relationships between elements in a portfolio. B.C.G. Analysis, for example, was developed by the Boston Consulting Group in the early 1970s. This was the theory that gave us the wonderful image of a CEO sitting on a stool milking a cash cow. Shortly after that the G.E. multi factoral model was developed by General Electric. Companies continued to diversify until the 1980s when it was realized that in many cases a portfolio of operating divisions was worth more as separate completely independent companies.

The Marketing Revolution

The 1970s also saw the rise of the marketing oriented firm. From the beginnings of capitalism it was assumed that the key requirement of business success was a product of high technical quality. If you produced a product that worked well and was durable, it was assumed you would have no difficulty selling them at a profit. This was called the production orientation and it was generally true that good products could be sold without effort, encapsulated in the saying "Build a better mousetrap and the world will beat a path to your door." This was largely due to the growing numbers of affluent and middle class people that capitalism had created. But after the untapped demand caused by the second world war was saturated in the 1950s it became obvious that products were not selling as easily as they had been. The answer was to concentrate on selling.

The 1950s and 1960s is known as the sales era and the guiding philosophy of business of the time is today called the sales orientation. In the early 1970s Theodore Levitt and others at Harvard argued that the sales orientation had things backward. They claimed that instead of producing products then trying to sell them to the customer, businesses should start with the customer, find out what they wanted, and then produce it for them. The customer became the driving force behind all strategic business decisions. This marketing orientation, in the decades since its introduction, has been reformulated and repackaged under numerous names including customer orientation, marketing philosophy, customer intimacy, customer focus, customer driven, and market focused.

The Japanese Challenge

By the late 70s, Americans had started to notice how successful Japanese industry had become. In industry after industry, including steel, watches, ship building, cameras, autos, and electronics, the Japanese were surpassing American and European companies. Westerners wanted to know why. Numerous theories purported to explain the Japanese success including:

- Higher employee morale, dedication, and loyalty;
- Lower cost structure, including wages;
- Effective government industrial policy;
- Modernization after WWII leading to high capital intensity and productivity;
- Economies of scale associated with increased exporting;
- Relatively low value of the Yen leading to low interest rates and capital costs, low dividend expectations, and inexpensive exports;
- Superior quality control techniques such as Total Quality Management and other systems introduced by W. Edwards Deming in the 1950s and 60s.

Although there was some truth to all these potential explanations, there was clearly something missing. In fact by 1980 the Japanese cost structure was higher than the American. And post WWII reconstruction was nearly 40 years in the past. The first management theorist to suggest an explanation was Richard Pascale.

In 1981, Richard Pascale and Anthony Athos in *The Art of Japanese Management* claimed that the main reason for Japanese success was their superior management techniques. They divided management into 7 aspects (which are also known as McKinsey 7S Framework): Strategy, Structure, Systems, Skills, Staff, Style, and Supraordinate goals (which we would now call shared values). The first three of the 7 S's were called hard factors and this is where American companies excelled. The remaining four factors (skills, staff, style, and shared values) were called soft factors and were not well understood by American businesses of the time. Americans did not yet place great value on corporate culture, shared values and beliefs, and social cohesion in the workplace. In Japan the task of management was seen as managing the whole complex of human needs, economic, social, psychological, and spiritual. In America work was seen as something that was separate from the rest of one's life. It was quite common for Americans to exhibit a very different personality at work compared to the rest of their lives. Pascale also highlighted the difference between decision making styles; hierarchical in America, and consensus in Japan. He also claimed that American business lacked long term vision, preferring instead to apply management fads and theories in a piecemeal fashion.

One year later, *The Mind of the Strategist* was released in America by Kenichi Ohmae, the head of McKinsey & Co.'s Tokyo office. (It was originally published in Japan in 1975.) He claimed that strategy in America was too analytical. Strategy should be a creative art: It is a frame of mind that requires intuition and intellectual flexibility. He claimed that Americans constrained their strategic options by thinking in terms of analytical techniques, rote formula, and step-by-step processes. He compared the culture of Japan in which vagueness, ambiguity, and tentative decisions were acceptable, to American culture that valued fast decisions.

Also in 1982, Tom Peters and Robert Waterman released a study that would respond to the Japanese challenge head on. Peters and Waterman, who had several years earlier collaborated with Pascale and Athos at McKinsey & Co. asked "What makes an excellent company?". They looked at 62 companies that they thought were fairly successful. Each was subject to six performance criteria. To be classified as an excellent company, it had to be above the 50th percentile in 4 of the 6 performance metrics for 20 consecutive years. Forty-three companies passed the test. They then studied these successful companies and interviewed key executives. They concluded in *In Search of Excellence* that there were 8 keys to excellence that were shared by all 43 firms. They are:

- A bias for action — Do it. Try it. Don't waste time studying it with multiple reports and committees.
- Customer focus — Get close to the customer. Know your customer.
- Entrepreneurship — Even big companies act and think small by giving people the authority to take initiatives.
- Productivity through people — Treat your people with respect and they will reward you with productivity.
- Value-oriented CEOs—The CEO should actively propagate corporate values throughout the organization.
- Stick to the knitting—Do what you know well.
- Keep things simple and lean—Complexity encourages waste and confusion.
- Simultaneously centralized and decentralized—Have tight centralized control while also allowing maximum individual autonomy.

The basic blueprint on how to compete against the Japanese had been drawn. But as J.E. Rehfeld (1994) explains it is not a straight forward task due to differences in culture. A certain type of alchemy was required to transform knowledge from various cultures into a management style that allows a specific company to compete in a globally diverse world. He says, for example, that Japanese style kaizen (continuous improvement) techniques, although suitable for people socialized in Japanese culture, have not been successful when implemented in the U.S. unless they are modified significantly.

In 2009, industry consultants Mark Blaxill and Ralph Eckardt suggested that much of the Japanese business dominance that began in the mid 1970s was the direct result of competition enforcement efforts by the Federal Trade Commission (FTC) and U.S. Department of Justice (DOJ). In 1975 the FTC reached a settlement with Xerox Corporation in its anti-trust lawsuit. (At the time, the FTC was under the direction of Frederic M. Scherer). The 1975 Xerox consent decree forced the licensing of the company's entire patent portfolio, mainly to Japanese competitors. This action marked the start of an activist approach to managing competition by the FTC and DOJ, which resulted in the compulsory licensing of tens of thousands of patent from some of America's leading companies, including IBM, AT&T, DuPont, Bausch & Lomb, and Eastman Kodak.

Within four years of the consent decree, Xerox's share of the U.S. copier market dropped from nearly 100% to less than 14%. Between 1950 and 1980 Japanese companies consummated more than 35,000 foreign licensing agreements, mostly with U.S. companies, for free or low-cost licenses made possible by the FTC and DOJ. The post-1975 era of anti-trust initiatives by Washington D.C. economists at the FTC corresponded directly with the rapid, unprecedented rise in Japanese competitiveness and a simultaneous stalling of the U.S. manufacturing economy.

Gaining Competitive Advantage

The Japanese challenge shook the confidence of the western business elite, but detailed comparisons of the two management styles and examinations of successful businesses convinced westerners that they could overcome the challenge. The 1980s and early 1990s saw a plethora of theories explaining exactly how this could be done. They cannot all be detailed here, but some of the more important strategic advances of the decade are explained below.

Gary Hamel and C. K. Prahalad declared that strategy needs to be more active and interactive; less "arm-chair planning" was needed. They introduced terms like strategic intent and strategic architecture. Their most well known advance was the idea of core competency. They showed how important it was to know the one or two key things that your company does better than the competition.

Active strategic management required active information gathering and active problem solving. In the early days of Hewlett-Packard (H-P), Dave Packard and Bill Hewlett devised an active management style that they called *management by walking around* (MBWA). Senior H-P managers were seldom at their desks. They spent most of their days visiting employees, customers, and suppliers. This direct contact with key people provided them with a solid grounding from which viable strategies could be crafted. The MBWA concept was popularized in 1985 by a book by Tom Peters and Nancy Austin. Japanese managers employ a similar system, which originated at Honda, and is sometimes called the 3 G's (Genba, Genbutsu, and Genjitsu, which translate into "actual place", "actual thing", and "actual situation").

Probably the most influential strategist of the decade was Michael Porter. He introduced many new concepts including; 5 forces analysis, generic strategies, the value chain, strategic groups, and clusters. In 5 forces analysis he identifies the forces that shape a firm's strategic environment. It is like a SWOT analysis with structure and purpose. It shows how a firm can use these forces to obtain a sustainable competitive advantage. Porter modifies Chandler's dictum about structure following strategy by introducing a second level of structure: Organizational structure follows strategy, which in turn follows industry structure.

Porter's generic strategies detail the interaction between cost minimization strategies, product differentiation strategies, and market focus strategies. Although he did not introduce these terms, he showed the importance of choosing one of them rather than trying to position your company between them. He also challenged managers to see their industry in terms of a value chain. A firm will be successful only to the extent that it contributes to the industry's value chain. This forced management to look at its operations from the customer's point of view. Every operation should be examined in terms of what value it adds in the eyes of the final customer.

In 1993, John Kay took the idea of the value chain to a financial level claiming " Adding value is the central purpose of business activity", where adding value is defined as the difference between the market value of outputs and the cost of inputs including capital, all divided by the firm's net output. Borrowing from Gary Hamel and Michael Porter, Kay claims that the role of strategic management is to identify your core competencies, and then assemble a collection of assets that will increase value added and provide a competitive advantage. He claims that there are 3 types of capabilities that can do this; innovation, reputation, and organizational structure.

The 1980s also saw the widespread acceptance of positioning theory. Although the theory originated with Jack Trout in 1969, it didn't gain wide acceptance until Al Ries and Jack Trout wrote their classic book "Positioning: The Battle For Your Mind" (1979). The basic premise is that a strategy should not be judged by internal company factors but by the way customers see it relative to the competition. Crafting and implementing a strategy involves creating a position in the mind of the collective consumer. Several techniques were applied to positioning theory, some newly invented but most borrowed from other disciplines. Perceptual mapping for example, creates visual displays of the relationships between positions. Multidimensional scaling, discriminant analysis, factor analysis, and conjoint analysis are mathematical techniques used to determine the most relevant characteristics (called dimensions or factors) upon which positions should be based.

Preference regression can be used to determine vectors of ideal positions and cluster analysis can identify clusters of positions. Others felt that internal company resources were the key. In 1992, Jay Barney, for example, saw strategy as assembling the optimum mix of resources, including human, technology, and suppliers, and then configure them in unique and sustainable ways.

Michael Hammer and James Champy felt that these resources needed to be restructured. This process, that they labeled reengineering, involved organizing a firm's assets around whole processes rather than tasks. In this way a team of people saw a project through, from inception to completion. This avoided functional silos where isolated departments seldom talked to each other. It also eliminated waste due to functional overlap and interdepartmental communications.

In 1989 Richard Lester and the researchers at the MIT Industrial Performance Centre identified seven best practices and concluded that firms must accelerate the shift away from the mass production of low cost standardized products. The seven areas of best practice were:

- Simultaneous continuous improvement in cost, quality, service, and product innovation
- Breaking down organizational barriers between departments
- Eliminating layers of management creating flatter organizational hierarchies.
- Closer relationships with customers and suppliers
- Intelligent use of new technology
- Global focus
- Improving human resource skills.

The search for "best practices" is also called benchmarking. This involves determining where you need to improve, finding an organization that is exceptional in this area, then studying the company and applying its best practices in your firm.

A large group of theorists felt the area where western business was most lacking was product quality. People like W. Edwards Deming, Joseph M. Juran, A. Kearney, Philip Crosby, and Armand Feignbaum suggested quality improvement techniques like total quality management (TQM), continuous improvement (kaizen), lean manufacturing, Six Sigma, and return on quality (ROQ).

An equally large group of theorists felt that poor customer service was the problem. People like James Heskett (1988), Earl Sasser (1995), William Davidow, Len Schlesinger, A. Paraurgman (1988), Len Berry, Jane Kingman-Brundage, Christopher Hart, and Christopher Lovelock (1994), gave us fishbone diagramming, service charting, Total Customer Service (TCS), the service profit chain, service gaps analysis, the service encounter, strategic service vision, service mapping, and service teams. Their underlying assumption was that there is no better source of competitive advantage than a continuous stream of delighted customers.

Process management uses some of the techniques from product quality management and some of the techniques from customer service management. It looks at an activity as a sequential process. The objective is to find inefficiencies and make the process more effective. Although the procedures have a long history, dating back to Taylorism, the scope of their applicability has been greatly widened, leaving no aspect of the firm free from potential process improvements. Because of the broad applicability of process management techniques, they can be used as a basis for competitive advantage.

Some realized that businesses were spending much more on acquiring new customers than on retaining current ones. Carl Sewell, Frederick F. Reichheld, C. Gronroos, and Earl Sasser showed us how a competitive advantage could be found in ensuring that customers returned again and again. This has come to be known as the loyalty effect after Reicheld's book of the same name in which he broadens the concept to include employee loyalty, supplier loyalty, distributor loyalty, and shareholder loyalty. They also developed techniques for estimating the lifetime value of a loyal customer, called customer lifetime value (CLV). A significant movement started that attempted to recast selling and marketing techniques into a long term endeavour that created a sustained relationship with customers (called relationship selling, relationship marketing, and customer relationship management). Customer relationship management (CRM) software (and its many variants) became an integral tool that sustained this trend.

James Gilmore and Joseph Pine found competitive advantage in mass customization. Flexible manufacturing techniques allowed businesses to individualize products for each customer without losing economies of scale. This effectively turned the product into a service. They also realized that if a service is mass customized by creating a "performance" for each individual client, that service would be transformed into an "experience". Their book, *The Experience Economy*, along with the work of Bernd Schmitt convinced many to see service provision as a form of theatre. This school of thought is sometimes referred to as customer experience management (CEM).

Like Peters and Waterman a decade earlier, James Collins and Jerry Porras spent years conducting empirical research on what makes great companies. Six years of research uncovered a key underlying principle behind the 19 successful companies that they studied: They all encourage and preserve a core ideology that nurtures the company. Even though strategy and tactics change daily, the companies, nevertheless, were able to maintain a core set of values. These core values encourage employees to build an organization that lasts. In *Built To Last* (1994) they claim that short term profit goals, cost cutting, and restructuring will not stimulate dedicated employees to build a great company that will endure. In 2000 Collins coined the term "built to flip" to describe the prevailing business attitudes in Silicon Valley. It describes a business culture where technological change inhibits a long term focus. He also popularized the concept of the BHAG (Big Hairy Audacious Goal). Arie de Geus (1997) undertook a similar study and obtained similar results. He identified four key traits of companies that had prospered for 50 years or more. They are:

- Sensitivity to the business environment – the ability to learn and adjust
- Cohesion and identity – the ability to build a community with personality, vision, and purpose
- Tolerance and decentralization – the ability to build relationships
- Conservative financing.

A company with these key characteristics he called a living company because it is able to perpetuate itself. If a company emphasizes knowledge rather than finance, and sees itself as an ongoing community of human beings, it has the potential to become great and endure for decades. Such an organization is an organic entity capable of learning (he called it a "learning organization") and capable of creating its own processes, goals, and persona.

There are numerous ways by which a firm can try to create a competitive advantage-some will work but many will not. In order to help firms avoid a hit and miss approach to the creation of competitive advantage Will Mulcaster suggests that firms engage in a dialogue that centres around the question "Will the proposed competitive advantage create Perceived Differential Value?" The dialogue should raise a series of other pertinent questions, including:- "Will the proposed competitive advantage create something that is different from the competition?"

"Will the difference add value in the eyes of potential customers?"-This question will entail a discussion of the combined effects of price, product features and consumer perceptions.

"Will the product add value for the firm?"-Answering this question will require an examination of cost effectiveness and the pricing strategy.

The Military Theorists

In the 1980s some business strategists realized that there was a vast knowledge base stretching back thousands of years that they had barely examined. They turned to military strategy for guidance. Military strategy books such as *The Art of War* by Sun Tzu, *On War* by von Clausewitz, and *The Red Book* by Mao Zedong became instant business classics. From Sun Tzu, they learned the tactical side of military strategy and specific tactical prescriptions. From Von Clausewitz, they learned the dynamic and unpredictable nature of military strategy. From Mao Zedong, they learned the principles of guerrilla warfare. The main marketing warfare books were:

- *Business War Games* by Barrie James, 1984
- *Marketing Warfare* by Al Ries and Jack Trout, 1986
- Leadership Secrets of Attila the Hun by Wess Roberts, 1987

Philip Kotler was a well-known proponent of marketing warfare strategy.

There were generally thought to be four types of business warfare theories. They are:

- Offensive marketing warfare strategies
- Defensive marketing warfare strategies
- Flanking marketing warfare strategies
- Guerrilla marketing warfare strategies.

The marketing warfare literature also examined leadership and motivation, intelligence gathering, types of marketing weapons, logistics, and communications.

By the turn of the century marketing warfare strategies had gone out of favour. It was felt that they were limiting. There were many situations in which non-confrontational approaches were more appropriate. In 1989, Dudley Lynch and Paul L. Kordis published *Strategy of the Dolphin: Scoring a Win in a Chaotic World.*

"The Strategy of the Dolphin" was developed to give guidance as to when to use aggressive strategies and when to use passive strategies. A variety of aggressiveness strategies were developed.

In 1993, J. Moore used a similar metaphor. Instead of using military terms, he created an ecological theory of predators and prey, a sort of Darwinian management strategy in which market interactions mimic long term ecological stability.

Strategic Change

In 1970, Alvin Toffler in *Future Shock* described a trend towards accelerating rates of change. He illustrated how social and technological norms had shorter lifespans with each generation, and he questioned society's ability to cope with the resulting turmoil and anxiety. In past generations periods of change were always punctuated with times of stability. This allowed society to assimilate the change and deal with it before the next change arrived. But these periods of stability are getting shorter and by the late 20th century had all but disappeared.

In 1980 in *The Third Wave,* Toffler characterized this shift to relentless change as the defining feature of the third phase of civilization (the first two phases being the agricultural and industrial waves). He claimed that the dawn of this new phase will cause great anxiety for those that grew up in the previous phases, and will cause much conflict and opportunity in the business world. Hundreds of authors, particularly since the early 1990s, have attempted to explain what this means for business strategy. In 1997, Watts Wacker and Jim Taylor called this upheaval a "500 year delta." They claimed these major upheavals occur every 5 centuries. They said we are currently making the transition from the "Age of Reason" to a new chaotic Age of Access. Jeremy Rifkin (2000) popularized and expanded this term, "age of access" three years later in his book of the same name.

In 1968, Peter Drucker (1969) coined the phrase Age of Discontinuity to describe the way change forces disruptions into the continuity of our lives. In an age of continuity attempts to predict the future by extrapolating from the past can be somewhat accurate. But according to Drucker, we are now in an age of discontinuity and extrapolating from the past is hopelessly ineffective. We cannot assume that trends that exist today will continue into the future. He identifies four sources of discontinuity: new technologies, globalization, cultural pluralism, and knowledge capital.

In 2000, Gary Hamel discussed strategic decay, the notion that the value of all strategies, no matter how brilliant, decays over time.

In 1978, Dereck Abell (Abell, D. 1978) described strategic windows and stressed the importance of the timing (both entrance and exit) of any given strategy. This has led some strategic planners to build planned obsolescence into their strategies.

In 1989, Charles Handy identified two types of change. Strategic drift is a gradual change that occurs so subtly that it is not noticed until it is too late. By contrast, transformational change is sudden and radical. It is typically caused by discontinuities (or exogenous shocks) in the business environment. The point where a new trend is initiated is called a strategic inflection point by Andy Grove. Inflection points can be subtle or radical.

In 2000, Malcolm Gladwell discussed the importance of the tipping point, that point where a trend or fad acquires critical mass and takes off.

In 1983, Noel Tichy wrote that because we are all beings of habit we tend to repeat what we are comfortable with. He wrote that this is a trap that constrains our creativity, prevents us from exploring new ideas, and hampers our dealing with the full complexity of new issues. He developed a systematic method of dealing with change that involved looking at any new issue from three angles: technical and production, political and resource allocation, and corporate culture.

In 1990, Richard Pascale (Pascale, R. 1990) wrote that relentless change requires that businesses continuously reinvent themselves. His famous maxim is "Nothing fails like success" by which he means that what was a strength yesterday becomes the root of weakness today, We tend to depend on what worked yesterday and refuse to let go of what worked so well for us in the past. Prevailing strategies become self-confirming. In order to avoid this trap, businesses must stimulate a spirit of inquiry and healthy debate. They must encourage a creative process of self renewal based on constructive conflict.

In 1996, Art Kleiner (1996) claimed that to foster a corporate culture that embraces change, you have to hire the right people; heretics, heroes, outlaws, and visionaries. The conservative bureaucrat that made such a good middle manager in yesterday's hierarchical organizations is of little use today. A decade earlier Peters and Austin (1985) had stressed the importance of nurturing champions and heroes. They said we have a tendency to dismiss new ideas, so to overcome this, we should support those few people in the organization that have the courage to put their career and reputation on the line for an unproven idea.

In 1996, Adrian Slywotzky showed how changes in the business environment are reflected in value migrations between industries, between companies, and within companies. He claimed that recognizing the patterns behind these value migrations is necessary if we wish to understand the world of chaotic change. In "Profit Patterns" (1999) he described businesses as being in a state of strategic anticipation as they try to spot emerging patterns. Slywotsky and his team identified 30 patterns that have transformed industry after industry.

In 1997, Clayton Christensen (1997) took the position that great companies can fail precisely because they do everything right since the capabilities of the organization also defines its disabilities. Christensen's thesis is that outstanding companies lose their market leadership when confronted with disruptive technology. He called the approach to discovering the emerging markets for disruptive technologies agnostic marketing, i.e., marketing under the implicit assumption that no one-not the company, not the customers-can know how or in what quantities a disruptive product can or will be used before they have experience using it.

A number of strategists use scenario planning techniques to deal with change. Kees van der Heijden (1996), for example, says that change and uncertainty make "optimum strategy" determination impossible. We have neither the time nor the information required for such a calculation. The best we can hope for is what he calls "the most skillful process". The way Peter Schwartz put it in 1991 is that strategic outcomes cannot be known in advance so the sources of competitive advantage cannot be predetermined.

The fast changing business environment is too uncertain for us to find sustainable value in formulas of excellence or competitive advantage. Instead, scenario planning is a technique in which multiple outcomes can be developed, their implications assessed, and their likeliness of occurrence evaluated. According to Pierre Wack, scenario planning is about insight, complexity, and subtlety, not about formal analysis and numbers.

In 1988, Henry Mintzberg looked at the changing world around him and decided it was time to reexamine how strategic management was done. He examined the strategic process and concluded it was much more fluid and unpredictable than people had thought. Because of this, he could not point to one process that could be called strategic planning. Instead he concludes that there are five types of strategies. They are:

- Strategy as plan-a direction, guide, course of action-intention rather than actual
- Strategy as ploy-a maneuver intended to outwit a competitor
- Strategy as pattern-a consistent pattern of past behaviour-realized rather than intended
- Strategy as position-locating of brands, products, or companies within the conceptual framework of consumers or other stakeholders-strategy determined primarily by factors outside the firm
- Strategy as perspective-strategy determined primarily by a master strategist

In 1998, Mintzberg developed these five types of management strategy into 10 "schools of thought". These 10 schools are grouped into three categories. The first group is prescriptive or normative. It consists of the informal design and conception school, the formal planning school, and the analytical positioning school. The second group, consisting of six schools, is more concerned with how strategic management is actually done, rather than prescribing optimal plans or positions.

The six schools are the entrepreneurial, visionary, or great leader school, the cognitive or mental process school, the learning, adaptive, or emergent process school, the power or negotiation school, the corporate culture or collective process school, and the business environment or reactive school. The third and final group consists of one school, the configuration or transformation school, an hybrid of the other schools organized into stages, organizational life cycles, or "episodes".

In 1999, Constantinos Markides also wanted to reexamine the nature of strategic planning itself. He describes strategy formation and implementation as an on-going, never-ending, integrated process requiring continuous reassessment and reformation. Strategic management is planned and emergent, dynamic, and interactive. J. Moncrieff (1999) also stresses strategy dynamics. He recognized that strategy is partially deliberate and partially unplanned. The unplanned element comes from two sources: emergent strategies (result from the emergence of opportunities and threats in the environment) and Strategies in action (ad hoc actions by many people from all parts of the organization).

Some business planners are starting to use a complexity theory approach to strategy. Complexity can be thought of as chaos with a dash of order. Chaos theory deals with turbulent systems that rapidly become disordered. Complexity is not quite so unpredictable. It involves multiple agents interacting in such a way that a glimpse of structure may appear. Axelrod, R., Holland, J., and Kelly, S. and Allison, M.A., call these systems of multiple actions and reactions complex adaptive systems. Axelrod asserts that rather than fear complexity, business should harness it. He says this can best be done when "there are many participants, numerous interactions, much trial and error learning, and abundant attempts to imitate each others' successes". In 2000, E. Dudik wrote that an organization must develop a mechanism for understanding the source and level of complexity it will face in the future and then transform itself into a complex adaptive system in order to deal with it.

Information-and Technology-driven Strategy

Peter Drucker had theorized the rise of the "knowledge worker" back in the 1950s. He described how fewer workers would be doing physical labour, and more would be applying their minds. In 1984, John Nesbitt theorized that the future would be driven largely by information: companies that managed information well could obtain an advantage, however the profitability of what he calls the "information float" (information that the company had and others desired) would all but disappear as inexpensive computers made information more accessible. Daniel Bell (1985) examined the sociological consequences of information technology, while Gloria Schuck and Shoshana Zuboff looked at psychological factors. Zuboff, in her five year study of eight pioneering corporations made the important distinction between "automating technologies" and "infomating technologies". She studied the effect that both had on individual workers, managers, and organizational structures.

She largely confirmed Peter Drucker's predictions three decades earlier, about the importance of flexible decentralized structure, work teams, knowledge sharing, and the central role of the knowledge worker. Zuboff also detected a new basis for managerial authority, based not on position or hierarchy, but on knowledge (also predicted by Drucker) which she called "participative management".

In 1990, Peter Senge, who had collaborated with Arie de Geus at Dutch Shell, borrowed de Geus' notion of the learning organization, expanded it, and popularized it. The underlying theory is that a company's ability to gather, analyse, and use information is a necessary requirement for business success in the information age. In order to do this, Senge claimed that an organization would need to be structured such that:

- People can continuously expand their capacity to learn and be productive,
- New patterns of thinking are nurtured,
- Collective aspirations are encouraged, and
- People are encouraged to see the "whole picture" together.

Senge identified five disciplines of a learning organization. They are:

- Personal responsibility, self reliance, and mastery — We accept that we are the masters of our own destiny. We make decisions and live with the consequences of them. When a problem needs to be fixed, or an opportunity exploited, we take the initiative to learn the required skills to get it done.
- Mental models — We need to explore our personal mental models to understand the subtle effect they have on our behaviour.
- Shared vision — The vision of where we want to be in the future is discussed and communicated to all. It provides guidance and energy for the journey ahead.
- Team learning — We learn together in teams. This involves a shift from "a spirit of advocacy to a spirit of enquiry".
- Systems thinking — We look at the whole rather than the parts. This is what Senge calls the "Fifth discipline". It is the glue that integrates the other four into a coherent strategy. For an alternative approach to the "learning organization".

Since 1990 many theorists have written on the strategic importance of information, including J.B. Quinn, J. Carlos Jarillo, D.L. Barton, Manuel Castells, J.P. Lieleskin, Thomas Stewart, K.E. Sveiby, Gilbert J. Probst, and Shapiro and Varian to name just a few. Thomas A. Stewart, for example, uses the term intellectual capital to describe the investment an organization makes in knowledge. It is composed of human capital (the knowledge inside the heads of employees), customer capital (the knowledge inside the heads of customers that decide to buy from you), and structural capital (the knowledge that resides in the company itself).

Manuel Castells, describes a network society characterized by: globalization, organizations structured as a network, instability of employment, and a social divide between those with access to information technology and those without.

Geoffrey Moore (1991) and R. Frank and P. Cook also detected a shift in the nature of competition. In industries with high technology content, technical standards become established and this gives the dominant firm a near monopoly. The same is true of networked industries in which interoperability requires compatibility between users. An example is word processor documents.

Once a product has gained market dominance, other products, even far superior products, cannot compete. Moore showed how firms could attain this enviable position by using E.M. Rogers five stage adoption process and focusing on one group of customers at a time, using each group as a base for marketing to the next group. The most difficult step is making the transition between visionaries and pragmatists. If successful a firm can create a bandwagon effect in which the momentum builds and your product becomes a de facto standard.

Evans and Wurster describe how industries with a high information component are being transformed. They cite Encarta's demolition of the Encyclopedia Britannica (whose sales have plummeted 80% since their peak of $650 million in 1990).

Encarta's reign was speculated to be short-lived, eclipsed by collaborative encyclopedias like Wikipedia that can operate at very low marginal costs. Encarta's service was subsequently turned into an on-line service and dropped at the end of 2009. Evans also mentions the music industry which is desperately looking for a new business model. The upstart information savvy firms, unburdened by cumbersome physical assets, are changing the competitive landscape, redefining market segments, and disintermediating some channels. One manifestation of this is personalized marketing. Information technology allows marketers to treat each individual as its own market, a market of one. Traditional ideas of market segments will no longer be relevant if personalized marketing is successful.

The technology sector has provided some strategies directly. For example, from the software development industry agile software development provides a model for shared development processes. Access to information systems have allowed senior managers to take a much more comprehensive view of strategic management than ever before. The most notable of the comprehensive systems is the balanced scorecard approach developed in the early 1990s by Drs. Robert S. Kaplan (Harvard Business School) and David Norton (Kaplan, R. and Norton, D. 1992). It measures several factors financial, marketing, production, organizational development, and new product development in order to achieve a 'balanced' perspective.

Knowledge-driven Strategy

Most current approaches to business "strategy" focus on the mechanics of management – e.g., Drucker's operational "strategies" – and as such are not true business strategy. In a post-industrial world these operationally focused business strategies hinge on conventional sources of advantage have essentially been eliminated:

- Scale used to be very important. But now, with access to capital and a global marketplace, scale is achievable by multiple organizations simultaneously. In many cases, it can literally be rented.
- Process improvement or "best practices" were once a favoured source of advantage, but they were at best temporary, as they could be copied and adapted by competitors.
- Owning the customer had always been thought of as an important form of competitive advantage. Now, however, customer loyalty is far less important and difficult to maintain as new brands and products emerge all the time.

In such a world, differentiation, as elicudated by Michael Porter, Botten and McManus is the only way to maintain economic or market superiority (i.e., comparative advantage) over competitors. A company must OWN the thing that differentiates it from competitors. Without IP ownership and protection, any product, process or scale advantage can be compromised or entirely lost. Competitors can copy them without fear of economic or legal consequences, thereby eliminating the advantage.

Strategic Decision Making Processes

Will Mulcaster argues that whilst much research and creative thought has been devoted to generating alternative strategies, too little work has been done on what influences the quality of strategic decision making and the effectiveness with which strategies are implemented. For instance, in retrospect it can be seen that the financial crisis of 2008/9 could have been avoided if the banks had paid more attention to the risks associated with their investments, but how should banks change the way in which they make decisions in order to improve the quality of their decisions in the future? Mulcaster's Managing Forces framework addresses this issue by identifying 11 forces that should be incorporated into the processes of decision making and strategic implementation. The 11 forces are:-Time; Opposing forces; Politics; Perception; Holistic effects; Adding value; Incentives; Learning capabilities; Opportunity cost; Risk; Style. The mnemonic "TOPHAILORS" is used to assist in the memory of these forces.

The Psychology of Strategic Management

Several psychologists have conducted studies to determine the psychological patterns involved in strategic management. Typically senior managers have been asked how they go about making strategic decisions. A 1938 treatise by Chester Barnard, that was based on his own experience as a business executive, sees the process as informal, intuitive, non-routinized, and involving primarily oral, 2-way communications. Bernard says "The process is the sensing of the organization as a whole and the total situation relevant to it. It transcends the capacity of merely intellectual methods, and the techniques of discriminating the factors of the situation. The terms pertinent to it are "feeling", "judgement", "sense", "proportion", "balance", "appropriateness". It is a matter of art rather than science." In 1973, Henry Mintzberg found that senior managers typically deal with unpredictable situations so they strategize in *ad hoc,* flexible, dynamic, and implicit ways.. He says, "The job breeds adaptive information-manipulators who prefer the live concrete situation. The manager works in an environment of stimulous-response, and he develops in his work a clear preference for live action." In 1982, John Kotter studied the daily activities of 15 executives and concluded that they spent most of their time developing and working a network of relationships from which they gained general insights and specific details to be used in making strategic decisions. They tended to use "mental road maps" rather than systematic planning techniques.

Daniel Isenberg's 1984 study of senior managers found that their decisions were highly intuitive. Executives often sensed what they were going to do before they could explain why. He claimed in 1986 that one of the reasons for this is the complexity of strategic decisions and the resultant information uncertainty. Shoshana Zuboff (1988) claims that information technology is widening the divide between senior managers (who typically make strategic decisions) and operational level managers (who typically make routine decisions). She claims that prior to the widespread use of computer systems, managers, even at the most senior level, engaged in both strategic decisions and routine administration, but as computers facilitated (She called it "deskilled") routine processes, these activities were moved further down the hierarchy, leaving senior management free for strategic decions making.

In 1977, Abraham Zaleznik identified a difference between leaders and managers. He describes leadershipleaders as visionaries who inspire. They care about substance. Whereas managers are claimed to care about process, plans, and form. He also claimed in 1989 that the rise of the manager was the main factor that caused the decline of American business in the 1970s and 80s.The main difference between leader and manager is that, leader has followers and manager has subordinates. In capitalistic society leaders make decisions and manager usually follow or execute. Lack of leadership is most damaging at the level of strategic management where it can paralyze an entire organization.

According to Corner, Kinichi, and Keats, strategic decision making in organizations occurs at two levels: individual and aggregate. They have developed a model of parallel strategic decision making. The model identifies two parallel processes both of which involve getting attention, encoding information, storage and retrieval of information, strategic choice, strategic outcome, and feedback. The individual and organizational processes are not independent however. They interact at each stage of the process.

Reasons why Strategic Plans Fail

There are many reasons why strategic plans fail, especially:

- Failure to execute by overcoming the four key organizational hurdles:
  - o Cognitive hurdle
  - o Motivational hurdle
  - o Resource hurdle
  - o Political hurdle.
- Failure to understand the customer:
  - o Why do they buy
  - o Is there a real need for the product
  - o inadequate or incorrect marketing research.
- Inability to predict environmental reaction:
  - o What will competitors do:
    - Fighting brands
    - Price wars.
  - o Will government intervene.
- Over-estimation of resource competence:
  - o Can the staff, equipment, and processes handle the new strategy
  - o Failure to develop new employee and management skills.
- Failure to coordinate:
  - o Reporting and control relationships not adequate
  - o Organizational structure not flexible enough.
- Failure to obtain senior management commitment:
  - o Failure to get management involved right from the start
  - o Failure to obtain sufficient company resources to accomplish task.
- Failure to obtain employee commitment:
  - o New strategy not well explained to employees
  - o No incentives given to workers to embrace the new strategy.
- Under-estimation of time requirements:
  - o No critical path analysis done.

- Failure to follow the plan:
  - o No follow through after initial planning
  - o No tracking of progress against plan
  - o No consequences for above.
- Failure to manage change:
  - o Inadequate understanding of the internal resistance to change
  - o Lack of vision on the relationships between processes, technology and organization.
- Poor communications:
  - o Insufficient information sharing among stakeholders
  - o Exclusion of stakeholders and delegates.

Limitations of Strategic Management

Although a sense of direction is important, it can also stifle creativity, especially if it is rigidly enforced. In an uncertain and ambiguous world, fluidity can be more important than a finely tuned strategic compass. When a strategy becomes internalized into a corporate culture, it can lead to group think. It can also cause an organization to define itself too narrowly. An example of this is marketing myopia.

Many theories of strategic management tend to undergo only brief periods of popularity. A summary of these theories thus inevitably exhibits survivorship bias (itself an area of research in strategic management). Many theories tend either to be too narrow in focus to build a complete corporate strategy on, or too general and abstract to be applicable to specific situations.

Populism or faddishness can have an impact on a particular theory's life cycle and may see application in inappropriate circumstances. In 2000, Gary Hamel coined the term strategic convergence to explain the limited scope of the strategies being used by rivals in greatly differing circumstances. He lamented that strategies converge more than they should, because the more successful ones are imitated by firms that do not understand that the strategic process involves designing a custom strategy for the specifics of each situation.

Ram Charan, aligning with a popular marketing tagline, believes that strategic planning must not dominate action. "Just do it!", while not quite what he meant, is a phrase that nevertheless comes to mind when combatting analysis paralysis.

The Linearity Trap

It is tempting to think that the elements of strategic management – (i) reaching consensus on corporate objectives; (ii) developing a plan for achieving the objectives; and (iii) marshalling and allocating the resources required to implement the plan – can be approached sequentially. It would be convenient, in other words, if one could deal first with the noble question of ends, and then address the mundane question of means.

But in the world in which strategies have to be implemented, the three elements are interdependent. Means are as likely to determine ends as ends are to determine means. The objectives that an organization might wish to pursue are limited by the range of feasible approaches to implementation. (There will usually be only a small number of approaches that will not only be technically and administratively possible, but also satisfactory to the full range of organizational stakeholders.) In turn, the range of feasible implementation approaches is determined by the availability of resources.

And so, although participants in a typical "strategy session" may be asked to do "blue sky" thinking where they pretend that the usual constraints – resources, acceptability to stakeholders, administrative feasibility – have been lifted, the fact is that it rarely makes sense to divorce oneself from the environment in which a strategy will have to be implemented. It's probably impossible to think in any meaningful way about strategy in an unconstrained environment. Our brains can't process "boundless possibilities", and the very idea of strategy only has meaning in the context of challenges or obstacles to be overcome. It's at least as plausible to argue that acute awareness of constraints is the very thing that stimulates creativity by forcing us to constantly reassess both means and ends in light of circumstances.

The key question, then, is, "How can individuals, organizations and societies cope as well as possible with... issues too complex to be fully understood, given the fact that actions initiated on the basis of inadequate understanding may lead to significant regret?"

The answer is that the process of developing organizational strategy must be iterative. It involves toggling back and forth between questions about objectives, implementation planning and resources. An initial idea about corporate objectives may have to be altered if there is no feasible implementation plan that will meet with a sufficient level of acceptance among the full range of stakeholders, or because the necessary resources are not available, or both.

Even the most talented manager would no doubt agree that "comprehensive analysis is impossible" for complex problems. Formulation and implementation of strategy must thus occur side-by-side rather than sequentially, because strategies are built on assumptions which, in the absence of perfect knowledge, will never be perfectly correct. Strategic management is necessarily a "repetitive learning cycle [rather than] a linear progression towards a clearly defined final destination." While assumptions can and should be tested in advance, the ultimate test is implementation. You will inevitably need to adjust corporate objectives and/or your approach to pursuing outcomes and/or assumptions about required resources. Thus a strategy will get remade during implementation because "humans rarely can proceed satisfactorily except by learning from experience; and modest probes, serially modified on the basis of feedback, usually are the best method for such learning."

It serves little purpose (other than to provide a false aura of certainty sometimes demanded by corporate strategists and planners) to pretend to anticipate every possible consequence of a corporate decision, every possible constraining or enabling factor, and every possible point of view.

At the end of the day, what matters for the purposes of strategic management is having a clear view – based on the best available evidence and on defensible assumptions – of what it seems possible to accomplish within the constraints of a given set of circumstances.

As the situation changes, some opportunities for pursuing objectives will disappear and others arise. Some implementation approaches will become impossible, while others, previously impossible or unimagined, will become viable. The essence of being "strategic" thus lies in a capacity for "intelligent trial-and error" rather than linear adherence to finally honed and detailed strategic plans. Strategic management will add little value – indeed, it may well do harm – if organizational strategies are designed to be used as a detailed blueprints for managers. Strategy should be seen, rather, as laying out the general path-but not the precise steps-by which an organization intends to create value.

Strategic management is a question of interpreting, and continuously reinterpreting, the possibilities presented by shifting circumstances for advancing an organization's objectives. Doing so requires strategists to think *simultaneously* about desired objectives, the best approach for achieving them, and the resources implied by the chosen approach. It requires a frame of mind that admits of no boundary between means and ends.

Marketing Mix

The term "marketing mix" was first used in 1953 when Neil Borden, in his American Marketing Association presidential address, took the recipe idea one step further and coined the term "marketing-mix". A prominent marketer, E. Jerome McCarthy, proposed a 4 P classification in 1960, which has seen wide use. The four Ps concept is explained in most marketing textbooks and classes.

Four Ps

Elements of the marketing mix are often referred to as 'the four Ps':

- *Product*-A tangible object or an intangible service that is mass produced or manufactured on a large scale with a specific volume of units. Intangible products are service based like the tourism industry & the hotel industry or codes-based products like cellphone load and credits. Typical examples of a mass produced tangible object are the motor car and the disposable razor. A less obvious but ubiquitous mass produced service is a computer operating

- *Price* – The price is the amount a customer pays for the product. It is determined by a number of factors including market share, competition, material costs, product identity and the customer's perceived value of the product. The business may increase or decrease the price of product if other stores have the same product.
- *Place* – Place represents the location where a product can be purchased. It is often referred to as the distribution channel. It can include any physical store as well as virtual stores on the Internet.
- *Promotion* represents all of the communications that a marketer may use in the marketplace. Promotion has four distinct elements: advertising, public relations, word of mouth and point of sale. A certain amount of crossover occurs when promotion uses the four principal elements together, which is common in film promotion. Advertising covers any communication that is paid for, from cinema commercials, radio and Internet adverts through print media and billboards. Public relations are where the communication is not directly paid for and includes press releases, sponsorship deals, exhibitions, conferences, seminars or trade fairs and events. Word of mouth is any apparently informal communication about the product by ordinary individuals, satisfied customers or people specifically engaged to create word of mouth momentum. Sales staff often plays an important role in word of mouth and Public Relations.

Broadly defined, optimizing the marketing mix is the primary responsibility of marketing. By offering the product with the right combination of the four Ps marketers can improve their results and marketing effectiveness. Making small changes in the marketing mix is typically considered to be a tactical change. Parm Bains says making large changes in any of the four Ps can be considered strategic. For example, a large change in the price, say from $19.00 to $39.00 would be considered a strategic change in the position of the product. However a change of $130 to $129.99 would be considered a tactical change, potentially related to a promotional offer.

The term 'marketing mix' howevér, does not imply that the 4P elements represent options. They are not trade-offs but are fundamental marketing issues that always need to be addressed. They are the fundamental actions that marketing requires whether determined explicitly or by default.

Four Cs

A formal approach to this customer-focused marketing mix is known as Four Cs (Commodity, Cost, Channel, Communication). Koichi Shimizu proposed a four Cs classification in 1973.

The four elements are:

1. Commodity (Original meaning of Latin: Commodus= convenient) : the product for the consumers or citizens. Not product out.
2. Cost (Original meaning of Latin: Constare= It makes sacrifices) : producing cost, selling cost, purchasing cost and social cost.
3. Channel (Original meaning is a Canal) : Flow of commodity : marketing channels.
4. Communication (Original meaning of Latin:Communio= sharing of meaning) : marketing communication : It doesn't promote the sales.

The Four Cs can be compared to the Four Ps. This system is basically the four Ps renamed and reworded to provide a customer focus. The four Cs Model provides a demand/customer centric version alternative to the well-known four Ps supply side model (product, price, place, promotion) of marketing management.

The Four Cs model is more consumer-oriented and attempts to better fit the movement from mass marketing to niche marketing. The Product part of the Four Ps model is replaced by Consumer or Consumer Models, shifting the focus to satisfying the consumer needs. Another C replacement for Product is Capable. By defining offerings as individual capabilities that when combined and focused to a specific industry, creates a custom solution rather than pigeon-holing a customer into a product. Pricing is replaced by Cost reflecting the total cost of ownership. Many factors affect Cost, including but not limited to the customer's cost to change or implement the new product or service and the customer's cost for not selecting a competitor's product or service. Placement is replaced by Convenience. With the rise of internet and hybrid models of purchasing, Place is becoming less relevant. Convenience takes into account the ease of buying the product, finding the product, finding information about the product, and several other factors. Finally, the Promotions feature is replaced by Communication which represents a broader focus than simply Promotions. Communications can include advertising, public relations, personal selling, viral advertising, and any form of communication between the firm and the consumer.

The Four Cs model has been criticized for simply being nothing more than the Four Ps with different points of emphasis. In particular, the Four Cs inclusion of customers in the marketing mix is criticized, since customers are a *target* of marketing, while the other elements of the marketing mix are *tactics*. The Four Cs also exclude numerous strategies for product development, distribution, and pricing, while assuming that consumers want two-way communications with companies.

5

Advertising the Hospitality Industry

Yield Management

Yield management, also known as revenue management, is the process of understanding, anticipating and influencing consumer behavior in order to maximize revenue or profits from a fixed, perishable resource (such as airline seats or hotel room reservations).

The challenge is to sell the right resources to the right customer at the right time for the right price. This process can result in price discrimination, where a firm charges customers consuming otherwise identical goods or services a different price for doing so. Yield management is a large revenue generator for several major industries; Robert Crandall, former Chairman and CEO of American Airlines, has called yield management "the single most important technical development in transportation management since we entered deregulation."

Definition

Definition 1: Revenue Management, sometimes called yield management, has become part of mainstream business theory and practice over the last fifteen to twenty years. Whether we call it an emerging discipline or a new management science—it has been called both—revenue management is a set of revenue maximization strategies and tactics meant to improve the profitability of certain businesses. It is complex because it involves several aspects of management control, including rate management, revenue streams management, and distribution channel management, just to name a few. Revenue management is multidisciplinary because it blends elements of marketing, operations, and financial management into a highly successful new approach. A revenue manager frequently must work with one or more other departments when designing and implementing revenue management strategies. Revenue Management. Maximizing Revenue in Hospitality Operations. Dr. Gabor Forgacs, 2010.

Definition 2: Revenue Management is the application of disciplined tactics that predict consumer behavior at the micromarket level and optimize product availability and price to maximize revenue growth. Revenue Management. Hard-core tactics for market domination. Robert G. Cross, 1997.

Definition 3: Defining Revenue Management: Top Line to Bottom Line. Hospitality Sales and Marketing Association International. HSMAI online store at.

History

Deregulation is generally regarded as the catalyst for yield management in the airline industry, but this tends to overlook the role of Global Distribution Systems (GDS's). It is arguable that the fixed pricing paradigm occurs as a result of decentralized consumption. With mass production, pricing became a centralized management activity and customer contact staff focused on customer service exclusively. Electronic commerce, of which the GDS's were the first wave, created an environment where large volumes of sales could be managed without large numbers of customer service staff. They also gave management staff direct access to price at time of consumption and rich data capture for future decision-making.

On January 17, 1985, American Airlines launched Ultimate Super Saver fares in an effort to compete with low cost carrier PEOPLExpress. Donald Burr, the CEO of People Express, is quoted in the book "Revenue management" by Bob Cross saying "We were a vibrant, profitable company from 1981 to 1985, and then we tipped right over into losing $50 million a month...We had been profitable from the day we started until American came at us with Ultimate Super Savers." The Revenue management systems developed at American Airlines were recognized by the Edelman Prize committee of INFORMS for contributing $1.4 billion in a three year period at the airline.

Revenue management spread to other travel and transportation companies in the early 1990s. Notable was implementation of revenue management at National Car Rental. In 1993, General Motors Corporation was forced to take a $744 million charge against earnings related to its ownership of National Car Rental Systems.

In response, National's program expanded the definition of Revenue management to include capacity management, pricing and reservations control. As a result of this program, General Motors was able to sell National Car Rental Systems for an estimated $1.2 billion. Other notable Revenue management implementations include the NBC which credits its system with $200 million in improved ad sales from 1996 to 2000, the Target Pricing initiative at UPS, and Revenue management at Texas Children's Hospital. Since 2000, much of the dynamic pricing, promotions management and dynamic packaging that underlie e-commerce sites leverage Revenue management techniques. In 2002 GMAC launched an early implementation of web based revenue management in the financial services industry.

There have also been high profile failures and faux pas. Amazon.com was criticized for irrational price changes that resulted from a Revenue management software bug. The Coca-Cola Company's plans for a dynamic pricing vending machine were put on hold as a result of negative consumer reactions. Revenue management is also blamed for much of the financial difficulty currently experienced by legacy carriers. The reliance of the major carriers on high fares in captive markets arguably created the conditions for low cost carriers to thrive.

Use by Industry

There are three essential conditions for revenue management to be applicable:

- That there is a fixed amount of resources available for sale.

- That the resources sold are perishable. This means that there is a time limit to selling the resources, after which they cease to be of value.
- That different customers are willing to pay a different price for using the same amount of resources.

If the resources available are not fixed or not perishable, the problem is limited to logistics, i.e. inventory or production management. If all customers would pay the same price for using the same amount of resources, the challenge would perhaps be limited to selling as quickly as possible, e.g. if there are costs for holding inventory.

Yield management is of especially high relevance in cases where the constant costs are relatively high compared to the variable costs. The less variable cost there is, the more the additional revenue earned will contribute to the overall profit. This is because it focuses on maximizing expected marginal revenue for a given operation and planning horizon. It optimizes resource utilization by ensuring inventory availability to customers with the highest expected net revenue contribution and extracting the greatest level of 'willingness to pay' from the entire customer base. Revenue management practitioners typically claim 3% to 7% incremental revenue gains due to revenue management activity. In many industries this can equate to over 100% increase in profits. A competent revenue management analyst with good decision support tools can generate $10,000 per hour.

Yield management has significantly altered the travel and hospitality industry since its inception in the mid 1980s. It requires analysts with detailed market knowledge and advanced computing systems who implement sophisticated mathematical techniques to analyse market behavior and capture revenue opportunities. It has evolved from the system airlines invented as a response to deregulation and quickly spread to hotels, car rental firms, cruise lines, media, and energy to name a few. Its effectiveness in generating incremental revenues from an existing operation and customer base has made it particularly attractive to business leaders that prefer to generate return from revenue growth and enhanced capability rather than downsizing and cost cutting.

Airlines

In the passenger airline case, capacity is regarded fixed because changing what aircraft flies a certain service based on the demand is the exception rather than the rule. When the aircraft departs, the unsold seats cannot generate any revenue and thus can be said to have perished. Airlines use special software to monitor how seats are being reserved and react accordingly, for example by offering discounts when it appears that seats will remain unsold.

Another way of capturing varying willingness to pay is to attempt market segmentation. A firm may repackage its basic inventory into different products to this end. In the passenger airline case this means implementing purchase restrictions, length of stay requirements and requiring fees for changing or canceling tickets.

The airline needs to keep a specific number of seats in reserve to cater to the probable demand for high-fare seats. The price of each seat varies inversely with the number of seats reserved, that is, the more seats that are reserved for a particular category, the lower the price of each seat. This will continue till the price of seat in the premium class equals that of those in the concession class. Depending on this, a floor price (lower price) for the next seat to be sold is set.

Hotels

Hotels use this system in largely the same way, to calculate the rates, rooms and restrictions on sales in order to best maximize the return too. These systems measure constrained and unconstrained demand along with pace to gauge which restrictions e.g.. length of stay, non refundable rate, or close to arrival. Revenue Managers in the hotel industry have evolved tremendously over the last 10 years and in this global economy targeting the right distribution channels, controlling costs, and having the right market mix plays an important role in Yield Management. Revenue management in hotels is selling rooms and services at the right price, at the right time, to the right people.

Rental Cars

In the rental car industry, yield management deals with the

sale of optional insurance, damage waivers and vehicle upgrades. It accounts for a major portion of the rental company's profitability, and is monitored on a daily basis.

Inter City Buses

Yield management has moved into the bus industry with companies such as Megabus and BoltBus, which runs a low cost network in the UK and parts of the US, and more recently, nakedbus.com and Intercape, which have networks in New Zealand and South Africa.

Multifamily Housing

In the Multifamily residential industry, yield optimization is focused on producing supply and demand forecasts to determine rent recommendations for profit optimization. However, the use of the yield optimization systems is fairly new to the industry in the late 1990s, with Archstone Smith pioneering its use. The multifamily industry currently has two providers of yield management systems, the Rainmaker's revolution LRO Lease Optimizer, and the M/PF YieldStar Asset Optimization System from RealPage. There is also a third-party website devoted to educating the multifamily industry on revenue management systems and techniques, called Multifamily Revenue Management.

Econometrics

Revenue Management econometrics centres on detailed forecasting and mathematical optimization of marginal revenue opportunities. The opportunities arise from segmentation of consumer willingness to pay. If the market for a particular good follows the simple straight line Price/Demand relationship illustrated below, a single fixed price of $50 there is enough demand to sell 50 units of inventory. This results in $2,500 in revenues. However the same Price/Demand relationship yields $4,000 if consumers are presented with multiple prices.

In practice the segmentation approach relies on adequate fences between consumers so that everyone doesn't buy at the lowest price offered. The airlines use time of purchase to create this segmentation, with later booking customers paying the higher fares. The fashion industry uses time in the opposite direction, discounting later in the selling season once the item is out of fashion or inappropriate for the time of year. Other pproaches to fences involve attributes that create substantial value to the consumer at little or no cost to the seller. A backstage pass at a concert is a good example of this. Initially Revenue Management avoided the complexity caused by the interaction of absolute price and price position by using surrogates for price such as booking class. By the mid 1990s most implementation incorporated some measures of price elasticity. The airlines were exceptional in this case, preferring to focus on more detailed segmentation by implementing O&D (Origin and Destination) systems.

At the heart of the Revenue Management decision making process is the tradeoff of marginal revenues from segments that are competing for the same inventory. In capacity constrained cases there is a bird-in-the-hand decision that forces the seller to reject lower revenue generating customers in the hopes that the inventory can be sold in a higher valued segment. The tradeoff is sometimes mistakenly identified as occurring at the intersection of the marginal revenue curves for the competing segments. While this is accurate when it supports marketing decisions where access to both segments is equivalent, it is wrong for inventory control decisions. In these cases the intersection of the marginal revenue curve of the higher valued segment with the actual value of the lower segment is the point of interest.

Yield Management System

Firms that engage in yield management usually use computer yield management systems to do so. The Internet has greatly facilitated this process. Enterprises that use yield management periodically review transactions for goods or services already supplied and for goods or services to be supplied in the future. They may also review information (including statistics) about events (known future events such as holidays, or unexpected past events such as terrorist attacks), competitive information (including prices), seasonal patterns, and other pertinent factors that affect sales.

The models attempt to forecast total demand for all products/ services they provide, by market segment and price point. Since total demand normally exceeds what the particular firm can produce in that period, the models attempt to optimize the firm's outputs to maximize revenue.

The optimization attempts to answer the question: "Given our operating constraints, what is the best mix of products and/or services for us to produce and sell in the period, and at what prices, to generate the highest expected revenue?"

Optimization can help the firm adjust prices and to allocate capacity among market segments to maximize expected revenues. This can be done at different levels of detail:

- by goods (such as a seat on a flight or a seat at an opera production)
- by group of goods (such as the entire opera house or all the seats on a flight)
- by market (such as sales from Seattle and Minneapolis for a flight going Seattle-Minneapolis-Boston)
- overall (on all the routes an airline flies, or all the seats during an opera production season).

Yield management is particularly suitable when selling perishable products, i.e. goods that become unsellable at a point in time (for example air tickets just after a flight takes off). Industries that use yield management include airlines, hotels, stadiums and other venues with a fixed number of seats, and advertising. With an advance forecast of demand and pricing flexibility, buyers will self-sort based on their price sensitivity (using more power in off-peak hours or going to the theater mid-week), their demand sensitivity (must have the higher cost early morning flight or must go to the Saturday night opera) or their time of purchase (usually paying a premium for the luxury of booking late).

In this way, yield management's overall aim is to provide an optimal mix of goods at a variety of price points at different points in time or for different baskets of features. The system will try to maintain a distribution of purchases over time that is balanced as well as high.

Good yield management maximizes (or at least significantly increases) revenue production for the same number of units, by taking advantage of the forecast of high demand/low demand periods, effectively shifting demand from high demand periods to low demand periods and by charging a premium for late bookings. While yield management systems tend to generate higher revenues, the revenue streams tends to arrive later in the booking horizon as more capacity is held for late sale at premium prices.

Firms faced with lack of pricing power sometimes turn to yield management as a last resort. After a year or two using yield management, many of them are surprised to discover they have actually lowered prices for the majority of their opera seats or hotel rooms or other products. That is, they offer far higher discounts more frequently for off-peak times, while raising prices only marginally for peak times, resulting in higher revenue overall. By doing this, they have actually increased quantity demanded by selectively introducing many more price points, as they learn about and react to the diversity of interests and purchase drivers of their customers.

Ethical Issues and Questions of Effectiveness

Yield Management is a form of price discrimination, and as such faces predictable consumer resistance.

Some consumers are concerned that Yield Management could penalize them for conditions which cannot be helped and are unethical to penalize. For example, the formulas, algorithms, and neural networks that determine airline ticket prices could feasibly consider frequent flyer information, which includes a wealth of socioeconomic information such as age and home address. The airline then could charge higher prices to consumers who are between 30 and 65, or live in neighborhoods with higher average wealth, even if those neighborhoods also include poor households. Very few (if any) airlines using Yield Management are able to employ this level of price discrimination because prices are not set based on characteristics of the purchaser, which are in any case often not known at the time of purchase.

Some consumers also object that it is impossible for them to boycott yield management when buying some goods, such as airline tickets.

Yield Management also includes many noncontroversial and more prevalent practices, such as varying prices over time to reflect demand. This level of Yield Management makes up the majority of YM in the airline industry. For example airlines may make a ticket on the Sunday after Thanksgiving more expensive than the Sunday a week later. Alternatively, they may make tickets more expensive when bought at the last minute than when bought six months in advance. The goal of this level of yield management is essentially trying to get demand to equal supply.

When YM was introduced in the early 1990s, primarily in the airline industry, many suggested that despite the obvious immediate increase in revenues, it might harm customer satisfaction and loyalty, interfere with relationship marketing, and drive customers from firms that used YM to firms that did not. To some extent, frequent flier programs were developed as a response to regain customer loyalty and reward frequent & high yield passengers. Today, YM is nearly universal in many industries, including airlines.

Despite optimising revenue in theory, introduction of yield management can sometimes fail to achieve this in practice because of corporate image problems. In 2002, Deutsche Bahn, the German national railway company, experimented with yield management for frequent loyalty card passengers. The fixed pricing model that had existed for decades was replaced with a more demand-responsive pricing model, but this reform proved highly unpopular with passengers, leading to widespread protests and a decline in passenger numbers.

Experimental Studies of Yield Management Decisions

Recently, people working in the area of behavioural operations research have begun to study the yield management decisions of actual human decision makers. One question that this research addresses is: How much might revenues increase if managers relied on yield management systems rather than their own judgment when making pricing decisions?

Using methods from experimental economics, this work has revealed that yield management systems are likely to increase revenues significantly.

Further, this research reveals that "errors" in yield management decisions tend to be quite systematic. For instance, Bearden, Murphy, and Rapoport showed that with respect to expected revenue maximizing policies people tend to price too high when they have high levels of inventory and too low when their inventory levels are low.

Marketing Mix

The term "marketing mix" was first used in 1953 when Neil Borden, in his American Marketing Association presidential address, took the recipe idea one step further and coined the term "marketing-mix". A prominent marketer, E. Jerome McCarthy, proposed a 4 P classification in 1960, which has seen wide use. The four Ps concept is explained in most marketing textbooks and classes.

Four Ps

Elements of the marketing mix are often referred to as 'the four Ps':

- *Product*-A tangible object or an intangible service that is mass produced or manufactured on a large scale with a specific volume of units. Intangible products are service based like the tourism industry & the hotel industry or codes-based products like cellphone load and credits. Typical examples of a mass produced tangible object are the motor car and the disposable razor. A less obvious but ubiquitous mass produced service is a computer operating system.
- *Price* – The price is the amount a customer pays for the product. It is determined by a number of factors including market share, competition, material costs, product identity and the customer's perceived value of the product. The business may increase or decrease the price of product if other stores have the same product.
- *Place* – Place represents the location where a product can be purchased. It is often referred to as the distribution channel. It can include any physical store as well as virtual stores on the Internet.

- *Promotion* represents all of the communications that a marketer may use in the marketplace. Promotion has four distinct elements: advertising, public relations, word of mouth and point of sale. A certain amount of crossover occurs when promotion uses the four principal elements together, which is common in film promotion. Advertising covers any communication that is paid for, from cinema commercials, radio and Internet adverts through print media and billboards. Public relations are where the communication is not directly paid for and includes press releases, sponsorship deals, exhibitions, conferences, seminars or trade fairs and events. Word of mouth is any apparently informal communication about the product by ordinary individuals, satisfied customers or people specifically engaged to create word of mouth momentum. Sales staff often plays an important role in word of mouth and Public Relations.

Broadly defined, optimizing the marketing mix is the primary responsibility of marketing. By offering the product with the right combination of the four Ps marketers can improve their results and marketing effectiveness.

Making small changes in the marketing mix is typically considered to be a tactical change. Parm Bains says making large changes in any of the four Ps can be considered strategic. For example, a large change in the price, say from $19.00 to $39.00 would be considered a strategic change in the position of the product. However a change of $130 to $129.99 would be considered a tactical change, potentially related to a promotional offer.

The term 'marketing mix' however, does not imply that the 4P elements represent options. They are not trade-offs but are fundamental marketing issues that always need to be addressed. They are the fundamental actions that marketing requires whether determined explicitly or by default.

Four Cs

A formal approach to this customer-focused marketing mix is known as Four Cs (Commodity, Cost, Channel, Communication).

Koichi Shimizu proposed a four Cs classification in 1973. The four elements are:

1. Commodity (Original meaning of Latin: Commodus=convenient) : the product for the consumers or citizens. Not product out.
2. Cost (Original meaning of Latin: Constare= It makes sacrifices) : producing cost, selling cost, purchasing cost and social cost.
3. Channel (Original meaning is a Canal) : Flow of commodity : marketing channels.
4. Communication (Original meaning of Latin: Communio= sharing of meaning) : marketing communication : It doesn't promote the sales.

The Four Cs can be compared to the Four Ps. This system is basically the four Ps renamed and reworded to provide a customer focus. The four Cs Model provides a demand/customer centric version alternative to the well-known four Ps supply side model (product, price, place, promotion) of marketing management.

The Four Cs model is more consumer-oriented and attempts to better fit the movement from mass marketing to niche marketing. The Product part of the Four Ps model is replaced by Consumer or Consumer Models, shifting the focus to satisfying the consumer needs. Another C replacement for Product is Capable. By defining offerings as individual capabilities that when combined and focused to a specific industry, creates a custom solution rather than pigeon-holing a customer into a product.

Pricing is replaced by Cost reflecting the total cost of ownership. Many factors affect Cost, including but not limited to the customer's cost to change or implement the new product or service and the customer's cost for not selecting a competitor's product or service. Placement is replaced by Convenience.

With the rise of internet and hybrid models of purchasing, Place is becoming less relevant. Convenience takes into account the ease of buying the product, finding the product, finding information about the product, and several other factors. Finally, the Promotions feature is replaced by Communication which represents a broader focus than simply Promotions. Communications can include advertising, public relations, personal selling, viral advertising, and any form of communication between the firm and the consumer. The Four Cs model has been criticized for simply being nothing more than the Four Ps with different points of emphasis. In particular, the Four Cs inclusion of customers in the marketing mix is criticized, since customers are a *target* of marketing, while the other elements of the marketing mix are *tactics*. The Four Cs also exclude numerous strategies for product development, distribution, and pricing, while assuming that consumers want two-way communications with companies.

Four As

Acceptability: Product has to be its acceptability. As long as it is accepted by customers it is a product. If the offering is not acceptable by the customer it is not product. For example a family planning guy convinced a person not to get more than two child. Two child is good to maintain population stability. The person agreed. Than he again convinced that to have one child is better to control population.

The person agreed: Than he again convinced that no child is the best because we have over population and we have to decrease our population.

The person agreed: Than he again pursued that not to get marred is even better but the person denied. so the last one is not a product.

Affordability: Price have to be affordable by customers. If the price is too high than the product will be unsalable. Price is the customer cost that customer sacrifices to get the product. so it has to be affordable.

Accessibility: Place has to be accessible by the customer. If the place to too remote than customer will not go. place have to be convenience by customers.

Awareness: Customer have to be aware about the product otherwise customer will not buy. so, through promotional activities products features and benefits have to be communicated among customer to create awareness.

Reaching the Destination

Hotel Strategy

You're likely to spend more, on any given trip, for hotel accommodations than for air travel. So paying attention to hotel rates is worth your time.

Hotels and other accommodations are much better than airlines at providing a satisfactory experience for business travellers: A really bad night in a business hotel is about as rare as a really good flight in coach. Price generally correlates with quality, and even the low end of the quality spectrum provides adequate comfort and convenience.

The rules-Review the different hotel classes.

The strategy-Decide what will determine the way you choose a hotel.

Making the deal-Read up on the steps to maximum value.

The Rules

Instead of sticking strictly to price, you'll find it more useful to think about hotel categories that reflect a combination of price and features. Undoubtedly, you're most apt to stay in a business hotel. Sometimes, however, other options can provide either more value or a more pleasant experience. Here's my take on the main sorts of hotels you'll encounter.

Business Hotels

Upscale business hotels constitute the great middle ground of the hotel business, with a wide price/quality spectrum. Unless you've been travelling on some other planet, you know the names well: Crowne Plaza, Hilton, Hyatt, Inter Continental, Marriott, Omni, Ramada, Renaissance, Sheraton, Sofitel, Westin, Wyndham, and dozens of others, worldwide.

Midprice Hotels

One of the "hottest" hotel market niches these days provides almost all the facilities and services of a full-price business hotel but at a sharply lower price range. The midprice niche includes two sub-segments:

- Midprice full-service hotel chains are generally offshoots or variants on the big business-hotel chains, including Hilton Garden Inn, Holiday Inn, Courtyard by Marriott, Ramada, and Sheraton's Four Points.
- A closely related segment-midprice limited service-provides almost the same facilities but a tad fewer services. This sub-segment includes Drury, Fairfield, Hampton Inn, LaQuinta, and a dozen or so others.

Budget Motels

If you've ever had to stay in a small town along the highway, you've undoubtedly slept in a budget motel. They're becoming ubiquitous outside cities. Almost all recent growth has been from the large chains. However, you still see a few low-end independents along downtown highways bypassed by Interstates in some of the smaller cities.

Most of us know what we mean by a budget motel. Major brands include Comfort Inn, Days Inn, Econo Lodge, Holiday Inn Express, Motel 6, Shoney's, Super 8, Travelodge, and a bunch of others. Most of those brands are national throughout the U.S. and many are active in Canada, as well.

Boutique Hotels

The prototypical boutique hotel is an older city-centre property that has been refurbished to a degree that it can compete with newly constructed midprice and expensive business hotels. Rooms tend to be smaller than at newer competitors, and they usually have fewer business facilities than larger business hotels. However, many travellers have concluded that those disadvantages are more than offset by more individualized decor and especially a high degree of personal service from the staff.

Luxury Hotels

The top-of-the-line segment includes such hallowed chain names as Fairmont, Four Seasons, and Ritz-Carlton, some well known independents, and hotels that retain a unique individual name even when they're part of a chain. Everything is opulent: rooms, lobbies, restaurants, shops, with personal services and prices to match. They're located mainly in big cities. They provide everything you could possibly want in a hotel—and probably lots of stuff you don't care about at all.

Resort Hotels

Chances are that you'll encounter resort hotels, if at all, only when you're attending meetings or conventions at the resort. And in that case, your choice of hotel is made for you: Your only decision is whether to accept the official convention rate or try for a bigger discount through some other program.

All-suite Hotels

All-suite hotels have gained much popularity with business travellers, and for good reason. Typically, you get 400-600 square feet of room, with separate "living" and "bedroom" areas, as well as at least minimal kitchen facilities. The living area provides lots more space to spread out your work than you find in the conventional room. And if you want to entertain a business visitor, you can do it in a more businesslike living room or office setting rather than across a possibly unmade bed.

Extended-stay Hotels

A subset of the all-suite genre, extended-stay hotels cater to guests who stay five days or more. Compared with more conventional all-suite properties, most of them have more space, overall, plus larger, better equipped kitchens, often including a refrigerator, stove, and even a dishwasher. Most of the big chains have in-room Internet access, about three-quarters of it highspeed. Prices start at the high end of the budget motel range and go well up into the business hotel range.

Bibliography

Carl H. : *Internet Distribution of European Travel and Tourism Services,* Research Centre of Bornholm, Denmark, 1999.

Chakravarti B.K. : *Hotel and Hospitality Management,* A.P.H., Delhi, 2011.

David L: *International Tourism Policy, New York,* Van Nostrand and Reinhold, 1990.

Eberts, Marjorie: *Careers in Travel, Tourism, and Hospitality,* Lincolnwood, VGM Career Horizons, 1997.

Fesenmaier D., Klein, S. : *Information & Communication Technologies in Tourism,* Springer-Verlag, Wien-New York, 2000.

Graham M S: *Language of Tourism,* The, Wallingford, CAB International, 1996.

Harrison, Lyndon: *Tourism Means Jobs,* Chester, Lyndon Harrison, 1996.

Judi Radice: *Restaurant & Food Graphics,* Glen Cove, PBC International, 1994.

Judy A: *Tourism: Management of Facilities,* London, Pitman: M & E, 1993.

Karski, A: *Urban Tourism* - A Key to Urban Regeneration?, 1990.

Kotler, Philip: *Marketing for Hospitality and Tourism*: New Jersey, Prentice-Hall, 1998.

Larkham, P J: *Building a New Heritage: Tourism, Culture & Identity in the New Europe,* London, Routledge,1994.

Leivadi, S: *Sociology of Tourism, The: Theoretical And Empirical Investigations,* London, Retailed, 1996.

Lucas, Rosemary E.: *Managing Employee Relations in the Hotel and Catering Industry,* London, Cassell, 1995.

Madhukar Manoj : *Hospitality Industries in Next Millennium,* Rajat, Delhi, 2001.

Marcussen, Carl H. : *Internet Distribution of European Travel and Tourism Services*, Research Centre of Bornholm, Denmark, 1999.

Margaret Wade: *Medieval Travellers: The Rich and Restless*, London, Hamish Hamilton, 1982.

Martin, B.S. : *The Efficacy of Growth Machine Theory in Explaining Resident Perceptions of Community Tourism Development*, Clemson University, 1996.

Murphy, P.E. : *Tourism: A Community Approach*, London: Methuen, 1985.

Nancy, N.: *Choosing a Career in Hotels, Motels, and Resorts*, New York, Rosen Pub. Group, 1997.

Peters, M: *International Tourism*, London, Hutchinson, 1969.

Richards, G. : *Culture, Crafts and Tourism: A Vital Relationship*, Tilburg: Atlas, 1999.

Robert C.: *Cases in Hospitality Marketing and Management*, New York, John Wiley, 1997.

Rocco, M.: *An Introduction to Hospitality Today*, Orlando, Educational Institute, 1998.

Sabharwal Rajiv : *Tourism and Hospitality Management in Liberalised Era*, Pacific, Delhi, 2011.

Sharma Sunil : *Planning and Development of Tourism and Hospitality*, Rajat Pub, Delhi, 2007.

Shrivastava Atul : *Modern Hospitality and Tourism Management*, Centrum Press, Delhi, 2010.

Slinn, Judy A: *Tourism: Management of Facilities*, London, Pitman: M & E, 1993.

Smith, G. : *International Tourism and Hospitality Careers through Education and Training*, CHRIE Annual Conference, Washington DC, 1996.

Smith, V.L. : *Hosts and Guests: The Anthropology of Tourism*, Oxford: Blackwell, 1978.

Swarbrooke, J.: *Marketing Tourism, Hospitality and Leisure in Europe*, London, International Thomson Business Press, 1996.

Index

M

N

P

R

S

T

W

□□□